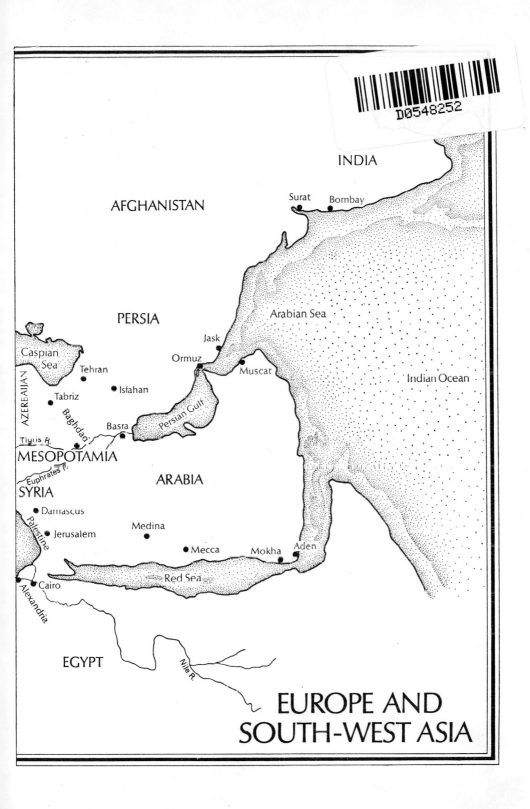

INDIA

AFGHANISTAN

Surat   Bombay

PERSIA

Caspian
Sea   Tehran

Jask

Arabian Sea

Ormuz

Indian Ocean

Muscat

AZEREAIJAN

Tabriz   Isfahan

Baghdad   Basra

Persian Gulf

Tigris R.

MESOPOTAMIA

Euphrates r.

ARABIA

SYRIA

Damascus

Medina

Palestine   Jerusalem

Mecca   Mokha   Aden

Cairo   Red Sea

Alexandria

EGYPT   Nile R.

EUROPE AND
SOUTH-WEST ASIA

THE BRITISH
IN THE
MIDDLE EAST

Sarah Searight

THE BRITISH
IN THE
MIDDLE EAST

EAST WEST PUBLICATIONS
LONDON AND THE HAGUE
In association with
LIVRES DE FRANCE, CAIRO

First published by George Weidenfeld and Nicolson Ltd. in
1969. This completely revised and updated edition published
in 1979.

ISBN 0 85692 018 5

Design and production services by Elron Press Ltd., London.
Printed and bound in Great Britain by
Butler & Tanner Ltd., Frome and London

Contents

Acknowledgements

The publishers wish to thank the following for permission to reproduce their photographs:

Country Life
Courtauld Institute of Art
Lady Lucas-Scudamore
National Portrait Gallery
The National Trust
Rodney Searight
Royal Geographical Society
Victoria and Albert Museum
'The Grand Vizier giving Audience to the English Ambassador' by Francis Smith reproduced by gracious permission of Her Majesty Queen Elizabeth II.

Jacket: 'A Frank Encampment in the Desert' by J. F. Lewis Yale Center for British Art, Paul Mellon Collection.

List of Illustrations

The Great Game

The Road to India

Luminous Vapours

Old Desolate Places

The Noisy, Odd, Capricious Stream

1. European visitors at Karnak, 1817, by F. Broughton
2. John Cartwright, British consul-general in Constantinople, from Wilkie's *Oriental Sketches*
3. View of Jouni, by W. H. Bartlett
4. Lady Hester Stanhope, frontispiece to Dr Meryon, *Memoir of Lady Hester Stanhope* (1845)
5. The Wailing Wall, Jerusalem, by William Simpson, 1869
6. Mount Tabor, from F. B. Spilsbury, *Picturesque Scenery*
7. The chapel of St Helena in the Church of the Holy Sepulchre, by David Roberts, 1839
8. The Khasne at Petra, by Lady Louisa Tenison, 1843
9. The Carmelite Convent on Mount Carmel, by A. Schranz, 1837

Artists in the Middle East

1. View from Alexandria Troas, from Sir William Gell, *The Topography of Troy* (1804)
2. A Graeco-Roman tomb in Asia Minor, by J. P. Gandy-Deering, c. 1812
3. Thomas Hope, by Sir William Beechey, 1798
4. Design for a chair, from Thomas Hope, *Household Furniture* (1807)
5. Design for an Egyptian room, from Hope's *Household Furniture*
6. Street scene in Cairo, by William Simpson, 1865
7. Francis Arundale, frontispiece to Arundale's *Illustrations of Jerusalem and Mount Sinai* (1837)
8. Sketches in pencil and watercolour, by David Roberts, 1833
9. Tomb of Al-Adel Tuman Bey in Old Cairo, by Owen Jones
10. Blind Arab with a teasel, by Egron Lundgren
11. A Halt in the Desert, by J. F. Lewis
12. The Silk Mart at Bursa, from J. F. Lewis, *Illustration of Constantinople*, (1837)
13. Street scene in Bab el-Luk, Cairo, by J. F. Lewis
14. Halaku Mirza, from Wilkie's *Oriental Sketches*
15. Study for 'Ecce Homo', from Wilkie's *Oriental Sketches*
16. Head of an Arab, by Frederick Lord Leighton
17. Bayazit on the slopes of Mount Ararat, by F. C. Lewis Jr.
18. The monastery of Mar Saba, by Hercules Brabazon

The Plaint of the Reed

1. The grand procession of the sacred camel, from the Rev. Cooper Willyam, *A Selection of Views in Egypt, Palestine, etc.* (1822)
2. Egyptian dancing girls, from E. W. Lane, *Manners and Customs of the Modern Egyptians* (1836)
3. The whirling dervishes, by an unknown artist
4. Persian musicians, from Morier's *Second Journey*
5. Gertrude Bell, water-colour by Flora Russell, 1887
6. A room in the house of the Mufti, Cairo, by Frank Dillon, c. 1860
7. The Sweet Waters of Asia, by William Purser

Foreword

'A quibble is to Shakespeare what luminous vapours are to the traveller; he follows it at all adventures; it is sure to lead him out of his way and sure to engulf him in the mire.' The Middle East has always offered plenty of scope to Dr Johnson's traveller and it is the luminous vapours I am often concerned with here, rather more than the subtleties of trade and the niceties of diplomacy.

This is a study of the British who lived in or were associated with the Middle East between the middle of the sixteenth century and the outbreak of World War I. British involvement in the area over the last four hundred years has been a mixture of hard-headed realism on the one hand – whether related to trade or to politics – and a pursuit of luminous vapours on the other. Dr Johnson is polite neither to Shakespeare and his quibble nor to the traveller and the same intolerant cynicism is detectable in many accounts of the Middle East of whatever date. It is more rewarding to study the development of understanding of the area, with all its ramifications, all its red herrings; it is the traveller who is prepared to engulf himself in the mire, to be led out of his way who will enlighten us most, the man who makes an organ for a terrifying sultan, the woman who brings back to England the Turkish secret of small-pox innoculation, the man wandering for no very explicit reason in Arabia – who give depth and perspective to that understanding. The element of fantasy that often adds luminosity to the vapour is encouraged even today by the vast increase in the wealth of Middle Eastern oil states: crime and detective fiction flourish in a Middle Eastern setting and there is a ready market for the more highly-coloured non-fiction, almost in the tradition of Sir John Mandeville's *Travels*. But an important part of the tradition of British involvement has been the penetration of the vapour, the revelation of cultures and civilisations hitherto virtually unknown, for which there has always been an equally avid public.

I have tried to steer as clear of politics as possible except in so far as they are needed to provide a setting for describing individuals. There is already abundant material on the politics of the period and the area. In the nineteenth century Britain was interested politically in the Middle East mainly as a vital link in Anglo-Indian communications; imperial considerations shaped the British political view of the Middle East and men trained in the imperial arena of India were often responsible for the practical application of British involvement – Persian telegraph, Egyptian irrigation, Jerusalem sewage and so on. The tendency to regard the Middle East, or certain parts of it, as having belonged to the British Empire is not surprising therefore, however mistaken: only Aden and its hinterland were ever part of the Empire. To counter the imperial view I have emphasised in this book the individual rather than the national character of the enterprises which brought the British to the area, and the follower of luminous vapours at the expense of the more practically employed. It seems to me that less credit has been given to the former's discovery of the Middle East although it has contributed as much as other expert views to our modern comprehension of the area and of the layer upon layer of diverse cultures which have been unearthed over the last two hundred years.

The book is divided into two parts for convenience rather than accuracy; the change in politics and attitudes regarding trade, antiquities and so on between the eighteenth and nineteenth centuries was more gradual than will appear here, although Napoleon's Egyptian expedition of 1798 acted as a catalyst for many existing trends.

The transliteration of place and personal names from Arabic, Persian and Turkish is always a sore topic with anyone writing about the Middle East; I have tried to use the established spelling for all the better known names and for lesser known ones have followed the transliteration most generally accepted today. Iran is referred to throughout as Persia since the older name was not revived until 1935. Syria is usually used to include Lebanon and Jordan except where specifically stated and Palestine for the area now occupied by Israel.

There are many people I should like to thank for their help on various subjects about which they know so much more than I do but I am particularly grateful to Mr Robin Fedden, Miss Mary Rowlatt, Mr John Marlowe and Mr Maurice Lush for valuable information, to my husband for help over Arabic and to my father as a bountiful source of illustrations. I also thank the library staffs of the School of Oriental and African Studies, the British Museum, the Public Records Office and the India Office.

Part One

1 The Middle East: Ottomans and Safavids

The term 'Middle East' was originally coined at the beginning of this century to refer to the coastal areas of the Persian Gulf, that strategic region between the Near East and India which was so vital to British communications. It is now used to cover a far wider area including the whole of south-west Asia and Egypt. In this book it does not include Afghanistan or North Africa west of Egypt. For the period of this book it was divided between the Ottoman Empire and Persia; today it consists of Turkey, Syria, Lebanon, Palestine/Israel, Jordan, Egypt, the countries of the Arabian peninsular, Iraq and Iran. The imposition of national boundaries after World War I has paradoxically given a more homogeneous appearance to the area than actually exists. The nineteenth century traveller in much of the Middle East was all too aware of the conflicting rivalries between such racial groups as Kurd, Armenian, Qashkai, Greek and Druze to name but a few; between societies such as settled and nomadic peoples, indeed between different nomadic tribes whose territories still cross international boundaries; and between different Muslim sects.

The north and east – Anatolia and Persia – is a mountainous plateau. There are few rivers in this region and the climate is harsh, varying from torrid heat in summer to extreme cold in winter. Vegetation is sparse except in certain areas such as the lush, semi-tropical southern shore of the Caspian Sea and the eastern shore of the Black Sea. Much of the plateau is semi-desert and the centres of population have tended to be either round the coast, as in Turkey, or in oases watered by springs or by streams of melted snow from the mountains.

The most productive area in the Middle East is the Fertile Crescent, a name coined by desert Arabs and dating from the earliest Islamic invasions. It describes the great river valley of the Tigris and Euphrates in Iraq, the foothills of the Turkish mountains skirting the Syrian Desert and Syria. It is the richest agricultural region in the Middle East and – for the period of this book – the most populous. The valley of the Tigris and Euphrates is in fact less reliably fertile than the Nile Valley; the flood is not so regular as that of the Nile and, because of the unremitting flatness of the land on either side of the rivers, the regulation of the flood has always depended on an efficiently run canal system. At the height of Abbasid power, during the eighth and ninth centuries, Mesopotamia (as the lower river valley was called) was indeed fertile: the route of the great Nahrawan Canal and its dependent system can still be seen today as one flies over the Abbasid capital of Samarra to the north of Baghdad. But under the anarchy which persisted intermittently throughout the Ottoman period the canals fell into disuse and the wealth of Mesopotamia evaporated.

Syria consists of a rich Mediterranean coastal plain, a range of mountains running from north to south and a narrow valley which follows the Orontes and Litani rivers to Lake Tiberias (the Sea of Galilee) and the Jordan River to the Dead Sea and the Gulf of Aqaba beyond. A range of hills cuts off the valley from the expanse of the Syrian Desert. The climate of Syria is the most moderate in the Middle East; the fact that it is a land of plenty has always attracted outsiders – political or commercial – to its welcoming valleys and villages.

The third area, Arabia, is a low desert plateau running southwards from the Syrian Desert. The Syrian Desert is less inhospitable than the Arabian; many tribes take their flocks there in the summer and for centuries nomad tribes, such as the Shammar and the Anaizah, have migrated there from Arabia when their grazing failed. In Arabia there are few settled areas except along the coasts. Yemen in the south-west has been called Arabia Felix, the richest agricultural area of a peninsula which otherwise varies only from semi-desert to waterless, plantless expanse.

The thin strip of green in a waste of brown desert is a familiar image of the Nile valley. The delta of Lower Egypt is densely populated and cultivated, although by the sixteenth century it had declined in population and productivity since its heyday as one of the so-called granaries of Rome. Upper Egypt – as the country south of Cairo is called – is indeed a strip of green, wider now because of its elaborate system of dams than it used to be but, until the completion of the Aswan High Dam, still dependent on the annual flood to revive its strength.

Until very recently it would have been easy to use the present tense in such a brief description of the Middle East. Time had little effect on the meagrely self-sufficient existence of the peasantry and nomads of these areas; most families subsisted for generations as small-scale agriculturalists or nomadic pasturalists. Little had changed since the days of the early travellers and even now it will be some time before the dramatic rise in oil income affects the extremes of poverty and wealth, the contrast of green oases and river valleys with stark mountain ridges and harsh desert. The political instability of a racially and geographically diverse region remains much the same today as four hundred years ago when the first Englishmen came to live there.

The Ottoman Turks were one of many Turkish tribes displaced from their homeland in the steppes of Turkestan by the Mongol invasions of the thirteenth century. They eventually settled in Anatolia and under a succession of able warrior rulers gradually acquired the hegemony of the area, Anatolia, expanding later by conquest into Rumelia (the lands of the Rumi or Greeks) including the Balkans and much of the north coast of the Black Sea. Interrupted by the invasions and conquests of Timur Lang (Tamurlane) at the end of the fourteenth century, the Ottomans soon recovered after his death. In 1453 they captured Constantinople, a major disaster in the eyes of European rulers of the time, but in fact of little strategic importance since the city had been an island within Ottoman territory for several years. The Black Sea became an Ottoman lake, Anatolia an Ottoman stronghold.

By the sixteenth century the Ottoman sultanate confronted that of the Mamluks based on Cairo, across the southern foothills of Anatolia. The Mamluk dynasty was descended from Circassian slaves; it included Egypt and Syria in its empire and exercised suzerainty over the Hijaz. Territorial rivalry with the Ottomans led to conflict in which the Mamluks were defeated first in Syria in 1516 and the following years decisively outside Cairo. The Hijaz offered its allegiance to the Turks and the Ottoman conqueror of the Mamluks, Selim I (the Grim), carried back to Constantinople the sacred sword and cloak of Muhammad. Selim also conquered the north of Iraq, including Mosul, but it was left to his great successor, Suleyman the Magnificent, to wrest it wholly from the hands of the Safavid rulers of Persia.

Recent historians have conveniently divided the Ottoman state into two spheres: the Ruling Institution and the Learned Institution. The Ruling Institution, 'the military-political elite',* was based on the warrior society of the early Ottomans, elaborated by the later addition of converted slaves or conscripted troops and officials. It was concerned with the civil and military administration of the state – the Sultan's household and bodyguard and his state officials and troops. A system known as *devshirme* (recruitment) was devised for the recruitment of Balkan slaves into the Sultan's service, at

* P. M. Holt, *Egypt and the Fertile Crescent*, p. 29.

1. The Sultans Selim I, 'the Grim' (1512–20) (left), and Suleyman I the 'Magnificent' (1520–66) (right). These sultans established the territorial power of the Ottoman Empire in the sixteenth century. Engraving from Richard Knolles, *A General History of the Turks* (1603)

the head of which was the grand vezir, second only to the Sultan; and dependent only on him for his authority. The power of the grand vezir was so all-embracing that the gateway to his palace in Constantinople became known as the Bab al-Aali, the Sublime Porte, from the eighteenth century synonymous to Europeans with the Ottoman government. The Learned Institution was composed of the *ulama* – the lawyers and theologians of a Muslim state – with the *mufti* of Constantinople, known as the *shaikh al-Islam*, at its head. Throughout the empire the *ulama*, in the person of the *qadi* (judge) of each town, administered the *sharia*, the sacred law of Islam as prescribed in the *Quran* and certain other early Islamic writings. The *sharia* was supplemented by *qanun* (law), issued by the Sultan only, which dealt with precedents not covered by the *sharia*. Janissaries, recruited under the *devshirme* system, were also garrisoned in every main town and became increasingly assimilated into the local population.

The Arab provinces of the Empire preserved a certain autonomy under governors appointed by the Sultan. Mount Lebanon, Kurdistan and the desert areas of Syria and Arabia were ruled by

local feudal leaders, such as the Maanids and Shihabs in Lebanon, in the desert Ottoman suzerainty was very lightly felt, being confined to fringe towns – Aleppo, Bir and Baghdad round the Syrian desert and Jiddah, Sanaa, Mokha and Aden in Arabia – and the protection of the pilgrimage route to Mecca. Baghdad and Basra, important as part of the frontier against Safavid power, were repeatedly attacked and harassed by Arab tribes to the south and west; this the Ottoman authorities could check but never eradicate.

Egypt was even less integrated into the Empire than the Syrian provinces. The Sultan appointed a viceroy but the failure of the Ottoman authorities to control sea communications with Egypt meant that their rule in Egypt was regularly challenged, either by the permanent garrison of Janissaries, or by the Egyptian *beys*, many of them of Mamluk origin, who were the dominant power in Egypt until the nineteenth century.

Although the Arab provinces were left much to themselves, initiative was discouraged, taxation heavy and by the eighteenth century the financial burden of corruption often intolerable. There were frequent periods of anarchy, leading to a gradual impoverishment from which the area has yet to recover. While Constantinople today presents an image of a once rich, luxury-loving, thriving capital, other towns formerly in the Ottoman Empire have little to show in the way of grand buildings from the sixteenth century onwards. European travellers frequently commented on the decay evident in the towns and countryside.

The Ottoman dynasty reached its zenith in Suleyman the Magnificent and the seeds of decline were already discernible at the time of his death in 1566. A vast over-centralised bureaucracy, financed by bribes, was based on Constantinople. By the seventeenth century the problem of peaceful succession was aggravated by the heir – the eldest male relative – having to spend all his life until his accession immured in one of the *qafas* (cages or kiosks) in the gardens of the Serail, to remove the threat of sedition. The Janissaries became a constant threat to authority throughout the Empire; their organisation, privileges and right to carry arms made them a dangerous rival to the civil authorities. Between the middle of the sixteenth and the end of the eighteenth centuries six sultans either abdicated or were deposed, usually by the Janissaries, and in the provincial cities their restlessness often led to rioting and disturbances. 'The deposeinge and placinge great rulers [and] the contention of the soldiers many times' was noted as early as 1592 by a Levant merchant.

Suleyman himself, the last of a remarkable series of Ottoman rulers, was the first Sultan to betray his warrior background for that of an oriental despot. Delusions of grandeur set in with his conquest of Iraq. Successive victories and the acquisition of new territories deceived the rulers of the Empire into believing that their wealth was continually growing. Their way of life became ever more luxurious and remote from the people. Moreover the seventeenth century was a period of general inflation throughout Europe, caused by the influx of precious metals from America. In Turkey as elsewhere this led to regular debasements of the coinage, and the situation was aggravated by imports of debased coins from Europe – a chronic source of worry to the over-honest servants of the Levant Company. The first part of this book is concerned with the period when this stagnation and deterioration was particularly evident.

The Safavid dynasty which ruled Persia for some two hundred and fifty years – from the end of the fifteenth century until the Afghan invasions and the defeat of the Safavid Shah Sultan Husain in 1722 – rose to ascendancy on the basis of the Shia sect of Islam. The founder of the dynasty, Ismail, who asserted his rule of Persia after he defeated the Turkish Ak-Kuyunlu dynasty in 1499, claimed descent from Ali, Muhammad's son-in-law, as well as from a celebrated mystic of the fourteenth century, Shaikh Safi al-Din, eponym of the Safavid dynasty. Ismail was able to unite the dissident Shia tribesmen of Persia as previous dynasties had not: by such measures as granting land to tribal chiefs converted to Shia Islam (thereby laying the foundations of a feudal society) and organising the military units (known as the Qizilbash because of their red hats), he managed to integrate the tribes into a new Persian state and to quell their chronic restlessness.

The success of the Safavids in uniting Persia soon attracted the attention of the Ottomans who became increasingly worried about the effect that the nationalist religion of the new state would have on the turbulent mountain tribes of eastern Anatolia. Defeated by the Turks in 1514, the Persians sought help from Europe, which was also being menaced by the Ottomans. Anthony Jenkinson, probably the first Englishman to visit Persia, arrived in 1561 just as the Safavid Shah Tahmasp was making peace with the Turks. During Tahmasp's reign Safavid control over the country was relaxed and Shah Abbas, who succeeded in 1587, found Persia invaded and the spiritual authority of the Shah undermined by the feebleness and debaucheries of his predecessors. He recaptured Baghdad from the Turks, as well as the highly prized Shia shrines at Najaf and Karbala in Iraq, and broke the growing power of the feudal military leaders by reorganizing his army (reportedly with the help of Anthony and Robert Sherley) supplementing feudal levies with mercenary troops.

The administration of the Safavid state – from the capital in Qazvin and later in Isfahan – bore many resemblances to that of its Ottoman neighbour. An absolute ruler governed the country through an intricate bureaucracy in which functions often overlapped to prevent any one official becoming too powerful. The *itimad al-daula*, similar to the Turkish grand vezir, was the principal minister and chief adviser to the Shah; he presided over a council of state and was responsible for foreign and military affairs, finance and certain aspects of provincial administration. Working under him were four military leaders, originally the heads of various sections of the army to whom other duties had later been entrusted. Civil departments were headed by various household appointments which by the seventeenth century had become the chief instruments of a national administration. As in the Ottoman Empire the law was administered by religious leaders in each town and district supplemented by decrees from the Shah.

Isfahan poets used to say that when King Solomon died, his body was propped up on his wooden staff so that the king could continue to oversee the completion of the temple in Jerusalem; but woodworm eventually ate through the staff and the decaying king fell to the ground. It is a sad anecdote, illustrative perhaps of the Safavid dynasty during the second quarter of the seventeenth century. In 1629 Abbas the Great died, but the effects of his death were staved off for several years, though the roots of the Safavid decline were already spreading through the country while he was alive. Like the Ottoman sultans the shahs who succeeded Abbas segregated themselves from the people by a costly paraphernalia of luxury and ritual. The Safavids never really secured Persia's frontiers in spite of their appeal through a national religion, and their Shia proselytisation alienated Sunni border tribes such as the Afghan Ghalzais and Abdalis and the Uzbeqs in the north-east. The original enrolling of the Qizilbash only ensured the allegiance of certain tribes and even their allegiance was weakened by the decreasing authority of the Shah; other tribes remained semi-independent, discontented and powerful, their allegiance to the Shah dependent on the dubious loyalty of local governors who themselves were often tempted to usurp the Shah's authority.

The later shahs of the Safavid dynasty maintained the splendour of the court of Abbas without being interested in the country over which they ruled and on which they depended for their luxuries. The recapture of Baghdad by the Turks in 1638 – attributed by some to the fact that the Shah had executed his ablest military leaders – was followed a year later by an uneasy peace with Turkey which nevertheless still called for the maintenance of a large, increasingly expensive and undisciplined, standing army. Sir John Chardin, a French Huguenot who was in Persia during the reign of Shah Sultan Husain at the beginning of the eighteenth century, complained of the difference between the Persia of Abbas the Great and that of Husain: 'the long peace enjoyed by [Persia] and the bloodthirsty administration of his predecessors have defeated their courage. Luxury, Sensuality, Licentiousness on the one hand, Scholasticism and Literature on the other, have made the Persians effeminate.' There speaks the mercantile mind: for others the art of the Safavids is one of their saving graces. This late flowering of the Persian artistic genius is one of its finest – the exquisite miniatures, the perfection of the rugs in the shrines at Qum and Ardabil, the ceramics, the architecture – these are some compensation for the lust and cruelty recorded by European visitors. Even Chardin allowed that they were 'the most civilised people of the East'.

The inroads of Russians in the north-west, Uzbeqs in the north-east and Afghans in the east, completely undermined the shallow security of the state which ultimately collapsed before the Afghans at the Battle of Gulnabad outside Isfahan in 1722. The Afghan conquest unleashed the anarchy to which so many of the frontier areas of Persia had already been reduced, but the inability of the Afghans to replace the Safavids with anything like a national administration accounts for their relatively easy defeats by Nadir Quli Khan, later

Nadir Shah, in 1729 and 1730. Nadir Quli Khan, a tribal leader from Khurasan, has been described as the last great Asiatic warrior.* He 'accepted' the throne in 1736 after denouncing Shah Tahmasp, last of the Safavids, for making peace with the Turks. He declared Sunni the official religion and made Meshed in the north-east his capital. The country was temporarily subdued at an appalling cost in lives: it was common to see pyramids of human heads outside main towns that Nadir Shah had passed through. Various claimants seized the throne after his assassination in 1747, the most notable of whom was Karim Khan, founder of the short-lived Zand dynasty which shone brilliantly for a few years from its capital in Shiraz. But not until the accession of Aga Muhammad Khan, leader of the Qajar tribe from the south-west corner of the Caspian Sea, did Persia once again become a united country.

Whether under Ottoman or Safavid rule, life was much the same in Cairo, Constantinople or Aleppo, Qazvin, Isfahan or Shiraz. In the countryside, whether in Turkey or Persia, Syria or Egypt, the life of the peasant was dictated by the seasons, his livelihood dependent on his own produce. Interregional trade was limited by the poverty of the population, the heavy import-export dues and the neglect of communications, although much of the Middle East was the great highway for the passage of goods from the Far East to Europe. Throughout the Middle East towns were divided into exclusive quarters for different races and religions, among them Jewish, Armenian and Greek. In Isfahan, for instance, a large wealthy Armenian community lived in Julfa on the other side of the river from the main town. In Smyrna today it is still possible to see the Jewish quarter inhabited by descendants of the Spanish Jews who escaped from the Inquisition in the fifteenth and sixteenth centuries. Each craft also had its own quarter and in most oriental towns today members of the same occupation are usually grouped together along one or more streets. No European lived outside the towns much before the nineteenth century and within a town he was for the most part confined to the European quarter.

The largest towns were Constantinople, Aleppo, Cairo and Isfahan, each of them of a size and splendour to rival, if not surpass, any European town of the same period. Persia, as a whole, acquired more notable buildings than the Ottoman Empire, due

---

* P. M. Sykes, *History of Persia*, vol. 11, p. 240. Nadir made a great impression on British visitors of the period, many of whom believed his earlier name, Tahmasp Quli Khan, to have been a corruption of Thomas O'Kelly, and this 'second Alexander' an Irishman by birth.

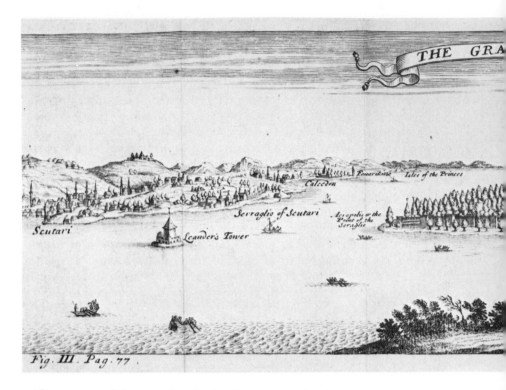

2. Panorama of Constantinople, looking across the Golden Horn to the
Sultan's palace and Santa Sophia. Engraving from Guillaume Joseph
Grelot, *A late voyage to Constantinople* (1683)

to the desire of the Safavids to glorify the shrines of their Shia saints,
at Meshed, Ardabil and Qum for instance, and to the changes of
capital during this period.

Constantinople and Isfahan are the most important architectural
examples of the period. Isfahan became the capital of Persia under
Abbas, and no other Persian ruler left such a monument to his
memory. It is considered by many to have been the most beautiful
city in the world in the middle of the seventeenth century. Its palaces
and mosques, gardens and bridges, fountains and squares dazzled
and fascinated generations of merchants and travellers from the more
familiar capitals of Europe. Isfahan lost its prestige after it was sacked
in 1722 by the Afghans but retained its beauty.

Constantinople was no less splendid than the Safavid capital. A
somewhat dilapidated prize in 1453 when the Turks captured it
from its impoverished Byzantine rulers, it soon regained its former
glory. The huge domed Byzantine churches became mosques; the
celebrated architect Sinan adapted Byzantine styles to build still

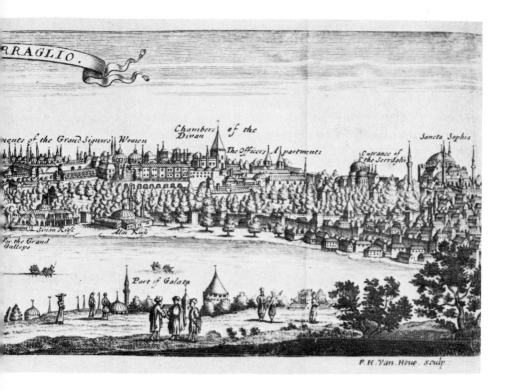

more mosques under the aegis of Suleyman the Magnificent; palaces crept out along the edge of the Bosphorus, while on the point of the Golden Horn the mysterious Serail in its ornamental gardens tantalised Europeans living in Pera on the other side of the channel.*

Both in Persia and the Ottoman Empire the other major towns are still easy to pick out as the main trade centres. In Persia there was Gilan, the centre of the silk industry, Qazvin, Tabriz, Kirman, Meshed and Shiraz. Further south along the Persian Gulf were Bushire, the East India Company's headquarters after they moved from Bandar Abbas (known to early merchants by its old name of Gombrun) and Ormuz, once known as the pearl of the Gulf and certainly its main emporium until the expulsion of the Portuguese from the island by a joint Anglo-Persian force in 1622. In the Ottoman Empire there was Cairo, with its forbidding mosques and

* The capital of the Ottoman Empire before the capture of Constantinople had been at Adrianople (Edirne) which the sultans continued to use as a summer camp and a base for expeditions into Europe. Although by no means as grand as Constantinople, it was sufficiently resplendent when filled with the Sultan's court to merit lengthy descriptions from visiting Europeans, in particular Lady Mary Wortley Montagu and Dr Covell.

bustling labyrinthine bazaars ('this Citye is so well peopled and frequented by reasons of its Commerce, that a Man can hardly pass the streets for Crowds of People,' wrote an English traveller, Veryard, in 1686); Damascus, fanatically Muslim, its desert character preserved by its hostility to infidels and scene of the annual gathering of Muslim pilgrims making the *hajj* to Mecca; Jerusalem, as sacred to Muslims as to Christians; Aleppo, the greatest market in Syria, where caravans from the east were met by merchants from Europe; Smyrna, one of the busiest ports in the eastern Mediterranean; Alexandria, with its prosperous Jewish and Christian quarters. Baghdad and Basra in Iraq were the starting points for caravans crossing the desert to Aleppo. Though few of these towns could boast buildings as magnificent as those of Constantinople and Isfahan, the wealthy classes built themselves elegant town houses

3. A Turkish wedding crossing the At Maidan, or Hippodrome, in Constantinople. This is an adaptation by William Hogarth of a number of drawings done on the spot by the Flemish artist J.-B. Vanmour, under the directions of the Frenchman Aubry de la Motraye. From Aubry de la Motraye, *Travels etc.* (1723–4)

whose sumptuous interiors – panelled and tiled, cooled by countless fountains and shaded by tinted glass – aroused the admiration of many a European merchant accustomed to the discomforts of contemporary houses in his own country.

The British who visited the Ottoman or Safavid Empires in the sixteenth or seventeenth centuries were justifiably afraid of the dreaded Turk, whose military exploits had sounded grimly in their ears for at least a hundred years before this book opens, and they were similarly wary of the Persians. Their fear was to some extent tempered by comparing the oriental despotism of Middle Eastern rulers with the politics of Renaissance Europe; to British travellers of the early seventeenth century, fear of the Spanish Inquisition was as great as capture by Barbary pirates and almost certain slavery. The organisation of the Ottoman or Safavid state was little more intolerant than that of Britain. Travellers by land in Britain ran the same risks as in the Middle East: plague and robbery were commonplace in both areas, roads were uncomfortable everywhere and eastern khans were hardly less comfortable than the average roadside inn in remote parts of Britain. In the towns where British merchants set up their factories European quarters were protected from the populace by gates and guards and their occupants managed to live isolated from much of the turbulence of the period as well as from its culture and achievements.

By the eighteenth century the luxury, ritual and grandiloquence of the Ottoman and Persian courts which had evoked such wide-mouthed admiration among the first British merchants to visit them were coming to be regarded with contempt by their successors. The anarchy into which so many Ottoman and Persian provinces now relapsed discouraged contact at a time when the gulf between the conservative despotism of the Middle East and the rational enquiring mind of Europe could still have been bridged.

2 The Lord of the Golden Horn

English relations with the Middle East until the mid-eighteenth century were mostly commercial. Trade with the Levant was by no means new to English merchants when the Levant company was founded in 1581. The first recorded English voyage to the Levant was in 1458, and the great historian of sixteenth-century travel, Richard Hakluyt, tells of 'divers tall ships' which 'had an ordinary and usuall trade to Sicilia, Cyprus, Chio and somewhiles to Crete, as also to Tripoli and Barutti in Syria' in 1511 and 1512, carrying cotton and woollen manufactures. They returned with an assortment of 'silks, chamlets, rubabe, malmesies, muskadels and other wines, sweet oyles, cotton woole, Turkie carpets, galles, pepper, cinnamon and some other spices'. Direct trade between England and the Levant lapsed in the 1560s and 1570s mainly because the war in the eastern Mediterranean between the Turks and Venice made most of that area unsafe to European shipping, but English goods still reached the Levant via Italy. In 1553 Anthony Jenkinson was given permission by the Sultan to trade throughout his dominions, but there is no evidence that he actually made use of the permission. The dangers of the trade demanded more capital and more protection than a single merchant could provide.

In the latter half of the century English access to the spices which were so much a necessity of life was threatened by Spanish annexation of Portugal and commercial quarrels with the Netherlands. By 1575, when an Englishman was first sent to Constantinople to investigate trading directly with the Ottomans, the fact that the French and Venetians were already established in the Levant proved to the hard-headed businessmen of London that trade with the dreaded Turk was not such a risk after all. The military success and legendary wealth of the Turks was bound sooner or later to attract the attention of merchants anxious to market their growing supplies of cloth.

In 1575 Joseph Clements was sent by two English merchants, Edward Osborne and Richard Staper, to Sultan Murad III. Queen Elizabeth is thought to have given her support to the venture in the hopes of obtaining the Sultan's alliance against Spain. Eighteen months after his arrival in Constantinople, Clements obtained a safe conduct for William Harborne to go to the Ottoman dominions. In 1580, after two years in Constantinople, Harborne won from the Sultan – in the face of strong French opposition – a grant of Capitulations governing relations between Turks and English trading in the Ottoman Empire, based on those granted to the French in 1535. These grants protected the foreigner from molestation of his person and goods and from imprisonment by the Turks; they exempted him from payment of taxes except 'our lawful toll and custom' on goods imported; and they allowed the appointment of consuls and other officials to govern the merchants, their trade and their relations with the Ottoman authorities. They were free to practise their own religion, to leave the country as and when they liked and to adjudicate in quarrels between their own nations (this, in the nineteenth century, became one of the major abuses of the Capitulations system, particularly in Egypt).

To begin with, Capitulations were renewed by each sultan on his accession, but this practice ceased after 1675, much to the relief of the ambassadors and companies concerned, who could ill afford the lavish presents and presentation ceremonies which became part of the ritual of renewal. The terms remained substantially the same throughout the life of the Levant Company. Although in theory they gave foreign merchants the maximum protection, in practice the authority of the Sultan, on which effective execution depended, was already declining and merchants found themselves dependent instead on the more temperamental authority of local governors and their officials.

In 1581 Queen Elizabeth granted Osborne, Staper and ten colleagues a seven-year monopoly in the Levant trade, thus establishing the Levant Company, otherwise known as the Turkey merchants. William Harborne was appointed the Company's agent in Constantinople and was given extra status by appointment as the Queen's 'messenger, deputie and agent' to the Ottoman court. In 1592 Elizabeth renewed the monopoly for twelve years in the form of a charter to the 'Governor and Company of Merchants of the Levant' with fifty-three members. The Levant monopoly now covered not only the lands of the Grand Signor, as the Sultan was called, but also those of 'Venice, including Zante, Cephalonia and Candia'.

Most of England's overseas trade at this period was conducted corporately: merchants trading overseas were obliged by political factors and hardships to be responsible for functions usually belonging to the state – appointing ambassadors to placate foreign potentates with presents, maintaining embassies, protecting themselves

against local and European piracy. At home, by operating as one
unit, they were often able to stand up to state interference in their
affairs. There were six new trading companies by the end of the
sixteenth century, compared with two in the earlier half of the
century. Each company dealt with a single area and merchants
could only trade with more than one area by belonging to more
than one company. The regulated company, of which the Levant
Company was an example, was a looser association than joint-stock
companies such as the East India Company, and each member
transacted his business through his own factors or agents.

Elizabethan merchants were governed mainly by self-interest, but
they firmly believed – and persuaded most of their contemporaries
to believe – that commerce was the best means to promote the
welfare of the community. 'Wherever the traders thrive the public
of which they are a part thrives also', wrote Dudley North, a Levant
merchant. The vital importance attached by the Elizabethans and
their successors to overseas trade as the life-blood of the nation gave
prestige and power to the merchant adventurers. Many were knighted
or became governors of one or more of the chartered trading companies, financial advisers to the Crown, large property owners or
lord mayors. Merchants such as Edward Osborne (one of the founders
of the Levant Company), Thomas Glover and Thomas Roe passed
through the gamut of civil life. 'Trade is now become the Lady,
which in this present Age is more courted and celebrated than in
any former', commented Roger Coke, a remark as true today as in
the seventeenth century.

International trade in the seventeenth century and even in the
eighteenth, was mainly in luxuries. Major exports to the Levant
were woollen and cotton cloths and by the end of the seventeenth
century the Turkey merchants were exporting to the Levant an
average of twenty thousand broadcloths a year. The Lancashire
cotton industry was said to have been founded on the Levant trade;
the Manchester cloth manufacturers 'buy cotton wool in London,
that comes first from Cyprus and Smyrna, and at home work such
stuffes, and then return it to London, where the same is vented and
sold into foreign parts, who have means at far easier terms, to provide themselves with the said first materials,' wrote Lewis Roberts,
a member of the Levant Company, in 1641. Fynes Moryson in
Tripoli in 1596 was offered a bed for the first time for months and
could hardly wait for supper he was so anxious to make full use of
this luxury: 'but after supper all this joy vanished by an event least
expected,' he recalled in his *Itinery*, 'for in this part of Asia great
store of cotton growes upon stalks like Cabbages . . . and these sheetes
being made thereof did so increase the perpetuall heat of this Coun-

trey, now most unsupportable ... as I was forced to leape out of bed and sleepe as I had formerly done' – on the floor.

Other exports were tin, spices and lead. George Sandys, a gentleman traveller who visited the Middle East in 1609, wrote of tin exports as being 'the most profitable, here exceedingly used and exceedingly wasted for they tinne the insides of their vessels and monethly renew it', a practice still common today. The spice trade became the salvation of the Levant Company in spite of gloomy forebodings to the contrary. William Aldrych, a real Job's comforter, wrote to the Company in 1599 on hearing of the arrival in Europe of Dutch ships laden with oriental spices coming by way of the Cape, that 'this tradynge to that Endyes have clean overthroughen our dealings to Aleppo as by experience ere longe we shall see'. In fact Aleppo maintained its position as 'the chief mart of all the East' partly because the Levant Company found it could buy spices from East India merchants in London, re-export them to the Middle East and sell them on the Aleppo market for less than produce coming overland.

In return the Turkey merchants brought back to England raw cotton and silk, currants, dyes, wines, brass and silverware – similar commodities to those mentioned earlier by Hakluyt. Most of these were paid for by exports, except for the currants from Zante where the market for English goods was limited; purchases there, and elsewhere when necessary, were usually paid for with Spanish dollars or pieces of eight, picked up from Lisbon or Cadiz in exchange for English goods. The Levant trade was always more popular with contemporary English economists than the East India trade because it seldom involved large-scale exports of bullion.

The main Levant Company factory was at Constantinople, home of the ambassador, who was responsible for relations with the Sultan and his officials. The significance of the Ottoman Empire in European politics inevitably involved the ambassador in diplomacy to some degree and it was only a matter of time before the Crown, under Charles I, took over the appointment. The Company still paid the ambassador, but they were loth to meet expenses incurred solely in state affairs; and if this included calling on the Sultan the sum could be astronomical. As a royal emissary the ambassador was obliged to live in more state than he would as the Company's representative. The first ambassador, William Harborne, lived down by the docks in Galata, but his successor, Edward Barton, moved up the hill to Pera, to a 'faire house within a large field and pleasant gardens compassed with a wall' – cooler and healthier and also more expensive. Much to its dislike the Company was responsible for maintaining the house and several ambassadors complained of its preference for frugal repairs to the thought of buying another. One inhabitant of the embassy, however, was quite satisfied with her accommodation: Lady Mary Wortley Montagu in 1717 went into rhapsodies about the embassy, in particular the view from her window which she described as the 'most beautiful in the world'. 'The unequal heights make it seem as large again as it is (though one of the largest cities in the world), showing an agreeable mixture of gardens, pines and cypress-trees, palaces, mosques and public buildings, raised one above another, with as much beauty and appearance of symmetry as your Ladyship [the Countess of Bristol] ever saw in a cabinet adorned by the most skilful hands.'

Barton shared his hill-top residence with John Sanderson, one of the few factors who has, through his letters and autobiography, left a picture of the early days of the Levant Company. Sanderson was typical of those truculent factors the ambassador so often had to deal with: Barton later accused him of having a 'cancar'd mind' and certainly Sanderson's abusive remarks justify this conclusion. He accused Barton of loose living and drunkenness, but this was complimentary compared to his remarks about poor Sir Henry Lello, ambassador when Sanderson was the factory's treasurer and the chief target for his scorn. In a letter home the factor described Lello calling on the sultan: he 'sat upon his horse with a ruddie downe looke as though he had been streyninge at a close-stoole; and when he came before the Grand Signor he stood with his hands handsomalie before him like a modest midwife and began a tremblinge speech in Inglishe, as you know, soundinge like the squeking of a goose divided into semiquavers.' Lello was not the only foreign representative to be reduced to quaking before the Ottoman ruler.

Lello's successor, Sir Thomas Glover, made full use of the embassy grounds as a haven for escaped Christian prisoners and slaves, whom he spent much of his time trying to persuade the Sultan to release. 'That red boar of an English ambassador', as a Turkish official described him, was one of the first ambassadors to learn the Turkish language, laws and customs.

After the middle of the seventeenth century the ambassadors nominated by the Crown were seldom merchants by profession, though none were adverse to making often substantial fortunes out of the Levant trade during their period of office. This indeed was recognised as part, or most, of the ambassador's salary, much to the annoyance of those ambassadors whose share of the trade was diminished by war or foreign competition. During the eighteenth century diplomatic duties came more and more to take precedence over commercial duties; Edward Wortley Montagu, for instance, was wholly preoccupied with diplomatic negotiations during his embassy from 1717 to 1718. In the last years of the Company's existence the Crown took over the payment as well as the appointment of the ambassador.

'When the Sultan entertaineth Embassadours, he sitteth in a roome of white Marble, glittring with gold and stones, upon a low throne, spred with curious carpets...', wrote Sanderson, 'It is now a custome that none doe come to his presence without presents.' Normally Europeans were not allowed to satisfy their curiosity about the Serail beyond the second court, and travellers to Constantinople would try to attach themselves to the ambassador's retinue on one of his expensive visits. After the interview, 'they go backward from him and never put off their hats; the showing of the head being held by the Turk to be an opprobrius indecency'. The time was yet to come when Europeans would deliberately sweep off their hats before a sultan.

When Henry Lello was to be confirmed as ambassador in 1599, the Company made a particular effort to present gifts worthy of the special pleas they had to make to the Sultan. The Sultana received a coach worth six hundred pounds, complete with coachman. But the most resplendent present – quite surpassing the French and Venetian efforts – was a unique clockwork organ, presented to the Sultan on behalf of the Company by its maker, Thomas Dallam, who later described his stay in Constantinople. He was sternly lectured by the ambassador on the seriousness of his task, in particular that the organ should perform perfectly lest the Company should lose all its privileges. At the presentation ceremony Dallam was kept in an ante-room; miraculously, as soon as the Sultan arrived in front of the organ its performance began: 'firste the clocke 22, then the chime of 16 bels went off, and played a songe of four partes. That beinge done, two personages which stood upon two corners of the second storie, holdinge silver trumpetes in their handes, did lift them to their heades, and sounded a tantarra. Then the musicke went offe and the organ played a songe of five partes twice over. In the top of the organ, being 16 foote hie, did stand a holly bushe full of blacke birds and thrushis, which at the end of the musicke did singe and shake their wynges.'

The Sultan was very excited by the instrument and asked if there was anyone in Constantinople who could play it. Immediately the grand vezir opened the door of the ante-room and produced poor Dallam before the Sultan and his assembled court – 'the sight whereof did make me almoste to thinke I was in another worlde', for there were more than four hundred of them, so splendidly dressed in gold and jewels that he would have fled if he could. At first he refused to

1. Thomas Dallam's organ, presented by him to Sultan Mehmed III on behalf of the Levant Company in 1599. Reconstruction drawn for *The Illustrated London News*

play, even for the Sultan: it would mean turning his back on the Grand Signor, which he had been warned could result in instant decapitation, if not worse. He yielded, however, at the Sultan's insistence, but remembered as he did so at least not to remove his cap. The Sultan was sitting so close to Dallam while he played that every time he moved the terrified organist 'thoughte he had been drawinge his sorde to cut of my heade'. Delighted with the organ and its maker the Sultan tried to persuade Dallam to stay, offering him two concubines, even two virgins, as an inducement. But Dallam refused and returned to England to design more organs, including that of King's College, Cambridge.

Dr Covell, a learned and verbose authority on the Greek Church, a collector of Turkish songs and music, amateur botanist and chaplain to the embassy from 1670 to 1677, gave an idea of the expense involved in the renewal of Capitulations in his description of the ambassador, Sir John Finch's visit to the Sultan at Adrianople for this purpose. An immense train of attendants* on bejewelled horses escorted Finch from Constantinople to Adrianople where the Sultan had gone for the summer. In Adrianople there was a round of visits at each of which, writes Covell, 'from the Grand Signior himself to the Kaimacham [mayor] of Stamboul, we give presents, viz. vests of cloth, silk, cloth of gold, silver, velvet, etc., and in most places we receive vests from them' – Covell later sold his for six and a half dollars. After a lavish meal with the vezir and his officials the ambassador was taken to his audience with the Sultan – the jewels inlaid in the furniture of the audience chamber and stitched to the Sultan's clothes convinced Finch that 'it was the richest room for certain in the whole world'. After four months in Adrianople the Sultan renewed the Capitulations and Sir John could return, considerably poorer, to the capital.

Even in the eighteenth century when Europeans were less in awe of the Sultan, a new ambassador, Abraham Stanyan, calling on the grand vezir for the first time, wrote that 'the retinue and pomp with which I am bound to appear in Turkish camps are greater and more expensive than I have ever known used by ambassadors in other courts'. Ambassadors, whatever their nationality, were expected to parade with as much pomp as if they were in fact the monarchs whom they were merely representing.

Constantinople was indeed a resplendent city for the Turkey merchants to find themselves in, especially in comparison with most

---

* Except for factors and Company officials these would have been Christians of Constantinople, such as Greeks and Armenians, as the embassy was not at this stage allowed to employ Muslims.

European cities of the period. Sandys was overjoyed at the sight as he arrived by boat, sailing up the Bosphorus from the Sea of Marmora early in the morning. 'Than this there is hardly in nature a more delicate object,' he recalled, 'if beheld from the sea or adjoyning mountains; the loftie and beautiful cypresse trees so intermixed with the buildings that it seems to present a citie in a wood to the pleased beholder'. He went on to describe this city, 'whose seven aspiring heads (for on so many hills and no more they say it is seated) are most of them crowned with magnificent Mosques, all of white Marble, being finished on the top with gilded spires that reflect the beames they receive with marvellous splendour', among them Santa Sophia, surrounded by the tombs of sultans and their families and haunted by beggars, and that of Sultan Ahmad, the so-called Blue Mosque, 'most magnificent of any in Constantinople'.

The Serail was the magnet that attracted all strangers, with its 'very fine gardens of all sorts of flowers' (specimens of which were brought home by amateur botanists such as George Wheler and Dr Covell) which partially hid the kiosks described as 'rooms of fair prospect, or (as we term them) banqueting houses into which the king sometimes goes alone, but most commonly with his concubines for his recreation'. Here 'luxury was the steward and treasure inexhaustible'. Lady Mary Wortley Montagu described the Serail to the Countess of Bristol soon after her arrival – its buildings 'all of white stone, leaded on top, with gilded turrets and spires, which look very magnificent, and indeed I believe there is no Christian king's palace half so large'.

The great aqueduct of Constantine also attracted the marvelling attention of English visitors. Suleyman the Magnificent had lengthened it and thereby, Sanderson wrote, 'increased the current of water in so great abundance, as they doe serve seven hundred and forty fountaines for the publique, not reckoning those which are drawne into diverse parts to furnish the great number of Baths which serve for delights'.

Most of the merchants in Constantinople commented on the famous Turkish baths, even more of a novelty in those days when bathing in England was still considered unhygienic. Turks were found to believe exactly the opposite. They built their baths near mosques because of the Islamic dictate of outer as well as inner cleanliness. According to George Wheler, 'they have a Roome without, with a sopha round it to undress themselves; and a large square Roome beyond that, covered with a Cuppola, through which the light is let by Belglasses; and about it are many little apartments covered with small Cuppolas, much resembling that built in London; only they usually have a great Bason in the middle, filled

2. Lady Mary Wortley Montagu, whose husband was ambassador in Constantinople 1717–18, discovered during her stay the Turkish practice of inoculation against small-pox by which she herself had been badly disfigured. She had her son inoculated and introduced the process to England. Portrait of Lady Mary and her son in Turkish dress attributed to J.-B. Vanmour

'with hot water into which they go to bathe themselves'. Some baths were segregated but in general special times or days were set aside for women. Lady Mary visited one in Sofia in 1717 on her way to Constantinople. 'It is the women's coffee house,' she wrote to Lady Rich, 'they take this diversion once a week, and stay there at least four or five hours without getting cold by immediately coming out of the hot bath into the cold room.'

One of the first Turkish baths (known as *bagnios* after the Venetian name) in London opened in 1679, probably the one to which Wheler referred. It was in Roman Bath Street, off Newgate Street, conveniently placed for the Turkey merchants in their various city premises. Scandal, in Congreve's *Love for Love*, was probably thinking of the new bagnio when he described 'a Beau, in a Bagnio, Cupping for a complexion, and Sweating for a shape'. It was described in 1720 as a 'neat contrived building after the Turkish mode for that purpose; seated in a handsome yard.... Much resorted into for Sweating, being found very good for aches, etc., and approved of by our Physicians.'* Known as the Royal Bagnio, it consisted of one large room with a cupola and several smaller ones lined with the fashionable Dutch oriental tiles. The water was heated, it cost four shillings per person and women were allowed in on special days. There was another bath in Chancery Lane and a third, Duke's Bagnio, in Long Acre. Turks were imported for 'champooing' or massage: ladies were allowed to wear masks for the ordeal if they were at all inclined to be embarrassed.

According to Peter Mundy, he and the other English merchants in Constantinople 'passe very commodiously with pleasure, love and Amitye among themselves, wearing our own Countrie habitt, Provision, fruit and wine very good varietye and plentye'. Ambassadors were sometimes accompanied by their wives, but few of the factors were married or had their wives in Constantinople. Still, as Sandys remarked, 'many of them will not be alone where women are so easily come by'. According to the eighteenth-century traveller, James Haynes, European merchants sometimes married local Christians in order to be able to infiltrate harems with their merchandise. During the seventeenth century, however, no official in the Levant was allowed to marry without the consent of the Company directors. In spite of Mundy's remark about dress, many factors wore Turkish costume whenever they went about the city; in Constantinople, a more cosmopolitan city than some, few incidents were reported involving Franks (as all Europeans were known), but elsewhere – in Cairo, Aleppo or Jerusalem for instance – Europeans dressed as such were often insulted and beaten. Lady Mary certainly wore Turkish dress during her stay in the east.†

Lady Mary Wortley Montagu was one of the wives who did accompany her husband on his embassy. This paragon of English elegance and learning described in one of her letters to Alexander Pope how she spent her week in Constantinople: 'Monday, setting of partridges – Tuesday, reading English – Wednesday, studying in the Turkish language (in which, by the way, I am already very learned) – Thursday, classical authors – Friday, spent in writing – Saturday, at my needle – and Sunday, admitting of visits and hearing of music'. How busy she must have seemed to her contemporaries, particularly to the poor little French ambassadress in Constantinople, who, according to Lady Mary, had never even ventured across the Golden Horn to Stambul and spent much of her time exclaiming

---

* John Strype, revised edition of Stowe's *Survey of London*, 1720.
† One of her costumes is now in the Victoria and Albert Museum.

with joy at the vast number of servants she had been allotted. In the summer the ambassador and his wife, in common with many other Europeans, left the heat and smells of the capital for the cool green forests called Belgrade on the slopes of the northern Bosphorus. Again to Pope she wrote, 'I am in the middle of a wood consisting chiefly of fruit trees, watered by a vast number of fountains ... and divided into many shady walks, upon short grass ... and within view of the Black Sea, from whence we perpetually enjoy the refreshment of cool breezes, that make us insensible of the heat of the summer.' 'The Elysian fields', she called the forests of Belgrade.

Characteristically, Lady Mary was more receptive to the customs of Muslim Turks than many of her contemporaries. She went to great pains to demonstrate the freedom Turkish women enjoyed through the protection of the harem and decided slaves were no worse treated than free servants. True to her time, she considered Islam little different from the rational deism admitted by many of her contemporaries.

It was during her years in Constantinople that she came across the practice of inoculation against smallpox, a disease she herself had contracted in 1715, and was considered to have been very disfigured by it. She had only been in Turkey a few months before she was writing to her friend Sarah Chiswell: 'A propos of distempers I am going to tell you a thing I am sure will make you wish yourself here. The smallpox, so fatal, and so general amongst us, is here entirely harmless by the invention of ingrafting, which is the term they give it.' Old women scratched a patient's vein, inserting a needle with smallpox venom on the head. The patient later developed two or three days' fever which soon disappeared leaving him immune. The practice was already known in England but only through the learned reports of the Royal Society. 'Every year thousands undergo this operation', Lady Mary went on, 'and the French ambassador says pleasantly, that they take the smallpox here by way of diversion, as they take the waters in other countries.' She had her six-year-old son inoculated in Constantinople and her daughter treated during an epidemic in England in 1721. A year later the Princess of Wales followed her example. Voltaire, in England between 1726 and 1729, described the operation in one of his *Lettres Philosophiques*, attributing its origin to the Circassians, famous for their beauty and highly prized for Turkish harems, so that a smallpox epidemic 'causait une notable diminution dans les serails de Perse et de Turquie'.

3 The Turkey Merchants

The ambassador was responsible for the supervision of the Levant Company's activities throughout the Ottoman Empire which were as important to the Company outside Constantinople as inside. Aleppo and Smyrna were the main centres of trading activity in the seventeenth and eighteenth centuries – apart from Constantinople – and the ambassador was responsible for the appointment of consuls and other officials to the factories there and elsewhere, subject to the approval of the Company in London.

Ambassadors journeying to take up their posts in the capital were allowed the extra expense of going overland, through France and Vienna to Adrianople and Constantinople. Other Company officials and factors went by sea through the hostile Mediterranean. There were three enemies: navies of European countries, depending on the state of war or peace (though at least if they were captured the unhappy merchants became honourable prisoners of war with the prospect of repatriation); Barbary pirates operating from North Africa; and English pirates using the Barbary coast as a base and when possible (but mistakes were frequent) avoiding their compatriots' ships. William Lithgow met Turkish pirates in the course of his *Peregrination* and describes the fight with characteristic vigour: 'in a furious spleene the first Hola of their courtesies was the prograce of a martiall conflict, thundring forth a terrible noise of Galley-roaring pieces. And we in a sad reply sent out a back-sounding echo of fiery-flying shots; which made an aequinox to the clouds, rebounding backward in our perturbed breasts the ambiguous sound of feare and hope.' Few travellers were as lucky as Veryard whose vessel was captured by Algerian pirates in 1686; after a three-day storm their Arab captors were so exhausted that the prisoners were able to escape from the hold ('in which Region of Darkness we lay smother'd for want of Air') and regain control.

Various attempts were made to deal with the pirates: the ambassador could ask the Sultan to intervene but he was powerless to do much as Sir Thomas Roe wrote to the Company from Constantinople in 1624; 'the pirates of Algiers and Tunis have cast off all obedience to this empire not only upon the sea where they are masters but presuming to do many insolences even upon the land and in the best ports of the grand signior'. With the gift of Tangier to Charles II by his Portuguese bride in 1661 the suppression of the Barbary pirates became the concern of the Restoration government though of the several expeditions fitted out for this purpose none had any lasting success. In the long run the only effective way of dealing with the pirates was to ensure that every vessel venturing into the Mediterranean was fully armed and to send merchant vessels as often as possible in convoy.

Henry Teonge, a chaplain with literary fancies, was with a convoy escorting merchant vessels in 1675. The convoy was expected to attack any sail sighted, whether hostile or not; if it was friendly, as happened on one occasion, 'our fight soone turned to a great deale of myrth'. Arriving at Tripoli (Libya) Teonge found that the English had successfully attacked the town for harbouring pirates; while his ship was blockading the port he composed *The Relation of this Combatte* ('for want of better employment before Trypolye'):

> Long lasted this same cruell fight,
> Which ran with bloody streames,
> Untill the sun, that western light,
> Withdrew his glorious beames.
>
> The Turks they took it in great snuff,
> And sorely were offended:
> But we did carry off their stuff
> And so the battell ended.
>
> ...God blesse King Charles; the Duke of York;
> The Royall Family;
> From Turkes and Jewes that eat no porke
> Good Lord deliver me.

Anchoring later in Iskenderun Teonge heard of the capture of the *Bristol Merchant*, with all her cargo and fourteen merchants, and of the Dartmouth pinnace which managed to get away with only two of her crew captured, who 'are now in a gally in Famagosta...which we intend to redeeme at our returne'. Slavery was the fate faced by most prisoners of the pirates. Some, such as Edward Webbe, were rescued from the galleys by the ambassador in Constantinople. Others were less fortunate. *The Camden Wonder* is a curious tale by Sir Thomas Overbury* showing how the pirates at the height of their power spread out from the Mediterranean. It is the history of one

---

* Son of the Sir Thomas Overbury who was murdered in the Tower of London in 1613.

John Harrison who was kidnapped by Barbary pirates from England and turned up two years later after his servant had been hanged for his murder, having spent the intervening period as a slave in Algiers and Smyrna. Joseph Pitts was another Barbary slave who contributed the most successful contemporary account of piracy in his *Faithful Account of the Religion and Manners of the Mahometans, with an account of the author's having been taken by his master on the pilgrimage to Mecca*; Pitts thus became the first Englishman, as far as is known, to visit Mecca and describe the *hajj*. In the early years of the seventeenth century there were reckoned to be some twelve thousand Christian prisoners in the hands of the pirates. A fund was set up in London after the Restoration by the Duchess of Dudley for the redemption of slaves, and the Levant Company on several occasions raised ransoms for its enslaved members or their employees.

Several Englishmen turned to piracy on the Barbary coast when the treaty signed between England and Spain on the accession of James I resulted in much of the English navy being disbanded. John Ward was the most notorious of these pirates, active in the Mediterranean from about 1607 to 1612, after which he retired to a palace he built himself outside Tunis. Lithgow met him there in 1615, describing the palace as 'beautified with rich Marbel and Alabaster stones; with him I found Domestick, some fifteene circumcised English Runagates, whose lives and countenances were both alike even as desperate as disdainful'.

Many writers describe the sighting of a hostile sail with great glee. Alexander Drummond, a Levant merchant who was on his way to the Levant during the Seven Years' War, described a sea trip he made from Smyrna to Iskenderun on which the captain was persuaded by his officers to chase a French ship and capture her. There was no great battle for 'we complimented her with some of our sugar plums and before noon she struck'. This was a more gentlemanly affair than those described by Teonge or Lithgow. 'Everything of value belonging to the captain and his brother was put in their chests that they might be preserved from the pillaging hands of the sailors; the gentlemen were carried on board, a ransom agreed upon and everything settled before night and the captain's brother left as hostage.'

Company officials and factors regarded their time in the Levant as limited; very rarely, before the eighteenth century, did they intend to spend their lives there if they could help it. One Levant factor in Aleppo wrote to his employer in London in 1745: 'You gentlemen will know that the inducements to a man living abroad and more especially in a country like this, are the hopes and expectations he has of gaining in his earlier days wherewithal to return to his native country to spend the latter part of his life with some comfort.'*

Dudley North was typical of the Turkey merchant who returned to England once he had made enough money to set up on his own. After leaving school, North went first to a writing school to learn 'merchants' accounts', serving as apprentice to a Turkey merchant for seven years. In 1661 he was sent to Smyrna. 'We live in a country admirably pleasant, and bringing forth all that is to be desired both for delicacy and ordinary food', he is quoted by his cousin Roger North. North lived frugally enough on the commissions he earned on his master's goods, refusing to keep a horse and hunting on an ass instead. After a few years in Smyrna quarrels with his master gave him the excuse to return to England, break off his employment and collect new and independent commissions. These took him to

1. A party of huntsmen setting out from the house of a merchant in Smyrna in 1684. Hounds like those in the picture were highly esteemed as gifts to appropriate Turkish or Persian officials. Engraving from de Bruyn, *A Voyage to the Levant* (1702)

Constantinople where he lived for the next ten years. He became a great authority on Turkish language and law, even planning to compile a Turkish dictionary, such a knowledge, he said, being the best assurance for financial success. He was said to have taken more than five hundred cases to the Turkish courts, where his great success was

* Robert Golightly to Edward Radcliffe, 28 April 1745, quoted in Ralph Davis, *Aleppo and Devonshire Square*, p. 75.

in behaving as the Turks – 'in a direct fact a false witness is a surer card than a true one; for if the judge has a mind to baffle a testimony, a harmless honest witness, that doth not know his play, cannot stand so well his many captious questions as a false witness, used to the trade will do', he wrote. He became Company treasurer in Constantinople in 1670 and built himself a new house – with a special room, proof against the notorious fires of the capital and another specially for entertaining Turks; he made loans to Turks at interest rates of 20–30 per cent, usury being forbidden to Muslims,* and dealt in jewels with the Ottoman court. From England his countrymen wrote to him for all kinds of advice, including Christopher Wren who wanted to know how the Turks covered the vast domes of their mosques.

North returned to England in 1680. Having no English clothes he was obliged to spend the first few days in his Turkish costume; this much amused his relatives, as did his management of his Turkish moustachios, 'for being apt to trespass upon the mouth, they were always habitually put by before drinking'.† He was knighted and appointed a sheriff of London; he sat in Parliament for three years; he employed apprentices ('I hope to place him with Sir Dudley North of whom I hear great commendations', wrote a merchant of his nephew in 1682, 'but he expects six hundred pounds... having so many offers'). In 1691 North published his *Discourses upon Trade*, a monotonous treatise in favour of monopolies, and died later the same year. Thus Turkey merchants 'live gentiley, become rich and get great estates in short time'.

In both Smyrna and Aleppo Company officials consisted of a consul, a treasurer, a chancellor and a physician. Dragomans – usually Italian or Greek – acted as interpreters and a scribe was employed to write any Turkish correspondence. The consul was responsible for the execution of the Company's regulations, for the conduct of the factors and for the harmony of relations with the local pasha. A consul at Smyrna in 1670, in one letter from the Company, was commended for his attempts to regulate the value of money as a remedy against the floods of cheap money, which were a great worry to the Company; he was advised to get the factors to agree only to accept money at its intrinsic value and to be diligent in preventing the import of false coinage; he was thanked for trying to

---

* North's usurious example had become a regular practice by the eighteenth century, fetching rates even then of around 12 per cent.

† Shakespeare aptly wrote: 'Farewell, Monsieur Traveller: look you lisp and wear strange suits, disable all the benefits of your own country, be out of love with your nativity, and almost chide God for making you that countenance you are, or I will scarce think you have swam in a gondola' (*As You Like It*).

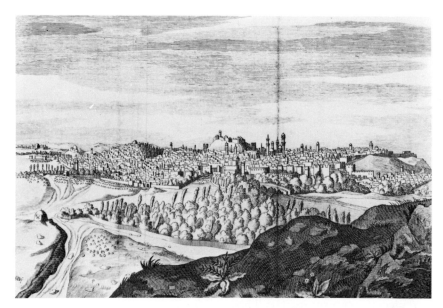

2. Aleppo, 'the chief mart of all the East', was the centre of the Levant Company's spice trade and an important terminus for Silk Road caravans. Engraving from Henry Maundrell, *A Journey from Aleppo to Jerusalem* (1703)

stop the abuses in the export of raw silk, a common complaint from English importers being the condition of the silk upon arrival in England; and he was warned against ships' captains trying to carry non-company goods, the Company recommending him to authorise a thorough search of each incoming and outgoing vessel.

Ships bringing merchandise for the great Aleppo market would anchor at Iskenderun, from which the small Levant Company factory would alert the Aleppo factory by pigeon of the ship's arrival. Iskenderun must have been the most unpopular spot in the Levant among the Turkey merchants. One of the earliest descriptions of it is Peter Mundy's: 'it is very unwholesome by reason of the huge hills hindringe the approache of the Sunne Beames, until nine or ten a Clocke in the mornings, lyeinge in a great Marsh full of boggs, Frogs and foggs'. None of the later visitors make Iskenderun sound any more attractive. Drummond described it as 'so wretched and vile as to be unworthy of notice'; both the town and the country around 'produce nothing but robberies, rapes and murders and every species of villainy'. The factory had a chapel attached to bury the many plague-stricken merchants and the traveller Fynes Moryson buried his brother Henry there in 1596. It was, however, the nearest port to Aleppo, the pigeon sometimes taking as little as two and a half hours to fly the sixty miles between them.

3. A seventeenth-century European merchant ship on its way up the Bosphorus. Few Christian ships were allowed into the Black Sea until the seventeenth century; in 1609 Thomas Glover received permission for the first English ship 'that ever swomme into those sease'. Engraving from de Bruyn, *Voyage to the Levant*

Aleppo was one of the pleasantest cities in the Levant. 'The chiefe beautie of this cytty is to be seene from the tip of a hill, which is about a mile or more west of the cytty', wrote Teonge; 'from hence all the cytty shows most beautiful; it stands rownd, the buildings all of stone and flatt on the topp... look white and very beautifull. Next you see the coopelows, which are in abundance not only on their moskeus, but on many of their greate buildings, rising up over the rest of the buildings like so many pretty mountains over the plaines.... Another adorning is the Cyprus trees, which are very high and greene, and all over the towne; which make a very pretty shew. And last of all the castle, which, though it stand on the south syde of the cytty, yet from the hill it seems to stand in the very midst of all the cytty.... About the towne are brave gardens, and pleasant plantations... being made more fruitfull by a small brooke which runs closse by the towne.'

In Aleppo, as in most Middle Eastern towns, the Company had its headquarters, or factory, in the English *khan*. 'These buildings', wrote Abraham Parsons, appointed consul in Iskenderun in 1767, 'are mostly square with a large area within, round which are magazines or warehouses, with a gallery running all round which leads to lodging rooms'; the gates are 'shut up every night after the manner of colleges', guarding the *khan* from the frequent street riots. Janissaries were also assigned to the factory for this purpose.

Life for the European in Aleppo was quite agreeable. Travellers could expect a most civilised welcome from the merchants there, French, Dutch and Venetian as well as English, who spent their spare time in feasting, hunting, games and picnics. Henry Maundrell, chaplain there at the end of the seventeenth century, described how they began the day with prayers and 'have our set times of Business, Meals and Recreation. In the winter we Hunt in the most delightful Campaign twice a week; and in the summer go as often to divert ourselves under our Tents in Bowling and other Exercises'. Teonge, whose first visit to Aleppo was a continual round of visits to other Europeans as well as to Turkish, Jewish and Armenian houses, was lavishly entertained in every place. Idyllic alfresco expeditions into the surrounding countryside were among his favourite occupations, 'where a princely tent was pitched and we had severall pastimes and sports, as duck-hunting, fishing, shooting, hand-ball, krickett and scrofilo; and then a noble dinner brought hither, with greate plenty of all sorts of wines, punch and lemonads; and at six wee returne all home in good order, but soundly tyred and weary'. Dr Alexander Russell, who as physician to the factory in the middle of the eighteenth century collected material for an exhaustive study of Aleppo, described the Europeans' tables as well stocked with a marvellous assortment of game and fish for which guests were prepared by draughts of weak punch before dinner. Teonge, whose appetite was usually foremost in his thoughts, sampled one dinner given by the consul for the English community which ran to more than thirty main dishes.

Smyrna was another important market for the Levant Company. 'Truly neere unto this Citty I saw such a long continuing Plaine,' wrote Lithgow, 'abounding in corns, wines, all sorts of fruitfull herbage, and so infinitely peopled, that mee thought, Nature seemed with the people's industrie to contend the one by propagating creatures, the other by admirable agriculture.' Smyrna 'hath so many advantages from its natural situation,' exclaimed the gentleman traveller George Wheler fifty years later, 'that notwithstanding the great calamities which have befallen it by war, and most prodigious earthquakes, . . . yet it hath still been thought worth the repairing and restoring to all the Beauty the Art of its inhabitants could contrive to adorn it with.'

Here the English merchants lived along the waterfront, their gardens reaching down to the sea where boats could be moored and loaded or unloaded. In summer the Europeans escaped the heat and ills of the bay by going to the hills of the hinterland, 'to course and hunt with their Greyhounds and Beagles of which they always keep a good pack'. Alexander Drummond, a member of the Levant

Company who founded the first freemason lodge in Smyrna in the eighteenth century, described the cheerful society of Smyrna which included an assembly at New Year, 'upon which it would be cruel to criticise, seeing the ladies are all natives of the country where gallantry and true politeness are but little known'. Freemasonry, Drummond hoped, would encourage the right society and he celebrated the opening of the first freemason lodge in verse:

> For ages past a savage race
> O'erspread these Asian plains,
> All nature wore a gloomy face,
> And pensive moved the swains.
>
> But now Britannia's generous sons
> A glorious lodge have raised,
> Near the famed banks where Meles runs,
> And Homer's cattle grazed;
>
> The bri'ery wilds to groves are changed,
> With orange trees around,
> And fragrant lemons fairly ranged,
> O'ershade the blissful ground.
>
> While safe within the sacred walls,
> Where heavenly friendship reigns,
> The jovial masons hear the calls
> Of all the needy swains.

It was a factor from Smyrna, Edward Daniels, who decided to set up his Ragusan servant, Pasquee Rosee, as proprietor of a coffee house in London; he had noticed on his return to England that there was no equivalent to these gathering places so popular in the Levant. Englishmen had first heard of the oriental habit of coffee-drinking from William Biddulph: 'it is accounted a great curtesie among them to give unto their friends a fin-ion [cup] or Scudella of Coffa, which is more wholesome than toothsome, for it causeth good concoction and driveth away drowsiness.... Their Coffa houses are more common than Ale houses in England; but they use not so much to sit in the houses as on Benches on both sides the streets ... every man his fin-ion full which being smoking hot, they use to put it to their Noses and Eares and then sup it up by leisure, being full of idel and Ale-house talk, whiles they are amongst themselves drinking of it.'

Rosee had a hand-bill printed to advertise his coffee house, whose extravagant language must have enticed many an innocent ale drinker to a new and at that time expensive addiction. 'It so incloseth the orifice of the stomach, and fortifies the heart within, that it is very good to help digestion; and therefore of great use to be taken about three or four o'clock afternoon, as well as in the morning. It much quickens the spirits and makes the heart lightsome; it is good against sore eyes, and the better if you hold your head over it and take in steam that way. It is excellent remedy against the spleen, hypochondrial winds and the life ... It is neither laxative nor restringent.' No wonder coffee houses became the rage of Restoration London. The East India Company began ordering consignments of coffee from Mokha in Yemen and the Levant Company sent it home from Aleppo. Coffee houses became centres for political meetings whose popularity increased with every effort of the government to suppress them. A poem published in 1665 described 'The Character of a Coffee-House':

> And if you see the great Murat
> With Shash on's head instead of hat,
> Or any Sultan in his dress,
> Or picture of a Sultaness,
> Or John's admired curl'd pate,
> Or the great Mogul in's Chair of State,
> Or Constantine the Grecian,
> Who fourteen years was th'only man
> That made Coffee for th'great Bashaw,
> Although the man he never saw;
> Or if you see a coffee-cup
> Filled from a Turkish pot, hung up
> Within the Clouds, and round it Pipes,
> Wax candles, stoppers, these are types
> And certain Signes (with many more
> Would be too longe to write the more)
> Which plainly do Spectators tell
> That in this house they Coffee sell.
> Some wiser than the rest (no doubt),
> Say they can by the smelle find out;
> In at a door (they say) but thrust
> Your nose, and if you scent burnt Crust
> Be sure there's Coffee sold that's good,
> For so by most 'tis understood.

One of the most famous coffee houses in London was the Sultaness' Head, proprietor Thomas Garway, whose family had for several generations traded with the Levant. Sir William Garway (or Garraway), whom John Sanderson had represented in the Levant in 1595, had seventeen children, several of whom became involved in the Levant trade. James Garway as a merchant in the Levant employed Peter Mundy; Anthony Garway was a merchant in Constantinople;

and Arthur Garway was imprisoned by the Turks so that it is likely he too traded with the area. Sir William's eldest son, poor 'crack'd' Sir Henry Garway, was sacked from his position as governor of the Levant Company because of royalist inclinations. The Thomas Garway who started the Sultaness' Head* was probably a grandson of Sir William.

Smyrna and Aleppo flourished as great trade centres throughout most of this early period, their fortunes and those of the factories there fluctuating with the tide of war or peace either in Europe or further east. Other factories in Turkey and the Levant were smaller and their operation dependent on favourable conditions. Such were those at Angora (Ankara) where the Turkey merchants were investing in mohair, and at Tripoli, another Levant port; at Beirut, Sidon, Tyre and Acre members of the Levant Company usually traded under the protection of the French factory since the volume of their trade was usually too small to merit an independent English factory.

Until the nineteenth century the Egyptian trade was neither very prosperous nor very popular with the Company, which thought it too hazardous and advised ambassadors not to appoint consuls or agents either to Cairo or to Alexandria. John Sanderson investigated the Egyptian market in 1586 but reported back gloomily on the high cost of living, the limited market for English wool and the high price of spices, even compared with Aleppo. Egypt as the great entrepot at the head of the Red Sea suffered more from the development of the Cape route than the rest of the Levant. Sandys pointed out that Egypt's Indian trade had already fallen since the first East Indian voyages, 'in so much as spices brought out of the Levant heretofore are now with profit brought hither by our Merchants'. The same crisis overtook the coffee trade in the eighteenth century when this staple import, brought by the Egyptians from Yemen, was ousted by cheaper West and East Indian transplanted coffee; Richard Pococke in 1738 noticed in Egypt that West Indian coffee 'sometimes, to deceive, is mixed' with Arabian and sold as the latter, which commanded a higher price.

The size of the Egyptian trade rarely justified the maintenance of a consulate. Benjamin Bishop was appointed consul in 1606, 'as badde a fellow as bad may be', who vanished from the scene after having become a Muslim. No one was appointed to replace him and William Lithgow in 1609 stayed with the French consul. English consuls were appointed from time to time between then and the end of the eighteenth century but for the most part the small amount

---

* The Sultaness' Head later became the first place in London to sell tea.

of English trade was conducted under French protection. Few consuls escaped the enmity or greed of the Turkish viceroy; the record of imprisonment, fines imposed and confiscation of property so far exceeded that of anywhere else in the Levant that the Company was with reason discouraged, though the ambassador in Constantinople occasionally found it helpful to have a representative in Cairo.

Only with the emergence of the problem of the route to India did interest in Egypt revive. Pococke found quite a large community of English merchants in Cairo in the middle of the eighteenth century, living 'agreeably enough among themselves... and in a plentiful country they do not want whatever may make life pass agreeably. The morning being spent in business, the remainder of the day is often passed in riding out to the fields and gardens to the north of Cairo... sometimes the whole day is spent in diversions that way.' Even this prosperity was short-lived, however.*

Early attempts by the Company to establish English factories along the North African coast failed because the feebleness of the Sultan's authority at that distance left factors little or no protection from Barbary greed. European merchants were discouraged by Muslim fanaticism from visiting, let alone settling in, the Red Sea ports of Arabia such as Jiddah, and Mecca and Medina were entirely out of bounds. The Danish traveller Karsten Niebuhr found an unnamed English merchant living in Jiddah when he was there in 1761, but local hostility generally warded off attempts by Europeans to develop trade with the Arabian hinterland and to take advantage of the prosperous pilgrim traffic flourishing in the Red Sea.

Outside the field of business there was little fraternisation between the Turks and the Europeans. The natural arrogance of the Turkish ruling class was heightened in the case of Europeans by its antipathy towards infidels. The governor at Bir on the Euphrates spurned Drummond's gifts when the latter tried to visit the castle there, remarking that no amount of gifts would induce him to admit the infidel Englishman. Dudley North was once timing a tightrope walker on his watch when the rope broke and the bystanders immediately accused him of causing the accident through the magic of his watch. Turkish dress was worn by Europeans in most parts of the empire to distract some of this attention from their alien religion and customs, although by the eighteenth century this was sometimes incongruously accompanied by a European wig or cloak.

The contempt, anyway, was mutual. Educated Englishmen such as George Sandys showed a typical ignorance and abhorrence of fundamental Muslim beliefs, and chaplains such as Teonge and

* See below, p. 118.

Maundrell made no attempt to bridge the gap between Islam and Christianity by investigating the differences; Teonge in particular accepted any number of crude contemporary suspicions about Islam, and Maundrell had no desire to mix with the Turks, whose conversation he found 'not the least entertaining'. Devastating outbreaks of plague regularly discouraged proximity, the Europeans soon discovering that the best way to survive was either by fleeing the stricken town or by rigid quarantine, shutting themselves in their *khans* sometimes for months on end, their only contact with the outside world being via a sterilising solution of vinegar, sulphur and water.

Occasionally English merchants broke through the social and religious barriers: Dudley North had several Turkish friends; Paul Rycaut, historian of the Ottoman Empire and consul in Smyrna in the 1660s, and the wearisome Dr Covell pursued their researches with the help of Turkish acquaintances, but even Rycaut admitted that 'a Turk is not capable of real friendship towards a Christian'. In general the Turkey merchants were anxious to make their fortunes and return to England as soon as possible.

The last years of the Company's life, from the beginning of the nineteenth century until its demise in 1824, saw an amazing recovery from the trade slump of the second half of the eighteenth century when war with the French had often prevented Company shipping from reaching the Levant for many months. The French Revolution and Napoleon's grandiose schemes of conquest soon damaged French trade supremacy. These were the years, too, when the development of the Lancashire industry, using ever greater supplies of Levant cotton, provided the Company with cheaper cloth to compete with the French.

Napoleon's ambition to partition the Ottoman Empire with Russian help, however, drew the British government's attention to the fact that Britain was still represented in the area by merchants whose main concern was the commercial interests of their employers, not the political aims of their government. A division of powers, political and commercial, weakened the Company's rights to monopolise the Levant trade, already under attack from anti-monopoly opinion. At a crucial meeting of the Company's General Court in 1824 even the governor, Lord Grenville, described the monopoly as an invidious restraint and persuaded the Company voluntarily to surrender its privileges. The government undertook to pay pensions to all officials in England who lost their jobs and in return the authority, property, money and effects of the Company were transferred to the Crown.

The importance of the Levant Company is often eclipsed by its rival, the East India Company. But its connections with the Ottoman Empire prepared the way for the greater political interest in the area in the nineteenth century. The Company's officials in the Empire were the early explorers of the area and the most reliable source of information. Among the Turks and their subjects in the Ottoman Empire they established a reputation for honest dealing, where corruption and deceit were eating away the heart of a once great empire – no small achievement when Muslim contempt for the Christian was still undimmed by any sense of political inferiority.

4 *The Grand Sophy*

The curiosity of Renaissance Europe about Persia was first aroused at the beginning of the fourteenth century by the travels of the Venetian merchant Marco Polo. He and his fellow Venetians were the first to explore the relatively unknown markets of the east which he described. English cloth reached the Far East and oriental goods found their way to England through the hands of many middlemen – Armenian, Indian and Arab as well as Venetian. The Venetians were joined at the beginning of the sixteenth century by the Portuguese after they had discovered the route round the Cape of Good Hope. But although Marco Polo's account was one of the first books printed by William Caxton, the English were in no hurry themselves to venture into what was clearly a hazardous, though potentially enriching, trade. Not until the 1560s did they venture beyond the Levant with their cloth.

These early travellers avoided the trap of comparing the bizarre society in which they found themselves with their own in England. Whereas in the Levant travellers condemned Turks and Arabs alike for not complying with European and Christian customs, the Persians for a long time were a source of wonder, close to admiration to Europeans; their clothes, their towns, their skills and their pleasures were often praised. Only later accounts, from merchants sweltering in the Persian Gulf, list the same complaints, discomforts and loneliness as their compatriots in the less pleasant towns of the Levant.

Direct trade between Persia and England was established on a regular basis by 1615. Earlier attempts to open up trade with Persia were made through either Russia or Syria, the southern routes being controlled by the Portuguese. Anthony Jenkinson, a member of the Muscovy Company which operated with Russia, who was already acquainted with the Levant and parts of central Asia, was the first Englishman to investigate the northern route. From Moscow Jenkinson sailed down the Volga to Astrakhan in 1561. He and his companions were nearly shipwrecked in a seven-day storm on the Caspian but eventually disembarked at Shabran (in modern Azerbaijan), whose ruler, Abdullah Khan, Jenkinson visited in his capital at Shamakha – the first time an Englishman saw for himself a

Persian court whose opulence must have compared favourably with the rougher standards of England.

The khan, 'a prince of mean stature, and of a fierce countenance', wrote Jenkinson, was 'richly apparelled with long garments of silke, and cloth of golde, imbrodred with pearles of stone; upon his head was a tolipane* with a sharp end standing upwards halfe a yard long, of rich cloth of golde, wrapped about with a piece of India silke of twentie yards long, wrought in golde, and on the left side of his tolipane stood a plume of feathers, set in a trunke of gold richly enameled, and set with precious stones; his earrings had pendants of gold a handfull long, with two rubies of great value, set in the ends thereof; all the ground within his pavilion was covered with rich carpets and under himself was spred a square carpet wrought with silver and golde.' So well acquainted was the khan with foreign habits that he courteously produced stools for Jenkinson and his party to sit on instead of the floor.

Jenkinson's reception at Qazvin, the capital, by the Grand Sophy† was very different from Abdullah Khan's. The Shah was on the point of concluding peace with the Turks who were strongly opposed to any diversion of the Persian silk and English cloth trades from Turkey to Russia, as Jenkinson was proposing. At his first audience with the Shah, 'in lighting from my horse at the Court gate, before my feete touched the ground, a paire of the Sophie's own shoes ... were put upon my feet, for without the same shoes I might not be suffered to tread upon his holy ground.' When he presented the queen's introductory letter to the Shah, written in Latin, English, Hebrew and Italian, the Shah curtly, if reasonably, retorted that no one in the country understood those languages. As Jenkinson left the precincts 'after me followed a man with a basinet of sand, sifting all the way that I had gone within the said pallace'.

Jenkinson's journey set a pattern for the next twenty years, but physical hazards and political uncertainties eventually defeated the possibility of trading with Persia by the northern route. Marlowe wrote all too accurately in *Tamburlaine*: 'Christian merchants that with Russian sterns Plow up huge furrows in the Caspian Sea, Shall vaile to us, as Lords of all the Lake';‡ the so-called Lords of

---

*The 'tolipane' was so called from its resemblance to the indigenous Persian flower, the tulip, the plant and name of which were introduced into Europe by the Dutch.

†The English corruption of Safi, the name of the dynasty.

‡ *Tamburlaine* was first produced in 1585, before Hakluyt's first edition of travels, containing accounts of Persia including Jenkinson's narrative, was published; it is thought Marlowe may have inserted these lines in a later edition of *Tamburlaine*. (see below, p. 90).

the Lake were more interested in battle honours than English kersies and agreements made by one expedition were seldom valid for the next. The trip across the Caspian was generally stormy and the boats unsuited to the stress; many merchants died of dysentery or plague (Persian silk came from the most unhealthy part of the country, the southern shore of the Caspian) or were waylaid and murdered by robbers; nor were expensive presents for local rulers justified by the returns of trade. Language was another problem, as Queen Elizabeth's letter showed. One merchant, Arthur Edwards, went down to Qazvin to investigate the market and wrote to the Muscovy Company recommending them to send to Persia someone who could at least speak Portuguese and could therefore buy a Portuguese-speaking slave who also knew Persian. How lonely he was, he sighed, in one letter home: 'God grant me in health to see your worships for I have had a carefull travell, with many a sorrowful day and unquiet sleepes. Neither had I the company of one English person to whome sometimes I might have eased my pensive heart.'

The last expedition at this time to try the northern route for Persian trade was in 1581, the same year as the foundation of the Levant Company. Unhampered by the risks of the overland route from the north, the Levant merchants were in a far stronger position to market English cloth in Persia, using Armenians as intermediaries, as well as in the Levant. They were also anxious to preserve the best possible relations with the Sultan, who would not be endeared to English merchants if their compatriots were trying to divert transit trade from Turkey to Russia.

English merchants in Aleppo were soon considering the possibility of a route to Persia from the eastern Mediterranean and Aleppo, a traditional caravan route across the desert and far shorter than the Russian route, if no less dangerous. Aleppo was an ideal starting point for any investigation and in 1581 John Newbery, an English merchant in Aleppo, set out from there for Persia with the encouragment of the Levant Company, afterwards producing an exhaustive survey of the area he covered. This is full of commercial details – customs dues, distances between towns, where luggage was searched, carriage rates, worthwhile imports, fashions and tastes. From Aleppo he went to Bir on the Euphrates ('as broad as the Thames at Lambeth,' he wrote to give a more precise picture) and thence to Baghdad and Basra. He sailed down the Gulf ('the Marines are all beasts', he complained, because they were too frightened to sail at night) to Ormuz, where he spent six weeks informing himself of the 'trade and custom of the place'. Across the water from Ormuz was Gombrun, later renamed Bandar Abbas, one day to be the main

English trading factory in Persia, but an insignificant and squalid village in Newbery's day. From there he went inland – to Lar and Shiraz, the latter one of the most beautiful towns in Persia, but Newbery was interested in trade not architecture. 'It is a towne that hath great store of victuals and fruits; Iron, Lead, Casder, Conchonille, Brasill, Linnen cloth and all wares that come out of India are very well sold here.' In Isfahan he paused long enough to list customs dues, then on via Kashan, Yezd, Qazvin, to Qum, one of the holy cities of Persia, to Tabriz, and finally, breathlessly, to Erivan, Erzerum and Erzinjan. And so back to Constantinople through the Taurus – 'with the greatest snow, frost and wind that ever I was in', – reaching the capital the day after a large fire had destroyed most of the Galata waterfront: Newbery makes no mention of the houses burnt down, only the merchandise destroyed.

Not content with a preliminary investigation of the route, in 1583 he was off again, this time accompanied by Ralph Fitch and John Eldred (also merchants who left accounts of their trip), a jeweller named William Leedes and a painter, James Story. Newbery died, probably in India, after leaving Fitch who wanted to press on further east; James Story is thought to have turned Jesuit when the party was imprisoned for a while by the Portuguese in Goa; and William Leedes set up as a jeweller at the Moghul court.*

The Reverend John Cartwright and his companion John Mildenhall also set out for Persia from Aleppo, following a slightly different and less frequented caravan route from Newbery's – across the southern valleys and mountains of the Taurus to Tabriz. Cartwright's account of his travels, published as *The Preacher's Travels* in 1611, was less valuable than Newbery's as a survey of Persian trade but infinitely more entertaining as a description of the country and its people. Tabriz was the principal market of north-west Persia by reason of its strategic position across the main route from Persia to the Black Sea (where Europeans were still forbidden to venture); Cartwright reckoned the population of Tabriz to be about two hundred thousand. From Tabriz he travelled to Qazvin, no longer the capital but still an important market with 'sundry Bassars, where in some you may buy Shashes and Tulipants, and Indian cloth of wonderfull finenesse; in others infinite furs, as Sables and Martine out of Muscovia.' 'I am persuaded', he concluded with more enthusiasm than business acumen, 'that any honest factor residing in Kazvin may vent a thousand cloaths yearly.'

---

* Several European jewellers, particularly French, found employment at the Persian and Moghul courts, where their expert stone-cutting was in advance of local techniques and where they had an abundance of material to work upon.

Travellers' tales of Persian opulence probably enticed the Sherley brothers, Anthony and Robert, to try their fortunes in that direction in 1598. Their eldest brother Thomas, also imbued with the family's adventurous spirit, had come to grief in the Levant where a prosperous career as a privateer had abruptly ended when he captured a Turkish vessel and was later found selling the loot in Constantinople. The Turks imprisoned him for two years and he was released only after repeated intercessions with the sultan by the English ambassador, Henry Lello. He returned to England to spend the rest of his life avoiding one debtors' prison after another, dying penniless and forlorn some time after 1625.

Anthony and Robert were more glamorous. Acting as the first English ambassadors to Persia – unaccredited, it need hardly be added – their acceptance of the Persian way of life, and their success in befriending the progressive Shah Abbas, made far more headway with the hedonistic Persians than their mercantile countrymen ever achieved.

1. Shah Abbas the Great (1571–1629) who rebuilt the Persian empire after the Turkish conquest of the sixteenth century. Engraving from Sir Thomas Herbert, *Some Yeares Travail* (1634)

Setting off from Venice in 1598 accompanied by a group of like-minded Englishmen, they sailed to Tripoli and travelled to Antioch (where one of the party, John Mainwaring, was seized by the ear by a Turkish janissary and marched up and down the street while onlookers threw stones at him) and Aleppo. They crossed the Syrian Desert to Bir and sailed down the Euphrates to Baghdad; here Anthony's presents for the Shah were confiscated by the Turks who had spotted the lavish jewels with which Anthony had hoped to tempt Abbas. The party eventually reached Qazvin in a pilgrim caravan returning from the Shia shrines of Mesopotamia.

The Englishmen were warmly welcomed by Abbas 'whose entertaynment was so great, that the Persians did admire, that the King should vouchsafe such high favour to a meere stranger, without desert or tryall of his worth'. Abbas probably saw in the brothers the very instrument he needed for the reform of the Persian army to defeat the Turks. Travelling to Isfahan with Abbas the following year, Anthony persuaded the Shah that he was equipped to cope with any innovation: he would put Abbas in touch with the Levant Company, he knew the new military techniques of Europe. Perhaps

2. The Royal Palace, Isfahan, built by Shah Abbas. Engraving from J. S. Buckingham, *Travels in Assyria, Media and Persia* (1829)

he did; Abbas was shrewd enough to have seen through any im-
postor, but he insured himself, when eventually persuaded by
Anthony to send him as his envoy to Europe, by keeping Robert
in Persia.

Anthony's mission to Europe was disastrous; his credentials were
never quite good enough for him to be accepted as an official envoy
– English or Persian – and he ended his days in Spain, as penniless
as Thomas. Robert, left in Persia, wrote unhappy letters to his
brother complaining of being abandoned to heavens knows what
fate. 'I am almost distracted from the thought of anie helpe for my
delivery out of this countrye.' In fact he was busy with the Shah's
army, though there is little historical justification for Samuel
Purchas' eulogy in *Purchas his Pilgrims*: 'The mightie Ottoman, terror
of the Christian world, quaketh of a Sherley fever.... The prevailing
Persian hath learned Sherleian Arts of War...'. For a while he was
appointed governor of a fort guarding one of the eastern approaches
to Isfahan, which implies reward for some service (probably at the
capture of Baghdad), and consoled himself for the departure of his
companions by marrying a Circassian, Teresa Sanpsonia, allegedly
a relation of one of the Shah's wives.

At last he too was sent to Europe by Abbas to encourage European rulers to wage war against the Turks. In 1609 he arrived in
Rome wearing a crucifix-adorned turban – the crucifix an earlier
gift from the Pope. From there he went to Spain where he tried to
interest the Spaniards in the Persian silk trade. In England his reception by officials of the Levant and East India Companies was far
from warm; Sir Thomas Roe in particular was as strongly opposed
to Sherley personally as he was to his proposals.

At court, however, he was received with all the curiosity and
deference his vanity required. The sight of this resplendent figure,
dressed in Persian costume from head to foot, refusing to doff his cap
in the King's presence, titillated interest in the land of the Sophy
as much as Hakluyt's tales. Cartwright's *Preacher's Travels* came out
in 1611, the year of Sherley's arrival in England.* It described the
Shah's court and the Sherleys at home in Isfahan, where Cartwright
had met them surrounded by pomp and splendour. No amount of
cold-shouldering by London merchants could lessen Sir Robert's
glamour.†

---

* William Parry, a companion of Anthony Sherley, had already published his
Discourse upon the Travels of Sir Anthony Sherley in 1601; *Three English Brothers* was a
pamphlet produced by a famous pamphleteer, Anthony Nixon, in 1607 and in the
same year a play on the Sherleys – *Travailes of Three English Brothers* – was also staged.

† Robert Sherley was knighted in 1609 by the Austrian emperor when in Prague
on his way to Rome, and also made a Count Palatine of the Empire.

3. View towards the town of Shiraz, a town instantly recognisable, reported
one English traveller, as that claimed as Paradise by all Persians and
extolled by the Persian poet Hafiz. Engraving from Cornelius de Bruyn,
Travels into Muscovy, Persia etc. (1737)

But the adulation palled and fashion changed. The Sherleys
returned to Persia in 1616 (calling on the Moghul emperor on the
way) and left again almost immediately for Europe, on one more
vain attempt to interest European powers in Persia. Stopping in
Rome on the way to England, Robert and Teresa were painted by
Van Dyk. Robert is standing defiant but paunchy in a huge turban,
a Persian cloak and tunic richly embroidered with scenes from
Persian life; Teresa is sitting on a low divan or 'sopha', dressed in
Persian silks of a lightness and grace rare among the heavy brocades
of contemporary Europe. Van Dyk painted a self-portrait at about
the same time, in the guise of Paris, wild and exotic; perhaps he
was ensnared by this glimpse of strange lands as he saw them in

4. Sir Robert Sherley, painted by Sir Anthony van Dyk in Persian costume in 1662 as befitted one who claimed to be the emissary of the Shah

Robert and Teresa. But arriving again in London in 1624, they were as coldly received as before. In 1625 a certain Naqd Ali Beg arrived in London claiming that he was the Shah's ambassador and not Robert whom he branded as an imposter; he even went so far as to hit the Englishman on the face in public when Sir Robert went to his lodgings to pay his respects. Charles I decided to send them both back to Persia, Sir Robert accompanied by England's first official ambassador to the Shah, Sir Dodmore Cotton.

The party reached Bandar Abbas in 1627 and began the long trek northwards; its adventures were recorded by one of the members, Thomas Herbert. By the time they reached Isfahan the Shah had already left for his summer quarters at Ashraf on the shores of the Caspian. In Ashraf they were presented to Abbas with little ceremony, soon after following him to Qazvin. Here the Shah's streak of cruelty revealed itself. Prompted by a jealous courtier he publicly rejected Sir Robert as ever having represented him in other countries, 'wishing Sir Robert Sherley to depart his kingdom, as old and troublesome'. So the Sherleys had outlived their uses. Broken by his disgrace Robert Sherley died a month later. 'He was the greatest traveller of his time, and no man had eaten more salt than he, none had more relisht the mutabilities of fortune. He had a heart as free as any man: his patience was more philosophicall than his intellect, having small acquaintances with the Muses . . . from the Persian Monarch had enricht himself by many meriting services: but obtained least . . . when he best deserved, and most expected it.' He was buried under the threshold of the house where he died in Isfahan. Teresa fled to a Carmelite convent for protection and later went to Rome. Ten days later Cotton died as well. The embassy hurried south to the coast as fast as it could and embarked for England. No other English ambassador was sent to the Shah until the beginning of the nineteenth century.

Meanwhile the East India Company was trying to establish a foothold in the Persian and Red Sea trade, to offset the imbalance of trade with India. The Company was founded in 1600. Many of its sponsors were members of the Levant Company; the management of the seventeen 'committees' included Thomas Smythe, governor of the Levant Company, and John Eldred who was now treasurer of the Levant Company, and both companies shared the same secretary. At first funds for trading were raised by voluntary subscription among members for special voyages. Later the capital was raised for 'joint stocks' which operated over longer periods. The Company began trading in the East Indies, later moving to Surat on the Indian mainland in spite of Portuguese opposition. Sales in India of English cloth, however, would obviously always be limited by the climate and the Company began looking for other ways to avoid exporting bullion to pay for commodities bought in the east.

Two ill-fated attempts were made in 1609 and 1610 to open trade in the Red Sea, in particular with Mokha, the principal market which thrived on the annual pilgrim traffic to Mecca and attracted merchants from Egypt, the Levant and India. The Company sent a ship to Mokha in 1609 but had little success in persuading the Turkish authorities to trade. The following year Sir Henry Middleton, calling at Aden, found the Turks unfriendly and their colleagues at Mokha hostile to the point of enticing him and several of his companions on shore where they were imprisoned for six months before managing to escape back to their ships.

Middleton's misfortunes resulted in one of the first published accounts in English of Yemen,* but they also discouraged the Company from sending any more expeditions up the Red Sea for another eight years. Sir Thomas Roe, ambassador to the court of the Moghul emperor, in 1618 revived the suggestion that the dearth of markets for English cloth in India and the Far East could be met in the Red Sea: one ship from the yearly fleet to Surat should be sent from Surat to the Red Sea, laden partly with Indian goods and partly with English cloth to be sold in Mokha and the proceeds invested in India, in spices and other commodities, for the return journey to England. An expedition to Mokha in 1618 found the authorities there far more friendly than had poor Middleton and it was decided to persevere with the trade. From the middle of the seventeenth century a regular factory was established at Mokha to cope with the growing demand for coffee in Europe as well as in India.

All coffee drunk in Europe in the seventeenth century came from Mokha. Turkey merchants, yearning for the hot fortifying drink they had sipped in shady cafés in Smyrna and Aleppo, popularised the drink in England where it was imported from Mokha at first through Holland and later by way of India. European merchants in Yemen were obliged by Turkish fanaticism to keep their factories in this insalubrious port – few of them agreed with the description of the Danish traveller, Niebuhr, that he had not seen 'a sweeter, cleaner, better governed Towne than this of Mokha' – but most of the coffee was in fact grown some two hundred miles north near Bait al-Fakih.† In the eighteenth century Niebuhr found Bait al-Fakih a large

---

* Middleton's account was published by Samuel Purchas in 1625. John Jourdain, who was on the 1609 voyage to the Red Sea, kept a journal of his experiences which included descriptions of Sanaa and Aden, but it was not published until 1945 (by the Hakluyt Society).

† Beetlefuck in the Company's jargon.

sprawling town about half a day's journey from the coffee plantations up on the cooler hillsides. This was the legendary Arabia Felix where, thanks to an adequate rainfall, 'the trees grow so thick together, that the rays of the sun can hardly enter among their branches'.

So popular did the drink become in England that the Company's imbalance of trade was momentarily corrected. The pirate John Avery complained of several colleagues who abandoned piracy in favour of trading coffee between Mokha and Alexandria. But a hundred years later Yemen coffee was meeting serious competition in the markets of Europe, and even Egypt and the Levant, from coffee transplanted to the West Indies and the Far East. Soon trade for English merchants at Mokha was reduced to consignments for India. When Eyles Irwin passed through in 1777 he found a single English agent recently appointed to deal with Arab boats taking coffee to Bombay.

The same need to save bullion prompted the Surat factory to investigate the Persian trade, so exhaustively studied by Newbery, Fitch, Cartwright and their fellow adventurers but hitherto avoided because of Portuguese opposition based at the entrance to the Gulf at Ormuz. In 1615 Richard Steele and John Crowther were sent overland to Persia. In Isfahan they introduced themselves to Robert Sherley, much to his embarrassment and irritation in view of his own hostile reception by officials of the Company in London. 'It was too late to look after that business of our Nation', he told the two merchants, 'and seemed discontented with the company, and the Master and Merchants. . . . But at last said he was an Englishman and promised to effect our desires', to be presented to the Shah, who gave the Company permission to trade from any port in his dominions. Jask was chosen as a suitable port for the first factory.

For the next hundred years England's only links with Persia were through the unhappy Company merchants living mostly in Jask, later in Bandar Abbas (Gombrun) – subject to the Surat factory. The Portuguese menace was far less than had been feared: as their hold over the entrance to the Persian Gulf weakened, so the desire of the Persians, especially Abbas, to dislodge them increased. The English were obvious allies for an attack on Ormuz, which was captured in 1622. The Portuguese garrison was driven out to Muscat on the south-eastern point of the Gulf. As a reward for their help the English were allowed to establish themselves at Bandar Abbas and a few merchants also lived in Isfahan. The Persian trade was never substantial and the total number of merchants involved in it in Persia at any one time was seldom more than twenty. East India Company merchants in Persia often complained of English cloth imported by

Armenians from Aleppo underselling their own imports. After the initial enthusiasm aroused by the early travellers had died down English interest in the land of the Grand Sophy was very slight compared with that in the Ottoman Empire. As a result of Steele and Crowther's visit a yearly quantity of cloth, iron, lead and other goods arrived at Jask or Bandar Abbas and the proceeds were invested in silk, wool (a kind of mohair from Kirman) and occasionally other Persian goods.

There was little to recommend Bandar Abbas to the English living there – 'but an inch-deal between Gombrun and hell', thought Herbert – except that it was eight days' journey nearer Isfahan than Jask and factors had to travel to Isfahan twice a year to collect the silk. Herbert in 1628 found it already a thriving port and deplored the number of prostitutes who flocked there in winter. The Dutch were the only other Europeans to have a factory at Bandar Abbas. There are no tales of festivities, nostalgic picnics and games; the factory had its own fruit and vegetable garden a couple of miles outside the town and Dr John Fryer, a factory physician, declared the local oysters to be second only to the British variety, but the 'intolerably hot' climate forbade the delicacies the Levant factories enjoyed. The death rate among the factors was every bit as high as in plague-infested Iskenderun; 'blubber-fish' washed up on the beach in great quantities at certain times of the year were thought to cause its unhealthiness.* Some died from dysentery, some from cholera, others on the road between Bandar Abbas and Isfahan, violently or naturally. Small wonder that the Persian factories were considered outposts of the Indian trading system and in the eyes of most factors, who seldom spent more than a few years there, lacking in any of the amenities which made life tolerable in India or the Levant.

The road from Bandar Abbas to Isfahan wound inland through the mountains to Lar – 'up hill and down hill, through broken Rocks and unsteady stones, through kindled Fires from sulphurious caverns and the more raging effects of the burning Orb', wrote the hyperbolic Fryer who met most hazards during his journey to Isfahan: flooding and impassable torrents, heat, thieves and the ordinary discomforts of travelling by mule over rough roads for

---

* Fryer described the 'Gombrun' boils in picturesque detail: 'upon their first appearance they carry with them the presence of Imposthumations, but presently after suppuration a long white filament like a small chit comes forth, which gently caught by the head is wound over a Tender Twig, which while it increases is turned round, and fed with Rose water, by a Clout dipped there in to keep it moist, lest becoming dry it should dye; . . . it is rebellious to all Medecines and must be nourished with Milk and Butter or else a Poultice of the Patient's own Ordure.'

several weeks, though it was compensated in his case by an insatiable curiosity about his surroundings. Every traveller paused in Shiraz, instantly recognisable, said Fryer, as the town claimed as Paradise by all Persians. Its markets overflowing with sumptuous merchandise, its palaces, above all its gardens to greet the weary traveller on the outskirts of the town, delighted the eye and greatly impressed the English, accustomed to the formal gardens of the period: 'the loftiest cypress trees in the universe ... under whose shelter thrive the underwoods ... these, with the water courses, make the whole design of the Perspective; in which promiscuously are included Philberts, Haslenuts, Pistachios, Sweet Almonds, Cherries of both sorts, Peach, Apricot, Prunella, figs, prunes, grannet, chestnut, nectarines, quince and all those we call wall-fruit; oranges and limes begin to flag here, rejoycing more where cold is less felt, for tho' it is very hot now, it has a short but severe winter, for which cause Roses, Lillies and Jassemin, are shaded under all these to defend them from each extreme; and below these the violet and the Primrose, with what exalt not their Heads above the Grass.'

Isfahan was still more splendid. Isfahan nusf-i Jihan, said the Persians of their capital: Isfahan is half the world. So rich and fertile were the gardens round Isfahan, so ornamented with trees, that the Dutch traveller Cornelius de Bruyn had to wait until winter before he had a clear enough view to sketch the city. The great ornamental city of Shah Abbas was separated by the river Zayanda-Rud from the prosperous Armenian suburb of Julfa. From the palaces and gardens of the Julfa bank – 'all flourishing and beautifull replenished with a thousand kinds of grafte, trees and sweet smelling plants' – the traveller crossed the arcaded Allahverdi Khan bridge, built by one of Abbas' generals, and approached the great square of Maidan-i Shah.

Few Persian rulers left so many monuments as Abbas, who adorned Isfahan with the mosques and palaces that made it one of the most beautiful cities of its time. Of this city the Maidan was the centre. The nineteenth-century traveller James Silk Buckingham described it as at least four times as large as Grosvenor Square, Russell Square or Lincoln's Inn. On one side was the Lutfallah Mosque, built by Abbas and 'adorned with a fine dome covered on the outside with green and blue stones incrusted with gold'. The Masjid-i-Shah, which Abbas never saw completed, dominated the end of the square; along the other side was the Ali Qapu, the entrance to the royal palace – 'of great state and magnificence, far exceeding all other proud buildings on this citye', wrote Cartwright, in Isfahan not long after the palace was completed and wondering at arts unknown in England; 'the walls glister with red Marbel, and pargeting of divers

5. The Great Maidan of Isfahan where Persians used to play polo at festival times. Original drawing in sepia wash attributed to Sir Robert Ker Porter, similar to a larger view in his *Travels in Georgia, Persia etc.* (1821)

colours; yea, all the Palace is paved with Checker and Tesseled worke, and on the same is spread Carpets wrought with Silke and Gold; the windowes of Alabaster, white Marbel and much other spotted Marbel; the Poasts and Wickets of massy Ivory checkered with glistering blacke Ebony.' The Maidan itself was usually filled with 'shops and artificers', crowded with merchants, 'buffoons and mountebanks'. At festival times it became a sports arena where the Persians would play *chughan* or polo, hitting the ball between pairs of pillars erected for the purpose at either end of the Maidan.* Inside the palace the rooms, decorated with paintings and gold and enamelled work, furnished with the finest, softest Persian carpets, faced on to courtyards with gardens, blossoming trees and over-flowing fountains.

Life for European merchants in Isfahan was very different from that in Bandar Abbas and it is sad that there are no English accounts

---

* As with so many Persian ideas that were brought to England it is impossible to tell whether they were originally encountered and made their greatest impression in Persia or in northern India. But there were so few English in Persia compared with the number in India, even in the seventeenth century, that the Indian influence was almost certainly stronger.

of the factory there, apart from Fryer's and those in the India Office papers which are mostly concerned with day-by-day trading. Most of the Europeans readily adopted Persian dress, customs and amusements – why not when living in the heart of a civilised world? 'The chief exercises', wrote de Bruyn, 'are riding and darting the cane; shooting with the bow, and fowling, and their usual pastimes are tobacco and conversation. They are great lovers of chess and play it perfectly well.' Summer evenings were spent in the gardens by Persians and Europeans alike, 'where you see an infinite number of persons of both sexes taking the air ... some on horseback, some on foot, smoking and drinking coffee'. Foreigners entertained each other lavishly, attended each other's feast-days (and those of the Armenians), weddings (a few agents had their wives with them or had married Armenians) and funerals, and escorted each other in and out of the city at the end or start of long journeys. For their colleagues in Europe they countered the gloomy tales from the Gulf with a rosier picture of a decadent, hedonistic society.

The fact that the goods imported from Persia were largely luxury goods contributed to this image. James I had tried to set up a silk farm in Chelsea, hopefully planting mulberry trees, but unfortunately the fruit turned out to be the red variety and less digestible than the leaves of the white variety preferred by silk worms. The custom of nurturing and hatching the silk worm eggs in womens' bosoms, as practised in the Levant and Italy, may also have been hard to root in English soil. The project was a failure. Through the East India Company, however, England gained access to a regular source of raw and wrought silk. The rich Persian silks sold by the Company came into their own during the luxury-loving years of the Restoration; the puritanical Protectorate saw a serious lapse in the Persian silk trade but Charles II, brought up on the fringe of the French court, preferred the ornate damasks, velvets, brocades and silk gauzes fashionable in France. Silk manufacture was encouraged by the large number of French Huguenots (among them Sir John Chardin) who immigrated to England after the Edict of Nantes in 1685, including skilled silk weavers who settled in the Spitalfields area of London.

Many courtiers must have shuddered when, as Pepys wrote in September 1666, 'the King hath yesterday in Council declared his resolution of setting a fashion for clothes which he will never alter'. A month later the news was out. 'To Court,' wrote Evelyn in his diary, 18 October, 'it being the first time his Majesty put himself solemnly into the Eastern fashion of vest, changeing doublet, stiff collar, bands and cloake, into a comely vest after the Persian fashion, with girdle or straps and shoe stringe and buckles of which some were sette with precious stones.' Evelyn was delighted: as a good patriot he had particularly disliked the court's slavish imitation of French fashions, and both he and Pepys had new Persian vests promptly made.

Persian silk had excited interest among English clothiers since the first journeys to Persia and Richard Hakluyt the elder commissioned a London dyer, Morgan Hubblethorne, to go on the last 'northern' expedition to Persia, in 1581, to investigate Persian dyeing methods. Many of the influential merchants of Charles ii's reign, such as Dudley North, had themselves spent several years in the East and they played as important a part as Charles himself in popularising the more exotic clothes and fashions of the East. Paintings of the period often show their subjects wearing huge oriental turbans and robed in the long, loose coats worn by their counterparts in the Middle East. Typically Persian colours appear: the vivid blue-green of Persian ceramics was popularly known in Europe as 'pers'; an elaborately embroidered silk was called 'persienne'; 'persian' described a fine silk used for lining. Persian flower designs such as roses, carnations and hyacinths were common. Other Persian motifs, such as the hats of the Qizilbash, mall players (polo-players) and minarets, popularised first through imported materials, were later copied in a bastardised form on English cloth.*

Persian wrought-silk imports fell during the eighteenth century, partly because of the confusion in Persia and partly because of restrictive measures to protect the struggling English silk weavers. The market for English cloth in Persia was also diminished by war and from early in the century the Company could no longer count on the Persian trade to offset its imports from India.

The Company came increasingly to depend on Basra at the head of the Gulf as a vital link in its chain of communications with Europe, as well as being a safer and more reliable market than most of the traditional Persian markets. Basra and Baghdad had always been important stages in communications between India and Europe, and by employing Arabs or Turks as couriers the Company avoided some of the hazards of the desert crossing which had made it too risky as a trade route. Soon after the establishment of the Company in Persia, its first agent, Edward Connock, was writing to Aleppo arranging a regular mail service via Baghdad with suggestions reminiscent of the pigeon post, asking the consul to send him 'two footmen of the Arab nation, and such as have

---

*Again it is difficult to distinguish specifically Persian influences among the trends brought to England by East India Company imports; the Paisley pattern is the most famous of all Indo-Persian designs, this so-called tear of Allah appearing in the earliest Islamic designs found in Persia, but it is just as likely to have been introduced to England from Indian printed calicos.

wife and children or parents in that your city of Aleppo' which would ensure the swiftest return of the footman once assigned his despatches. Letters took nine to eleven months to arrive, of which the desert trip, some seven hundred and eighty miles long, took about thirty-eight days.

Company employees also began to use the overland route when travelling to and from India, and the Company's agent in Basra was responsible for contacting caravans for the desert crossing. Dr Edward Ives returned from India with despatches by this route in 1720. He and his eight companions joined a caravan at Basra – always advisable – taking with them by way of provisions 'one Bengal tent, two Arabian tents, 18 Arabian blankets, which, one with another, holds about 24 quart bottles'. They were to contain '72 bottles of Madeira wine, 58 of claret, 54 of Mango shrub, 15 of Arrack, 15 of cyder, 240 pounds of biscuits or rusk', and so on down to twelve quart bottles of common syrup clarified with whites of eggs and twenty camels hired to carry it all.

Occasionally the Company sent an agent to Baghdad. This once glorious city of the Abbasids was by this time smaller than Basra and most travellers reported it to have been very damaged by the intermittent civil wars of Mesopotamia. Despite its alleged 'most serene, temperate and wholesome air', Baghdad was particularly prone to devastating plagues, which discouraged its development as a permanent base until the nineteenth century.

The Persian factories themselves were only indirectly affected by the Afghan invasions, but the decline in the East India Company's trade was accentuated by the removal of the capital from Isfahan – a southern city relatively easily reached from the Persian Gulf – to Meshed, far away in the north-east. The full effect of this depression of trade is shown by Niebuhr's report that when he was in Bandar Abbas in 1767 he could not find a 'single European counting house in the city'. It was a factor of the Muscovy Company, John Elton, however, who pointed out that Meshed was within easy reach of the Caspian; it was also close to the centre of the silk industry in Gilan. In 1739 a determined Elton shipped goods across the Caspian to Reshd where he was granted a firman to trade by Nadir's son, Riza Quli. Back in England Elton conducted a persuasive campaign of promotion for his trade route in the *Gentleman's Magazine*, before returning to Moscow to win Russian permission to bring the silk back through Russia. In Reshd again, however, he quarrelled with the Russian consul and entered the service of the Shah, having been asked by Nadir to fulfil the Shah's life dream – the building of a Persian fleet.

An anxious Muscovy Company sent out Jonas Hanway, merchant

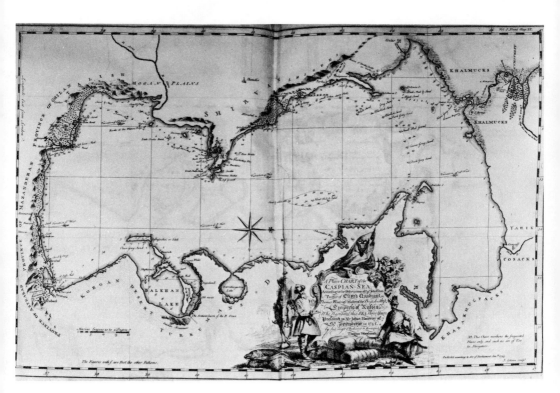

6. Chart of the Caspian Sea, from Jonas Hanway, *An Account of British Trade over the Caspian Sea* (1753). Hanway was sent to Persia in 1745 by the Muscovy Company

and philanthropist,* to investigate the position. On his way Hanway visited Elton working on the Shah's fleet at Langarud on the Caspian shore: 'as Gilan is generally esteemed the sink of Persia, so Langarud is considered the sink of Gilan', was Hanway's acid comment. He reached Astrabad just before it was captured by the rebel Qajars (later to be the ruling dynasty), who confiscated his goods and confined him to his lodgings where he wrote imploring prayers to pass the time: 'if thy gracious providence has ordained that my life now be brought to an end by these unthinking men, thy will be done. Avert, O Lord, the destruction that threatens them, and lay not my blood to their charge.'

After he was released he made his way to Hamadan (assailed on the road by robbers who threatened to enslave him), where the

---

* Hanway later conducted a fiery campaign against the drinking of tea, meeting his match in Dr Johnson who was a firm advocate of the drink. He is also known as one of the first people to walk around London using an umbrella.

7. Jones Hanway in Astrabad, 1745. Here he appears to be trying to placate local Qajar rebels. Engraving from Hanway's *Account*

Shah promised him full compensation for the loss of his goods, but he could only claim it by returning to 'that wretched place' Astrabad. 'How happy Persia might be, if a general depravity of manners did not involve her inhabitants in such an inextricable confusion,' he mused as he returned through the mountains to Astrabad, an opinion which was to become increasingly prevalent among visitors to Persia. Stone pyramids outside Astrabad covered with niches in each of which was a human head informed him of Nadir's defeat of the Qajars. He got his compensation, though not before the Shah's officials had tried to make him accept it in the form of concubines, which Hanway would have none of. Although Hanway returned to England fully persuaded that trade by the northern route was as impracticable as in the sixteenth century, and for much the same reasons, English merchants continued to trade at Reshd until the assassination of Nadir Shah in 1747, after which Qajar rebels plundered them of some eighty thousand pounds – an indication that the trade was not a complete failure.

La Ville de
SCHAMACHIE.
en Perse.

8. Shamakha in Persia, the residence of Abdullah Khan, ruler of Azerbaijan, who welcomed Anthony Jenkinson and his colleagues so warmly in 1561. Engraving by Pieter van der Aa

Elton never completed his fleet. He managed to launch one ship of twenty three-pounders but he himself was killed in a local rebellion in 1751 and the scheme collapsed. Nadir had been assassinated four years previously. Nadir also tried to build a fleet in the Gulf to protect Persian shores from marauding Arab pirates. He built a dockyard and had timber transported across Persia but again the plan fell through after his death. A so-called admiral of his fleet, Mullah Ali Shah, was found by Niebuhr in possession of Ormuz in 1767.

Bandar Abbas and the surrounding country had been unsettled for much of the century. In 1721 the town was attacked by four thousand Baluchi tribesmen who were beaten off with some difficulty by the English and Dutch factors. Pirates from the opposite side of the Gulf attacked the town on several occasions. In 1759, during the Seven Years' War, a French naval expedition bombarded the English factory and took the factors prisoner. The Company decided to abandon Bandar Abbas in favour of Basra where a British consulate was recognised by the Ottoman sultan in 1767. Mean-

while an agreement had been reached in 1763 with the local ruler of
Bushire for the English to establish a factory there, and the shaikh
had granted the Company a site for the factory, a garden and a
burial ground. Karim Khan in Shiraz (for which Bushire acted as
port) preserved a certain amount of peace and prosperity and it is
to this brief period of calm, under one of the more enlightened
despots of recent Persian history, that Shiraz owes its present
reputation as one of the most beautiful of Persian cities. In spite of
the favourable terms granted by Karim Khan in his firman to the
Company, trade was blighted by the instability of the north. No one
could afford to buy English products and Persian silk was replaced
on the English market by Bengal silk. Trade and relations with Persia
did not really recover until the firm establishment of the Qajar
dynasty and fear for India's security led to the embassies of Sir John
Malcolm and of Sir Harford Jones Brydges at the beginning of the
nineteenth century.

5 Not for Trafficking Alone

'An insatiable Desire for Liberty, of giving [men's] thoughts a larger field to expatiate in and an Occasion of actually viewing and contemplating such things in the Original as they had often admired in the bare Copy' – such were the emotions described by the traveller Veryard which inspired Jenkinson, Newbery and their mercantile contemporaries to venture so far afield in search of markets for English cloth: 'for lust of knowing what should not be known', as Flecker's court poet sang as he set out from Baghdad for Samarkand.

The sixteenth century was a period of expansion of knowledge in all directions – artistic, scientific and geographical. Bacon in his essay on travel wrote that 'travel in the younger set, is a part of education: in the elder, a part of experience.' Veryard believed that it was a man's duty to travel: nature had placed him upon a stage to be an actor, not a mere spectator, and he must learn to 'contact new worlds and with the Spartans fix the Bounds of our Empire as far as we can pitch our Spears'. The superficial traveller was condemned by Samuel Purchas as returning home with 'a few smattering terms, flattering garbes, Apish cringes, foppish fancies, foolish guises and disguises, the vanities of Neighbour Nations ... without furthering of their knowledge of God, the world or themselves'. And as a measure of occasional broad-mindedness, one of the most intelligent travellers of this period, Sir Henry Blount, had the temerity to wonder if the Turks were really as barbarous as travellers and historians made out, or were they governed 'by another kinde of civilitie, different from ours, but no lesse pretending'? Blount, more inquisitive than some, decided to see for himself, for 'an eye witness of things conceives them with an imagination more compleat, strong and intuitive than he can either apprehend or deliver by way of relation'.

English literature on the Middle East began in earnest with the publication of Richard Hakluyt's *Principal Navigations* in 1598. As a young man, Hakluyt was taken to visit his elder cousin, another Richard Hakluyt, a merchant with interests in eastern trade,* who so inspired him with the new geographical discoveries that he re-

* See above, p. 58.

solved 'if I ever were preferred to the University ... I would by God's assistance prosecute that knowledge and kinde of literature, the doors whereof were so happily opened to me'. In 1598 and over the next three years he published an enlarged three-volume edition of *Navigations*. 'After great charges and infinite cares,' he wrote in his introduction, 'after many watchings, toils and travels, and wearying out of my weak body, at length I have collected three severall volumes of the English Navigations, Traffiques and Dis-coveries, to strange, remote and farre distant countreys.'

Hakluyt preserved a mass of material, including accounts by English pioneers in Persia and the Levant, which would otherwise have perished. His successor, Samuel Purchas, continued his work in *Hakluytus Posthumous, or Purchas His Pilgrims*, published in 1625. No one is left out of the *Pilgrims*; the title page alone contains small wood-cut portraits of most travellers from Abraham to Menelaus, to Mandeville and onwards. He described his collection as 'pilgrim-guides', enabling his readers to travel to 'the most uncouth countries of the world' without the actual discomfort. 'These vast Volumes', he wrote, 'are contracted and Epitomised, that the nicer Reader might not be cloyed.' Purchas is more verbose and glib than the painstaking Hakluyt; though he might write that 'the Actors are the Authors themselves, each presenting his own actions and passions', he had no hesitation in omitting parts he considered un-suitable and inserting his own opinions in the margin.

Few of the early travels published by Hakluyt or Purchas have any literary pretensions. They describe unfamiliar scenes with little of the feeling for indigenous society and tradition which distinguishes the classic travelogues. Their authors were strangers to the languages as well as to the countries through which they travelled and often used heavy irony to hide their ignorance of an outlandish society. Their ponderous style was modelled on classical authors – Herodotus, Ptolemy and Pliny were the most popular – from whom they cribbed outrageously to fill the gaps in their own observations. Congreve puts these entertaining but biased writers in their places in *Love for Love*: 'I know the length of the Emperor of China's foot,' says Sir Sampson Legend of the East India Company, 'have kissed the Great Moghul's slipper, and rid a hunting upon an Elephant with the Cham of Turkey – Body o' me, I have made a Cuckold of a King, and the present Majesty of Bantam is the issue of these Loins.' Answers old Foresight: 'I know when travellers lye or speak the Truth, when they don't know it themselves.'

But the greatest contribution of Hakluyt's and Purchas's volumes – Hakluyt's especially – was their stimulation of further voyaging. Several accounts of the Levant and Persia, collected by Purchas or published on their own, show a greater interest in the history and society of the area than those collected by Hakluyt, their authors inspired as much by desire to see places described by Hakluyt's authors as to investigate trade. Tom Coryate, for instance, who with a mixture of what Johnson called 'learning, wit and buffoonery' had entertained his contemporaries with verses on his travels in Europe early in the seventeenth century, travelled on foot through the Levant, Persia and further east from 1612 to 1617, dying at Surat in 1617. All we know of his travels in the Middle East are a few letters and some fragments published by Purchas. Coryate it was who wrote:

> I loathe to live long in a private place,
> Myself I love, but I am born to wander,
> And I am glad when I extremes embrace,
> Sweet sour delight must my contentment render,
> So, so I walk to view hills, towns and plains,
> Each day new sights, new sights consume all pains.

William Lithgow was another sturdy pedestrian sight-seer, with a more vitriolic pen than the gentle Coryate's: 'I scorne to draw my pen to the ignorant fools, neither shall it stoop to the proud Knave, for I contemne both'. He was violently anti-Papist and gleefully abused Catholics as 'snakish Papists', 'that snarling crew', whose 'despightful waspishness' he found round many corners. George Sandys and Henry Blount, gentlemen travellers who toured the Ottoman Empire in the first half of the seventeenth century, are interesting to compare: Sandys, the scholarly son of a bishop, always ready to defend Christianity against Islam, while Blount, a remarkably tolerant observer, wrote one of the best seventeenth-century accounts of the Ottoman Empire and excused his tolerance by maintaining that the hasty traveller, such as he, often had a fresh and sincere impression which a longer residence might turn to a 'biased love or hatred'.

Descriptions of pilgrimages to Palestine form a distinct class within early travel literature of the Middle East. Pilgrims were among the earliest visitors to the area. They used to sail from Venice to Jaffa on special pilgrim galleys, were met in Jaffa by the warden of San Salvatore, the Franciscan monastery which housed most European pilgrims in Jerusalem, and escorted to the Holy City. The galley fell into disuse, however, during the Venetian wars with the Turks and post-Reformation pilgrims from England preferred to include the Holy Land (which they now claimed to scorn) in a general tour of the Levant. Some, such as Henry Timberlake and George Sandys, came by camel from Cairo; Sandys crossed the 'forsaken' Sinai Desert with a party of Italians and elderly Jews going to Jerusalem to die or to bury their dead. Fynes and Henry Moryson came by

sea, disastrously as it happened; for on landing Henry was in such
ecstasy that he flung himself on the ground, hit his nose and had
a violent nose bleed and 'howsoever this be a superstitious sign of
ill, yet the event was to us tragicall by his death shortly after happen-
ing' – in Iskenderun.

But the commonest route, especially after the establishment of the
Levant Company, was from northern Syria, either inland through
Damascus or along the Mediterranean shore. Travelling in the
Levant was hazardous, though it seemed less so at this period than
in the nineteenth century when the contrast between travel in the
Middle East and in England was greater. A prefatory poem to
Lithgow's *Peregrination* praised him for his courage in the face of
adversity – 'by Sea, land, alone in cold and raine, Through Bandits,
Pirats and Arabian Theeves'.

A pilgrim was obliged to pay an entrance fee to Jerusalem (and
to the Holy Sepulchre), his weapons were removed to be returned
on departure because the Turks were justifiably afraid of religious
strife, and he was forbidden to ride anything except donkeys.*

---

*John Sanderson got away with riding a horse because he knew the Greek
Patriarch.

1. Interior of the Church of the Holy Sepulchre, one of the earliest European
depictions of the Sepulchre. Engraving from de Bruyn, *Voyage*

Jerusalem itself was 'a verie desolate place', according to Henry
Timberlake, much of it 'grasse, mosse, and weedes, like as to a piece
of ranke or moist ground'. The pilgrim was taken round the sights
(divided by the Aleppo chaplain William Biddulph into three
categories: Apparent Truths, Manifest Truths and Things Doubtful),
by one of the San Salvatore monks. A later pilgrim, James Silk
Buckingham, reckoned that the authority of the monks counted for
more than that of the Bible when it came to establishing holy sites,
but when he suggested this to a monk he was implored to keep his
doubts to himself lest he should upset his fellow pilgrims. Sanderson
warned his compatriots to learn some Italian before they went to
Jerusalem because no other European language was spoken.

Most pilgrims also undertook the dangerous and wearying trip
to the River Jordan through the mountains of Judaea. 'A most
miserable dry barren place it is,' wrote Henry Maundrell of the
route, 'consisting of high rocky mountains, so torn and disordered
as if the earth here had suffered some great convulsion, in which
its very bounds had been turned outwards.' In the Jordan valley
'some stripp'd and bath'd themselves in the River; others cut down
boughs from the trees; every man was employed one way or another
to make a memorial of this famous stream'. Sanderson and Lithgow,
for instance, took branches of the turpentine tree, Lithgow presenting his to James I.

The Dead Sea inspired some of the more fantastic tales of the
Holy Land. Even such prosaic travellers as Lithgow and Teonge
subscribed to some of them, for instance that birds flying over its
salt waters would die from the fumes they exuded, or that apples
growing beside the lake crumbled to dust and ashes when bitten.
The apples in fact are likely to have been a kind of gall-nut whose
flesh does indeed disintegrate into a kind of powder.

The pilgrim who had visited the right number of holy places was
given a certificate and could then be made a Knight of the Holy
Sepulchre by the abbot, 'but no good English subject will accept
that order of knighthood', scoffed Lithgow, as it also involved swear-
ing allegiance to the Pope. There were various other souvenirs.
Tattooing was a favourite and the Jerusalem cross the commonest
design; Lithgow caused an uproar when he had the English royal
arms tattooed underneath the cross, thereby polluting the Holy
Sepulchre 'with the name of such an Arch-enemy of the Roman
church'. Others brought home Jerusalem garters embroidered with
their names and the date of their visits.

One of the best accounts of a pilgrimage was by Henry Maundrell,
Aleppo chaplain at the end of the seventeenth century – 'the chaste,
the accurate and the pious Maundrell', as Buckingham called him.
Conscious of his position as a representative of the English church,

Maundrell was suitably scathing about the various legends of the Holy Land, 'only kept up, as my Lord Bacon observes many false notions are, because it serves as a good allusion and helps the Poets to a similitude'. English pilgrims approached the Holy Land with curiosity tempered by scepticism, but most left impressed by the devotion which surrounded the holy places. As Fynes Moryson remarked, 'the very places struck me with a religious horror and filled my mind, prepared to devotion, with holy motives'.

Maundrell's account is a good example of the change that gradually took place, from the end of the seventeenth century, in the attitude of travellers to the countries which they visited. To begin with there was little interest in the remains of classical antiquity which littered the shores of the eastern Mediterranean. The magnificent ruins of Baalbek, standing so conspicuously in the Bekaa valley, are rarely mentioned in English accounts before Maundrell visited them on his return from Jerusalem. George Wheler a few years earlier showed a similar almost unprecedented interest in the ruins near Smyrna. Members of the Levant Company living in the Middle East occasionally collected inscriptions, coins or manuscripts and East India Company merchants travelling between Bandar Abbas and Isfahan occasionally diverged from the path to visit the massive ruins of Persepolis near Shiraz. But Tom Coryate and William Lithgow were exceptional in battling their way to the Troad, which they both believed was Troy (eventually proved to have been about twelve miles to the south), and both were immensely proud of their effort. Coryate made himself a knight of Troy:

> Brave Brute of our best English Wits commended;
> True Trojan from Aeneas race descended;
> Rise top of wit, the honour of our Nation,
> And to old Ilium make a new Oration.

while Lithgow thought his visit important enough to publish a picture of himself astride the ruins, inscribed, 'Loe here's mine effigie, and Turkish suit, Placed in old Ilium.'

Thomas Roe, ambassador in Constantinople from 1621 to 1628, was among the first of a long line of European diplomats to enrich their native lands with classical relics, beginning with inscribed slabs or carved capitals and increasing until in the nineteenth century whole temples and tombs were being removed. A predecessor of Roe's, Sir Thomas Glover, set the fashion for buying antiques and manuscripts for the English aristocracy, employing a team of agents throughout the Levant for this purpose. On his appointment as ambassador Roe was asked by both the Earl of Arundel and the Duke of Buckingham to help them in their searches by getting permits from the Turks to remove objects from

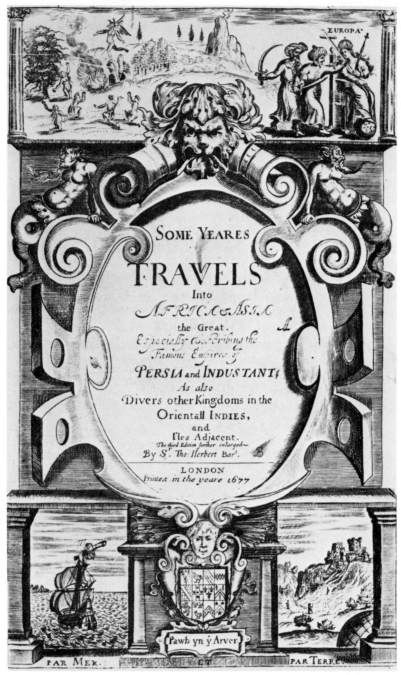

2. Title page of Sir Thomas Herbert's *Some Yeares Travail* (1634). It is interesting to compare Herbert's images of the Middle East with Thomas Fuller's
more fanciful ideas, illustrated on p. 81

the Empire. Roe was reluctant, but wanted to insure against a prolonged stay in the Ottoman capital by keeping his powerful friends.

Roe was contacted in the Levant by an agent of Arundel's, first John Markham, who died soon after arriving ('statues, columns, or antique works in stone, Mr Markham, while he lived, hath ransacked the country', wrote Roe to Arundel), and later William Petty, whom Roe found a dangerous rival in his own efforts to satisfy Buckingham. Much to Roe's annoyance Petty refused to use his expertise for Buckingham's benefit as well as Arundel's. Buckingham and Roe were agreed in being interested in objects of aesthetic more than historical value. Referring to Petty's and Arundel's enthusiasm for the crumbling statues over the Golden Gate in Constantinople Roe wrote to Buckingham: 'They are in my eye extremely decayed; but Mr Petty doth so praise them, as that he hath not seen much better in the great and costly collections of Italy.' Roe's attempts to get permission to remove these statues finally awoke the Turks to the value of their antiquities and they began to be more wary of European depredations.

Petty was indefatigable; even after he had been shipwrecked off the coast of Smyrna and lost a whole cargo of statuary, he hurried back to Pergamon, Ephesus and other sites, 'where he hath made your Lordship great provision', Roe told Arundel. Arundel followed contemporary fashion in arranging the statuary round his house and garden; portraits of himself and his wife show them seated at the entrance to the gallery which stretches into the distance, a vista of marble gods and goddesses. No doubt the hero of the seventeenth-century play, *The Antiquary*, was modelled on Arundel and his friends when he was described as one who sits 'all day in contemplation of a statue with ne'er a nose'.

Arundel and Buckingham might set about their depredations with a semblance of legality by working through Roe, but not all early antiquarians were as scrupulous. Sir Kenelm Digby, on a privateering expedition in the eastern Mediterranean in 1628, considered the collection of marble antiquities as profitable as hunting down richly laden ships. On Delos – 'to avayle myself of the convenience of carrying away some antiquities there' – Digby put his men to work rolling enormous pieces of marble down to the shore. They regarded this as a challenge – 'one stone, the greatest and fairest of them all, containing four statues, they gave over after they had bin, three hundred men, a whole day about it'.

By the eighteenth century Horace Walpole, on his interminable tours of the stately homes of England, was describing the fashion for Graeco-Roman statuary from Asia Minor without which no land-

scaped garden was complete:* at Easton Newton for instance there
was a statue of Tully 'haranguing a numerous assembly of decayed
Emperors, vestal virgins with new noses, Collussus's, Venus's, head-
less carcasses and carcaseless heads, pieces of tombs and hieroglyphs'.

Roe himself was more enthusiastic about collecting coins and
manuscripts, if his ruthlessness in acquiring the latter is anything to
go by. 'I have begun to deal plainly with the Patriarch,' he wrote
to the Archbishop of Canterbury, 'who hath made a great collection,
that his olde books rott and rust by him among ignorant Greeks,
that will never understand, nor make use of them; that in right they
belong to the Church of God, that will publish them.' This last point
Roe used most persuasively. In urging the Greeks to send their
manuscripts to England where they could be printed and returned
multiplied to Constantinople, Roe and his contemporaries acquired
a number of documents dealing with the early Christian Church,
including the Codex Alexandrinus which Roe's friend the Greek
Patriarch ostensibly presented to James I. Soon Oxford and Cambridge were besieged by vagrant Greek priests trying to sell their
manuscripts themselves.† The oriental scholar, Edward Pococke,
bought a large collection when he was in the Levant. John Greaves,
another scholar, was among the many who believed that there was a
library of Greek manuscripts in the Serail, and, like Roe, pursued
the Greek Patriarch for his treasures until the unfortunate man was
unexpectedly arrested and 'as a traytor strangled and his body thrown
into the sea'.

The discovery of Palmyra at the end of the seventeenth century
resulted eventually in one of the most famous antiquarian publications of the following century, Robert Wood's *Palmyra*. The vast
desert city, founded by the Greeks and prospering until the defeat of
its rebellious Queen Zenobia in the third century by the Romans,
remained hidden from the inquisitive gaze of merchants and
travellers for many years. In 1678 two English merchants in Aleppo
decided to trace the rumours picked up from local *beduin* of a ruined
city to the east of Aleppo. On their first attempt they were turned
back by hostile Arabs, but a second better-armed party in 1691
reached Palmyra about two weeks after leaving Aleppo. The journal
of their discovery was published in the Royal Society's *Philosophical
Transactions*, an unsatisfactory account by any standard, giving no

---

* The taste for classical Greek sculpture had yet to be acquired: even Elgin's
Parthenon marbles, when first displayed in London, were abused as too true to life
and lacking in imagination.

† These same Greek priests were the first to introduce coffee-drinking into
England and one of the first coffee houses in England, the Angel Inn, was
opened in Oxford in 1650.

3. James Dawkins and Robert Wood first discovering a sight of Palmyra. The only concessions to an oriental atmosphere made in this severely classical scene is the turban worn by Giovanni Battista Borra, the artist who accompanied Wood and Dawkins to Syria and who is seen drawing in the righthand corner, and the Turkish horsemen hired to protect the party. Engraving by John Hall, 1773, from a painting by Gavin Hamilton

record of their impressions of Palmyra where they seem to have spent only a few days. Nevertheless their description of the extensive panorama of ruined temples, tower tombs and wide arcaded streets – however blown and weathered by centuries of sand – was enough to stimulate theorising and conjecture.* Various scholars tried their hand at interpreting Palmyra, in the light of ancient writers and the few inscriptions copied by the party, but they lacked any comprehensive account on which to base their calculations.

---

* Captains Irby and Mangles who visited Palmyra about 1820 were very disenchanted: 'not a single pediment, architrave or frieze worthy of admiration and we judged Palmyra to be hardly worthy of the time, expense, anxiety and the fatiguing journey – we suspect that it was the difficulty of getting to Tadmore [the Arab name] and the fact that few travellers have been there, that has given rise to the great renown of the ruins.'

Some seventy years passed before Robert Wood and his companions filled the gap.

Wood had visited the Middle East in 1743, and in 1749 he readily agreed to accompany two young gentlemen (one of whom died on the way at Magnesia) on a second visit. They spent some time in Asia Minor and in 1751 reached Palmyra, where they spent two weeks. On his return to England in 1753 Wood published one of the most superb examples of contemporary scholarship, on Palmyra, and a similar volume on Baalbek two years later, both illustrated with magnificent engravings from drawings by his companion artist, Giovanni Battista Borra. 'Of all works that distinguish this age,' wrote Horace Walpole, 'none perhaps excel those beautiful editions of Baalbek and Palmyra. ... The pomp of the buildings has not a nobler air than the simplicity of the narration.'

Antiquarianism was the great eighteenth-century hobby and innumerable societies were set up about this time for its study. The Earl of Sandwich and Dr William Stukeley (both of whom as young men had included the Levant in their grand tours) founded the Egyptian Club, 'to enquire into Egyptian antiquities' and to promote and preserve 'Egyptian and other learning'. Sandwich was the first president, known as the 'sheich'; other members called themselves 'philoaegyptians' and had themselves painted in Turkish costume. Sir William Jones, a celebrated Persian scholar, was a

4. Palmyra, visited by Wood and the artist Borra in 1751; the publication of their account, with engravings from Borra's drawings, was hailed as a masterpiece of the period. Engraving from Wood's *Ruins of Palmyra* (1753)

5. Measuring a statue in Egypt, at a time when very few foreigners risked a journey outside Cairo or Alexandria. Engraving from F. L. Norden, *Travels in Egypt and Nubia* (1757)

member of the Society of Antiquaries, as were the Bandar Abbas physician, John Fryer, and the antiquarian Richard Chandler. In 1769 Chandler produced a lavish volume – *Marmora Oxoniensis* – describing the Arundel marbles so carefully collected by Roe, Markham and Petty and acquired by Oxford University in 1735.

The Society of Dilettanti, formed about 1735 by classical and antiquary enthusiasts, was the most industrious of these societies. Sandwich was again one of the leading members. In 1764 the Society commissioned Chandler, Nicholas Revett, an architect, and a painter, William Pars, to undertake an expedition to Greece and Asia Minor, a project inspired by Robert Wood on the pattern of his own surveys of Palmyra and Baalbek. Using Smyrna as their headquarters they were told to 'collect information and to make observations relative to the ancient taste of these countries, and to such monuments of antiquity as are still remaining'. A copy of Chandler's journal (published in 1773) which Revett annotated indicates some strain between the antiquary, the architect and the painter and their various interests. None of this is apparent, however, in the official publication, *Ionian Antiquities*, which, together with Wood's publications, helped arouse the marked enthusiasm for Graeco-Roman art and architecture in the closing years of the century. Wood's Palmyrene Temple of the Sun had already been reproduced in Stourhead Park and Osterley; now it was the turn of Asia Minor and Lord le Dispenser had the Temple of Teos built under Revett's direction in his grounds near High Wycombe.

Perhaps it was the intrepid Lady Mary Wortley Montagu who irrefutably demonstrated to her countrymen that men and women of fashion, taste and education could survive travelling in the east, living among Turks and Muslims and deprived of the pleasures of London society.* Lord Sandwich embarked on the Grand Tour in 1738 with his tutor; discouraged by war from travelling in Europe they went instead to Constantinople, Asia Minor and Egypt. William Ponsonby also included Asia Minor on his Grand Tour. A more notorious visitor was Frederick Baltimore, who went to Turkey in 1763, accompanied by an artist as was increasingly the fashion. Baltimore's own account of his journey is brief and unpretentious, but five years later after a scandalous trial in which he was accused and acquitted of rape, the injured damsel published the *Memoirs of the Seraglio of the Bashaw of Merryland*† by a 'Discarded Sultana' in which Baltimore is described as having 'imported every species of Asiatic luxury, without consulting his own constitution or the climate of his mother country'. Old tales of oriental splendour died hard.

By the middle of the eighteenth century most published accounts of the area were far more serious and accurate than their predecessors. Hakluyt and Purchas had been succeeded by several huge editions of travels, sometimes running into as many as ten volumes, claiming to assemble every tale of travel ever written. Now in the eighteenth century came the large, expensive folios, often financed by one of the many societies which sprang up at the time, filling the well-stocked libraries which occupied such a prominent place in the new houses. The Society for the Encouragement of Learning was one of these, founded to assist authors to publish expensive books. 'A man must carry knowledge with him, if he would bring home knowledge,' said Johnson, an injunction obeyed by several of the erudite gentlemen who now visited the Middle East, no longer content, either, with touring the area in a few months.

Richard Pococke, author of the *Description of the East*, was a well-to-do clergyman who spent three years exploring the Middle East,

---

* Lady Mary herself collected several antiquarian mementos of her travels, though in her case – unlike her later countrymen – her depredations along the coast of Asia Minor were limited by the ship's captain's refusal to allow anything large on board.

† So called from the estate owned by Baltimore in Maryland.

from 1737–40. He apologises to those of his readers who might think his book a mere travelogue: 'such as delight only in ... the history of the several little accidents that happen, may pass over, with a transient view, the dry descriptions of plans, buildings, and statues which others may esteem the most valuable part of the book.' Gibbon praised his 'superior learning and dignity', though criticising him for too often confusing what he had seen with what he had heard. Pococke and Charles Perry were among the few travellers to go up the Nile beyond Cairo; Perry, who was in the Levant and Egypt between 1739 and 1740 and published his *View of the Levant* in 1743, declared that 'we are really sick and surfeited' of the endless discussions of the Pyramids, and turned his back on them to visit remoter parts of Egypt. His account is also one of the best contemporary descriptions of the eighteenth-century Ottoman Empire. James

6. James Bruce of Kinnaird, who travelled through Egypt to Abyssinia about 1770. Frontispiece portrait from his *Travels to discover the source of the Nile* (1768–73)

Bruce's *Travels* covered most of North Africa, one of the earliest and certainly one of the best accounts of a little-known area. Alexander Russell's *Natural History of Aleppo* (where Russell was doctor to the Levant Company from 1745 to 1753) is a delightful and exhaustive survey of the society, flora, fauna and particularly the plague (on which he became a recognised expert) of a major Ottoman city. These are only the better-known and better-written examples of the kind of erudite travelogue which fed, somewhat indigestibly, the growing curiosity in the eastern Mediterranean, the Levant and Egypt.

6 Flowers of Luxuriant Fancy

The interest aroused in England by the adventures and the adventurers described in the last chapters took a variety of forms. Academic appreciation of the Middle East grew from the study of the history and language of the area, also inspired by its greater proximity as it became known through travellers: historians could draw on their accounts for material and philologists could study the documents they brought back. Poets and playwrights reproduced the exotic scenes portrayed often with such rich imagery by those who had actually been there. Why indeed, asked one poet:

> ... Should we praise the venturing Merchant more
> That brings bright Pearls from th'Erythraean shore;
> Or Gold from Inde, t'enrich his countrymen,
> Than him that Traffiques with a skilful pen,
> T'adorn his Native land with Forrein Wit?*

Historians of the sixteenth and seventeenth centuries were attracted principally by the power and might of Turkey and its seeming invincibility. Sir Henry Blount was not alone in thinking that Turkey represented the height of contemporary civilisation and as such should be studied by all and sundry. Ponderous histories attempted to explain the Turks' success while also providing a background to the contemporary accounts published by Hakluyt, Purchas and their successors. The most popular of these was Richard Knolles' *General History of the Turks*, first published in 1603 and brought up to date in 1670 by Paul Rycaut. Dr Johnson thought the history incomparable, though unfortunately about 'a remote and barbarous people' about whom 'none desire to be informed'. Byron claimed it was one of the first books to amuse him as a child, affecting his later desire to visit the Levant, and 'gave me perhaps the oriental colouring which is observed in my poetry'. Gibbon on the other hand wondered more prosaically whether 'a partial and verbose compilation from Latin writers, 1300 pages of speeches and battles, can either instruct

* By Thomas Hay, published in John Greaves' edition of *The Seraglio* by Robert Withers, 1650.

or amuse an enlightened age'. It certainly amused and also instructed Knolles' own generation. As history it is prejudiced and inaccurate but there is a certain splendour about Knolles' sonorous prose and the grandiose scale of the history.

Paul Rycaut was another influential historian who besides editing later editions of Knolles' history also wrote one of his own, *The Present State of the Ottoman Empire*, which included an excellent review of its past state. Rycaut was unusual among early historians of the Ottoman Empire in that he had actually lived there: he first went to the Levant as secretary to the ambassador, Lord Winchilsea, in 1661 and during the following six years collected most of the material for his history, a lively account of the Empire and its background. In 1667 he was appointed consul in Smyrna where he lived until 1679. A number of other histories were also published in the sixteenth and seventeenth centuries, none comparable to those of Knolles or Rycaut, but each in its time a source of information and drama to contemporary writers.

The Ottoman Empire stimulated more interest than Persia because its presence was of greater concern to Europe. Histories of Persia were harder to come by. The history of ancient Persia was written from time to time, using standard biblical and classical authorities, but medieval Persia was virtually a blank in English historiography from the sixteenth to the eighteenth centuries and English writers drew almost exclusively on travel literature for their information. In this respect the works of Thomas Herbert, Sir John Chardin and the Dutchman Cornelius de Bruyn were particularly valuable, both for their perceptive comments on the present scene and for their summaries of the preceding Safavid shahs, supplying thereby a modicum of history for their contemporaries. Thomas Herbert, for instance, added an entertaining history to his account of Cotton's embassy (in spite of the delight he takes in dwelling on the more bloodthirsty aspects of Safavid rule) though he is at his best when describing contemporary Persia, often with reference to the past, as he journeyed through the country.

By far the best account of Safavid Persia is that of Sir John Chardin, the French jeweller with the 'eyes of a philosopher', who was in Persia at the coronation of Sulaiman III in 1667, and later from 1673 to 1676, and whose profession took him into the highest court circles. He is probably the only writer on Persia at this time who studied Persian in Persia for any length of time: 'I was so solicitous to know Persia', he wrote, 'that I knew Isfahan better than Paris ... the Persian language was as easie to me as French and I could currently read and write it.' His *Travels* were translated into English in 1686, five years after his Protestantism had led him to emigrate to England. Like Herbert, he prefixed his account of Persia with a brief history which became a popular source of information on that country, supplementing previous accounts by Herbert, merchants such as Newbery and biographers of the Sherleys. Cornelius de Bruyn's *Travels*, another detailed picture of the contemporary Persian scene, were published in English in 1737.

Most of the early historians of the Ottoman Empire were writing from secondary sources – earlier histories published in Europe and information supplied by travellers. The study of Arabic, Turkish or Persian documents was far outpaced by public interest in the countries concerned. Even Rycaut is unlikely to have consulted any Turkish documents, historical or otherwise. Some of the most valuable works of theology as well as of medicine and mathematics known to the medieval world were in Arabic and classical scholars of the early Renaissance discovered that much of Greek philosophy and literature was preserved only in medieval Arabic translations emanating from Islamic universities. But oriental languages were studied mainly for the light they would throw on the development of Christianity.

William Bedwell, the founder of Arabic studies in England, stressed the practical importance of the universality of Arabic as a *lingua franca* of religion, diplomacy and commerce from the Atlantic to the China Seas. One of Bedwell's publications, *The Arabian Trudgman*,* explained Arabic terms used by European writers, a useful guide to any reader of oriental travel literature in which these terms appear in countless forms and spellings bearing little relation to the original. Knowing the language did not immediately lead to understanding the religion and society, however. The fact that early Arabic scholars were generally clerics bedevilled English Arabic studies until the latitudinarian scholars of the eighteenth century adopted a gentler attitude. Bedwell subscribed to the general prejudice against Islam, referring to Muhammad as 'the name of that famous imposter and seducer of the Arabians or Saracens ... and inventour of the Alkoran and laws of that superstitious faction'.

Some of the strangest legends appearing in literature on the Middle East were inspired mainly by intolerance of Islam. Thomas Fuller, for instance, whose *Pisgah Sight of Palestine* is one of the more confusing collections of truth and superstition, repeats the well-known legend that 'Mahomet's tomb at Mecca is said strangely to hang up, attracted by some invisible loadstone'. Other writers held

* Probably few of Bedwell's readers appreciated the pun in *trudgman*, a word he derived from the Turkish word, *tarjuman*, meaning translator, and the origin of *dragoman*.

1. Title page from Thomas Fuller, *A Pisgah Sight of Palestine* (1650), showing some of the inaccuracies and myths about the Holy Land which books such as this helped to perpetuate.

as erroneously as Fuller that Muhammad was buried at Mecca, that on his death his flesh had been eaten by swine and that his coffin had been destroyed by lightning. Dudley North might be attacked by superstitious Turks for using his 'magic' watch to make a tight-rope walker fall, but equally Pietro della Valle, an Italian traveller, watching a snake-charmer in Cairo knew 'full well' that the devil was behind him as behind all things Muslim.

Sir Thomas Adams, a draper of London, endowed an Arabic lecture at Cambridge in 1632. The vice chancellor, thanking Adams, wrote that 'the work itself we conceive to tend not only to the advancement of good literature by bringing to light much knowledge that is lockt up in that learned tongue but also to the good service of the King and State in our commerce with those eastern nations'. Sir Thomas was presumably more interested in the latter consideration. He also paid for a translation of the Bible into Persian for proselytisation, inspired perhaps by the apocryphal tale in *The Preacher's Travels* that Shah Abbas had been converted to Christianity by Robert Sherley.

The study of Arabic for biblical research inevitably led to interest in the great wealth of Arabic literature for its own sake. Bedwell and a Dutch Arabist, Matthias Pasor, were responsible for the oriental education of the greatest of early Arabists, Edward Pococke, one of the few actually to have lived in the Middle East, where he was chaplain to the Levant Company in Aleppo from 1630 to 1636. He spent these years studying Arabic and Turkish, Chaldean and Syriac, in learned discussions with members of the many Christian sects still existing in Syria and in busily buying oriental manuscripts, some for Archbishop Laud and some for himself which he gave to the Bodleian Library. Laud later founded a chair for Arabic at Oxford and persuaded Pococke to occupy it for a year, after which he returned to the Levant – to Constantinople – for more manuscripts. Pococke's first-hand experience of Islam stood him in good stead when he produced a commentary on the Old Testament, but more important it helped to develop Arabic scholarship in a wider field than that of the Bible. In particular his *Specimen Historiae Arabum*, a series of Latin essays on Arab religion, literature and science, marked a new advance in oriental studies based on Pococke's own manuscripts. It is remarkable for the magnitude of its erudition. A pupil of Pococke's, Robert Boyle, who studied Arabic in order to be able to sweep away the 'groundless traditional conceptions' cluttering contemporary science, also paid for Pococke to translate into Arabic a tract by Grotius on Christianity, which it was optimistically hoped would convert Muslims.

As more Arabic documents were brought to Europe and translated, the earlier intolerance of Islam was tempered, under the guidance of scholars such as Pococke and later Arabists, by the development of an historical appreciation of the part played by the East in the growth of European civilisation. One of the most outstanding eighteenth-century historians of Islam was an Arabic scholar, Simon Ockley. Ockley's *History of the Saracens*, published in several editions in the eighteenth century, is in a different class from earlier histories, not merely because he wrote it in English, as opposed to Latin, and thereby made it available to the general reader. Ockley based his history on Islamic manuscripts in the Bodleian where he would

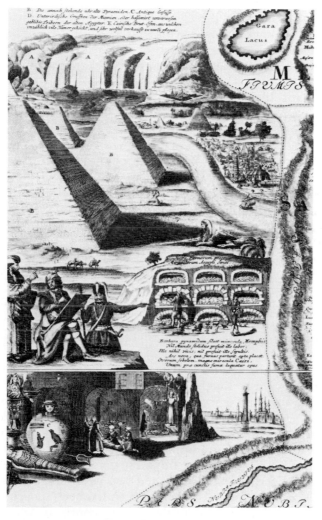

2. The Pyramids and the Nile, a fanciful map from *Le voyage du Sieur Paul Lucas* (1720)

abandon the duties of his parish to pore over the valuable collections of Pococke, John Greaves (a distinguished Arabic and Persian scholar, a contemporary of Pococke's whom he had accompanied to Constantinople in 1638) and Thomas Roe – inadequate collections in his opinion. As he wrote to his daughter, 'I wish that some public spirit would rise among us and cause these books to be bought in the East for us which we want...we are all swallowed up in politics; there is no room for letters; and it is to be feared that the next generation will not only inherit but improve the polite ignorance of the present.'

Ockley was wrong: the next generation produced not only a definitive translation of the *Quran* by George Sale, which was not bettered for another hundred years, but also a history of Islam even wider in scope than Ockley's – that of Edward Gibbon. Ockley had from time to time betrayed his priestly background in comparing Islam unfavourably with Christianity; Gibbon on the other hand praised Islam, if only to spite Christianity in the Byzantine form which he so heartily despised. ' 'Tis said he has been a Muslim,' mocked Johnson with some justification. Though Gibbon admitted his 'total ignorance of the oriental tongue', his encyclopaedic mind absorbed the accumulated knowledge of the eighteenth century – French, English and classical – often guided by Ockley's bibliography, using French and English translations of Islamic documents 'till I had ranged round the whole circle of oriental history'.

The British conquest of India during the eighteenth century gave a much needed impetus to the study of Persian, the poor relation of Arabic and Hebrew studies in England, but now recognised as the common tongue of northern India. William Jones – 'harmonious Jones' as Dr Johnson called him – achieved for Persian what Pococke had for Arabic, revealing for the first time the beauty of Persian literature in English. He also developed a more scientific approach to the study of oriental languages, thereby laying the foundations of modern philology.

Studying law in Oxford in 1764 Jones found an Arab to teach him Arabic while he taught himself Hebrew and Persian. In 1769 he listed his activities as writing poetry, planning an essay on education and an Aeschylean tragedy about Mustafa – the murdered son of Sultan Suleyman, a perennial tragic hero – and collecting materials for a Persian grammar and a treatise on Arabic poetry. The Persian grammar, one of the most persuasive arguments for a language ever written, was published two years later. 'The Persian language is rich, melodious and elegant; it has been spoken for many years by the greatest princes in the politest courts of Asia.... Some men never heard of Asiatic writings, and others will not be convinced that there is anything valuable in them. . . . [study of the language] has certainly been checked in its progress by the learned themselves; most of whom have confined their studies to the minute researches of verbal criticism; like men, who discover a precious stone, but instead of searching for the rich ore, or for gems, amuse themselves with collecting smooth pebbles and pieces of crystal.' The man of taste, he concluded, 'will undoubtedly be pleased to unlock the stores of native genius and to gather the flowers of unrestrained and luxuriant fancy.'

These were just some of the academic sources which poets and playwrights from the sixteenth to eighteenth centuries were able to draw on in portraying the oriental scenes and characters whose strangeness made them such popular subjects. The Middle East had throughout the Middle Ages been an abundant source for every kind of fantasy, fable and monstrosity. Most of these were assembled, together with some genuine accounts, in the thirteenth-century *Travels* of the legendary Sir John Mandeville. Many of the marvels reported by even the most reputable travellers were influenced by,

3. Bain public des femmes mahometanes. Turkish baths became fashionable in England in the eighteenth century though one of the first was opened in Newgate Street, London, as early as 1679. Lady Mary Wortley Montagu was greatly impressed by the beauty of the women when she visited them in Constantinople. Engraving from M. d'Ohsson, *Tableau Général de l'Empire Othoman* (1787)

if not copied from Sir John, who almost certainly never existed. Much of the *Travels* is concerned with a pilgrimage to the Holy Land and many of the Dead Sea tales, for instance, appeared for the first time in Mandeville, but the author also encompassed Egypt, Mesopotamia and much of Africa.

The line between fact and fiction was easily crossed, but nowhere more easily than in Egypt, descriptions of which – before the eighteenth century – are more relevantly included in this chapter on the legendary Middle East than in one on travel. The amount of attention given to early accounts of Egypt often obscures their relative scarcity (compared with accounts of the Levant) and also their limits. Before the eighteenth century very few travellers ventured south of Cairo and rarely east, except to cross the northern edge of the Sinai Peninsula to go to the Holy Land; the rest of Egypt was known only by hearsay. Mandeville's Egypt was a riot of fantasies, among them a desert monster which was half man, half goat, and the phoenix which immolated itself on a temple altar in Heliopolis every five hundred years and was reincarnated from the ashes; in Sinai the monks of St Catherine's monastery were kept supplied with olive oil by an annual pilgrimage of birds bearing olive branches in their beaks. But what could be more fantastic than John Sanderson's description of animals in Cairo: 'both wild and tame gattie pardie, dragons, live cocadrills', an ostrich going round and round in circles to lay her eggs and using her tail as a sunshade,

4. A fennec, or desert fox, from James Bruce, *Travels*

the dried musk glands of a female crocodile giving off scent – there was enough material here for a thousand legends.

Most conjectures about Egypt were based either on Mandeville or on ancient authorities such as Herodotus (who set a good example himself of elaborating fact with fancy), Diodorus Siculus, Pliny and Strabo whom few queried and whose conclusions were certainly not replaced by anything more accurate until the middle of the eighteenth century. The Turkish-Circassian ruling class and even the Egyptians themselves were not in the least interested in their past. Henry Blount wrote that 'because Egypt is held to have been the fountaine of all Science and Arts civill, therefore I did hope to finde some sparke of those cinders not yet put out', but he was disappointed as far as the past was concerned (hence his success in describing the present).

Cairo was outlandish enough, with its markets, its animals, its entertainers and above all its river. But the pyramids were the focal point of all visits to Egypt. 'To be but pyramidally extant is a fallacy in duration,' wrote Sir Thomas Browne: the antiquity of these strange piles was appreciated, but what was their purpose? One of the earliest descriptions in English is Edward Webbe's: 'They are seven mountaines builded on the outside, like unto the point of a Diamond, which mountains were builded in King Pharaoh's time to keep corne in, and they are mountains of great strength.' A common theory was that they had served as granaries, probably Joseph's.

5. A houbara, or Macqueen's bustard, from Bruce's *Travels*

Veryard thought they had been built by the Israelites 'to keepe them out of Idleness, the Nurse of all Sedition'. Some saw them for what they were eventually proved to be – sepulchres for Egypt's pharaohs. John Greaves, the oriental scholar, spent some weeks in 1638 measuring the pyramids; his observations are precise mathematical and astronomical data, carefully compared with similar observations he had made of buildings in Rome, but they failed satisfactorily to solve the riddle of the pyramids.

Another Egyptian attraction, equally mysterious and wonderful to those who had never seen them, were the mummies. John Sanderson was taken to a 'momia' in the desert beyond the pyramids – a cave where thousands of mummies had been discovered. 'We were lett downe by ropes as into a well, with waxe candles burninge in our hands, and so waulked upon bodies of all sorts and sizes, great and smaule, and some are embaulmed in little earthern pots... I broke off all parts of the bodies to see how the flesh was turned to drugge, and brought home divers heads, hands, arms and feete for a showe.' There was a long-established trade in powdered mummy (genuine or otherwise), which was supposed to be a particularly efficacious medicine and to have certain magical properties. Sir Sampson Legend, Congreve's exhaustive traveller, declared: 'I have a shoulder of an Egyptian King, that I purloined from one of the Pyramids, powder'd with Hieroglyphs, thou shalt have it brought home to thy house and make an Entertainment for all the Philomaths and Students in Physick and Astrology in and about London.'

Occasional glimpses of great beauty in all these accounts enable us to see instantly how contemporaries must have viewed these bizarre lands. Here is the Sultan's barge in Constantinople, described by Robert Withers – 'one of the delicatest and rarest presence that ever I beheld, for it is a quadrant of seven arches on a side cloisterwise... and in the midst riseth a core of three or four Rooms with Chimneys, all guilt over most gloriously. The whole frame soe set with Opalls, Rubies, Emeralds, burnisht with gold, painted with flowers and graced with Inlaid work of porphyry, marble, jet, jasper and delicate stones that I am persuaded there is not such a bird cage in the world.' Shakespeare's description of Cleopatra's barge (published the same year) was not more splendid. Here is Cartwright in a garden in Tabriz: 'a most beautiful and flourishing garden, large and spacious, replenished with sundry kinds of Trees and sweete smelling Plantes, and a thousand Fountaines and brooks, derived from a pretie River, which with his pleasant stream divides the Garden from the citie; and is of so great a beautie that for the delicacy thereof it is by the Countrey Inhabitants called Sechis-Genet, that is to say, the Eighth Paradise.' And here is Sandys among

6. Goat and fat-tailed sheep, from Alexander Russell, *A Natural history of Aleppo* (1794)

the beduin he met crossing Sinai: 'they dwell in Tents, which they remove like walking Cities, for opportunitie of prey, and benefit of pasturage. They acknowledge no Soveraigne, not worth the conquering, nor can they be conquered, retyring to places impossible for Armies, by reason of the rolling sands and penurie of all things.' There is no need of the fantastic to set the imagination working here.

Contemporary writers in England made good use of the strange tales told by these travellers. Othello tantalised Brabantio with tales of his travels:

> Wherein of Antars vast, and Deserts wide,
> Rough quarries, rocks, hills, whose head touched heaven,
> It was my hint to speak. Such was my process,
> And of the Cannibals that each other eat,
> The Anthropophagi, and men whose heads
> Do grow beneath their shoulders.

Various melodramatic episodes in Turkish and Persian history furnished themes for English writers – battles, conquerors, assassination and romance, usually full of Christian propaganda against the infidels. Tamburlaine was a popular hero in English drama of this period because of his defeat of the more menacing and therefore more infidel Turk. Marlowe revelled in the exotic names in his play on the conqueror:

> Is it not brave to be a king, Techelles?
> Umsucasane and Meridamas,
> Is it not brave to be a king,
> And ride in triumph through Persepolis?

Thomas Dekker, a great enthusiast for travel accounts (claiming he would know his way in the Serail as well as one of the Sultan's eunuchs, without ever having been there), was one of the few writers to take pity on Tamburlaine's Ottoman victim, Bajazet I, 'once the greatest monarch of the East'.

The succession problems of the Ottoman and Safavid dynasties provided abundant material. In *Henry IV*, Part II, when the new King Henry V consoles his brothers, Shakespeare refers to the early Ottoman custom of a sultan, on his accession, killing off all his brothers as possible rivals:

> Brothers, you mix your sadness with some fear:
> This is the English, not the Turkish Court;
> Not Amurath an Amurath succeeds,
> But Harry Harry.

In 1553 Suleyman the Magnificent was persuaded by a favourite wife to murder his heir Prince Mustafa, son by another wife. Fulke Greville delved into Knolles as the principal source for his *Tragedy of Mustafa*, first performed in 1609. A later version of Mustafa's fate was written by Roger Boyle (brother of Robert), the second performance of which coincided with, or was arranged to suit, Charles II's appearance in Persian costume in October 1666. Evelyn considered it 'exceeding well written' but 'did not approve of any such pastime in time of such judgements and calamities'.

A similar event in Persian history was Shah Abbas' treatment of his fourth son Khudabanda. The same cruelty, described in some detail by Thomas Herbert and observed in his treatment of Robert Sherley, was revealed in his murder of his eldest son and blinding of his third and fourth sons (the second only escaped by dying a natural death). Khudabanda revenged himself on Abbas by murdering his own daughter, Fatima, to whom Abbas was devoted, and then poisoning himself. Sir John Denham described this in *The Sophy* (using Herbert as his main authority), performed in 1642, into which he inserted many a topical allusion to absolute monarchs ill-advised by favourites.

Mehmet II, conqueror of Constantinople and therefore the Devil incarnate to most of Europe, was a popular subject and a favourite legend of this period was that of Irene, the beautiful Greek slave with whom Mehmet became so infatuated that he neglected his public duties; he only managed to conquer his love by slaying her in front of his nobles. There is no satisfactory evidence for the story, but it fitted in with other equally bloodthirsty legends about Mehmet. William Painter, in his *Palace of Pleasure* of 1566, describes Hyerenee, the heroine, 'of such rare and excellent beautie as she allured eyes of every wight to wonder and behold her'; who so bewitched Mehmet that 'he not onely consumed dayes and nights with her but burned with continual jealousie'. One of the least literary versions of the theme was Charles Goring's *Irene*, first performed in 1708:

> Jealous of Empire and my lost Renown
> I stabb'd a Mistress, to preserve my Crown;
> But had the faire returned my generous flame,
> I'd slighted Empire and embraced the Dame.

In the most famous version of the legend Irene did return the flame. Dr Johnson's *Irene* was produced for the first time in 1749 by his friend David Garrick who also acted in it. Here Irene, faced with the choice between temporal power and glory and the preservation of honour and loss of life, decides for the former. Johnson was much concerned with the moral content of the tale which he had found in Knolles, but as a play it was not a success.

During the eighteenth century the oriental fairy tale became the popular framework for contemporary fiction. The difference between eighteenth-century pseudo-oriental tales and nineteenth-century oriental romances, from William Beckford's *Vathek* onwards, was that the former concentrated on the moral content of the tale to the detriment of the oriental background; later writers used all the available orientalia to produce as authentic a tale as possible regardless of moral, except for the convention of the triumph of good over evil.

Edward Pococke (junior) translated into Latin *Hai Ibn Yuqdhan*, a philosophical romance by Ibn al-Tufail, part of which Ockley translated into English: it is this part which Defoe is thought to have used as a model for *Robinson Crusoe*. The *Arabian Nights* was translated into English from the French in 1712 and soon governed the form, though not the content, of all kinds of fiction. The allegorical or philosophical tale, with no religious implications, appealed to writers of the period and came into its own early in the century under the guidance of Addison and Steele in the *Spectator*. Addison in particular liked to use these fairy tales to point to the moral in his essays. 'The virtue of complaisance in friendly discourse is very prettily illustrated by a little wild Arabian tale', he explained. Johnson carried on the same tradition in the *Rambler*, elaborating tales such as *Hamlet and Rashid* and *Obidah and the Hermit* with 'the pompous style of the East'. Neither Addison nor Johnson was particularly suited to the oriental genre, Addison's style being too gentlemanly and Johnson's too didactic. Even Nicholas Hawkesworth's tales in the *Adventurer*, filled as they are with the monsters of the conventional Arabian fable, are mainly concerned with pointing a moral. France set the fashion for adapting the oriental tale to a satire on contemporary society; Voltaire wrote *Zadig* and Montesquieu *Lettres Persanes*. The latter was imitated by Lord Lyttelton in *Persian Letters*, in 1735, in which the Persian Selim in London writes letters to his friend Mirza in Isfahan, satirising English society and politics. Lyttelton had rather an affection for oriental tales; another of his literary efforts was *The Court Secret*, allegedly translated from the original Arabic but in fact a satire on the love affair of the Earl of Scarborough and the Duchess of Manchester.

'The late humour of reading oriental Romances...though I will not contend it has much better'd our Morals, has, however, extended our Notions, and made the Customs of the East much more familiar to us than they were before', wrote Addison. This was only partly true; the fantastic tales by Addison and others bore little relation to reality and Persia for instance was the most popular setting for the very reason that it was more unfamiliar and therefore more adaptable to the author's imagination. Fortunately the histories of Ockley and Gibbon, the erudite travels of the period and the elegant translations of poetry by William Jones contrived to balance these highly imaginative representations of the Middle East, though the contrast is still to be found throughout the following hundred and twenty years and some would say even today.

Part Two

7 The Middle East in the Nineteenth Century

The second part of this book covers the period between Napoleon's expedition to Egypt in 1798 and the outbreak of World War I in 1914. From 1798 onwards the Eastern Question grew into one of the thornier diplomatic issues of the nineteenth century. Politics are of little concern here except where they impinge upon other fields of activity. They form, however, an ubiquitous background to the development of awareness of the Middle East; this chapter attempts the perhaps impossible task of abridging into a few pages the domestic history of the area during more than a century of radical change.

More than one historian has pointed out that the French defeat of the Muslims in Egypt heralded an era marked by patronage on the part of Europe and a feeling of shame and self-consciousness on the part of the Muslims in Egypt, Turkey and the Levant and in Persia. The area became a chess board for diplomats and politicians to manipulate rulers and factions just as, paradoxically, scholars were beginning to appreciate the significance of its contribution to European civilisation.

Self-interest often prevented outright military invasion and the onslaught of European ideas was more sustained than any threatened belligerence. The French Revolution has been described as 'the first great movement of ideas in Western Christendom that had any effect on the world of Islam'.* Napoleon's invasion of Egypt failed in its military aims, but through education and through military missions there and elsewhere it introduced to the Middle East the revolutionary ideals of France which were later fostered by increasing westernisation.

A perceptive writer, Charles Perry, commented in 1743 on the 'present weak, feeble condition of the Turkish Empire'. During the eighteenth century a shrinking economy supported an expensive and cumbersome bureaucracy resistant to change. Isolated attempts to reform Ottoman institutions were made during the century, but with little success. Sultan Selim III tried to modernise his empire in

* Bernard Lewis, *The Emergence of Modern Turkey*, p. 40.

the 1790s: embassies were set up in European capitals and the first permanent Turkish ambassador to London was presented to George III in 1793; the army was reorganised; and contact with Europeans was encouraged. The reforms produced a violent reaction, however, in particular among the religious leaders and the Janissaries; the latter deposed Selim in 1807 and were later responsible for his murder. It was left to Selim's younger brother, Mahmud II, to set on foot the changes essential to the survival of the empire. Tentative attempts to reform both the Ottoman Empire and Egypt (now dealt with as an autonomous part of the Empire) began in the eighteenth century, but their continuous development was only successful in the nineteenth century.

Mahmud's success depended on his efforts to centralise his authority. By trying to eliminate all other sources of power he went a long way towards removing the causes of a century or more of internal unrest which had led to the impoverishment of the empire. To many historians his greatest achievement was his destruction of the Janissaries, whose barracks, and many of their inhabitants, were blown to pieces in 1826 – a day known in Ottoman history as the 'Auspicious Event'. This time the army was successfully remodelled on European lines, trained in the use of European tactics and weaponry by French instructors. The power of the conservative religious leaders was weakened and military and administrative reforms were backed by better educational facilities.

Mahmud died in 1839 but his policy of centralisation was continued by his successors in a series of reforms known as the *Tanzimat*, three of which are particularly notable. The first, the *Hatt-i Sharif* of Gulhane, was promulgated in 1839 at the time of the Convention of London when the Great Powers persuaded Muhammad Ali, ruler of Egypt, to surrender his claims to Syria which he had successfully invaded in 1831. The second, the *Hatt-i Humayun*, was promulgated in 1856 at the end of the Crimean War. The third was the Constitution of 1876, published on the eve of an international conference to debate a settlement in the Balkans. Of these the only fundamentally liberal reform was the last, which was revoked by the Sultan only two years later. The ordinances, timed to conciliate European statesmen principally concerned with the plight of non-Muslims in the Empire, affirmed and reaffirmed the equality of all religions in the Ottoman Empire. Beyond that the Sultan was able to take the opportunity to consolidate his power further with little or no outside interference.

In the latter part of the century concession hunters tempted the Turkish authorities into mortgaging the finances of the state in return for vague promises of railways, mines, forestry and banking, in the hopes that such modern developments would do something to alleviate the economic and nationalist strains which were pulling the empire apart. The seeds of a genuine liberalism, however, planted by the French Revolution, were watered by the greater proximity of Europe and the conflicting aims of European powers regarding the Ottoman Empire. The revolution when it came in 1908, instigated by the Young Turks, was already torn between nationalists who advocated an Ottoman Empire ruled by a central Turkish authority (embodied in the Committee of Union and Progress), and the liberals who favoured decentralisation with more rights for minorities. Nationalism among both the Young Turks and the subject races of the empire destroyed the liberal dream. From 1909 (when the despotic Sultan Abdul-Hamid was deposed) until 1913 the CUP ruled as tyrannically as any Ottoman sultan. The European powers at first welcomed the CUP and a delegation which visited England in 1909 was fêted and welcomed by members of parliament and the government. But by 1913 the British ambassador was writing that 'the Young Turk régime threatens to unite against itself all the elements which nothing else would bring together'.

During the nineteenth century the European powers were influenced primarily by the strategic importance of the Middle East across the path from Europe to the Far East, and used a variety of pretexts to interfere in the internal affairs of the area, particularly Egypt and the Levant, to secure the path. In Egypt after 1798 no European power could afford to ignore the message of the French occupation. The great moderniser of Egypt, Muhammad Ali, was a member of the Albanian contingent in the Ottoman army which helped the British drive the French out of Egypt. He seized power in Egypt in 1805 when the Turkish authorities in Constantinople were disconcerted by the deposition of Selim III, and he was firmly entrenched by the time Mahmud's policy of centralisation was under way. There are many similarities in the measures taken by these two rulers to enable their countries to meet the challenges of nineteenth-century Europe, as well as to consolidate their own power. During his forty years as dictator of Egypt, Muhammad Ali destroyed the Mamluk hierarchy which had ruled Egypt for so long, and replaced it with his own hereditary pashalik. He created a new army – the most modern in the Middle East according to Henry Layard who in 1839 compared it favourably with Mahmud's relatively ill-equipped and oddly dressed forces. In 1831 the Egyptian army invaded Syria under the generalship of Muhammad Ali's son Ibrahim, to create a buffer zone against the Ottoman authorities. The invasion was too successful, however; the European powers, faced with the prospect of an uncertain authority governing the strategic Syrian routes, stepped in to ward off what might have been a death blow to the Ottoman Empire. At the Convention of London, when the Egyptians had occupied Syria for nearly nine years, Muhammad Ali was persuaded to evacuate it in return for the Sultan's agreement to make the pashalik, or viceroyalty, of Egypt hereditary. A British and Austrian naval expedition enforced the settlement in Syria. In Egypt, meanwhile, Muhammad Ali reorganised taxation, introduced cotton and other agricultural industries and improved education. An expedition to Arabia, at the nominal bidding of the sultan, to suppress the Wahhabi revolt, restored the position of Egypt as the recognised protector of the holy cities of Mecca and Medina.

One of the more painful results of Muhammad Ali's and his successor's reforms in Egypt was a financial deficit. The appalling indebtedness of the country, which by 1876 owed some hundred million pounds of which some sixty-eight million was foreign debt, began under Muhammad Ali, but was accentuated by the expense of the Suez Canal, the collapse of cotton prices at the end of the American Civil War and the extravagance of Ismail, who ruled from 1863 until his deposition in 1879. Foreign intervention to right Egyptian finances became foreign control, leading ultimately to the British occupation of Egypt in 1882. Essentially a temporary move, in principal to protect the Khedive and the British community from the mutinous Egyptian army led by Colonel Arabi, it was soon realised – notably by Evelyn Baring, later Lord Cromer, who arrived in Egypt in 1884 as British Agent and Consul-General that Egypt would never achieve financial solvency and thence political stability if the British left. Nor for that matter would the British ever have felt secure in India unless they controlled the Suez Canal. No formal control of Egypt was set up till the country was declared a British protectorate in 1914 but the principle of withdrawal had been abandoned by 1890. Under Cromer's rigid financial discipline the country regained its prosperity at the expense of its independence. From the beginning of the twentieth century the British position was increasingly attacked by a fast-growing nationalist movement, inspired partly by movements of Islamic reform led by the Wahhabis in Arabia, by Jamal al-Din al-Afghani, the great nineteenth-century modernist, and his disciple Muhammad Abdu in Egypt, and partly by a new generation of Arab nationalists, many of them Christian Arabs from Syria, owing allegiance primarily to their Arab nationality rather than to their religion.

During the nineteenth century the traditional factional strife of Syria – between rival families in the towns, religious sects in the Holy Land (where Jewish immigration created new problems towards the end of the century) and feudal dynasties in Mount Lebanon – attracted the attention of Europe because of the important strategic position of Syria across the main channels of communications with India. Russia emerged as the champion of the Greek Orthodox, France of the Catholics and Maronites, Britain of the Druzes. For British statesmen the preservation of the Ottoman Empire was the best safeguard of the overland route to India and the Empire could not, in British opinion, survive the secession under French or Russian protection of so vital a part of her territory as Syria.

British and French agents fomented the uprising in 1840 of Christians and Druzes in Lebanon against the Egyptians and their ally, Bashir II Shihab, Druze ruler of Mount Lebanon. Over the next twenty years the power of the Druze chieftains gradually declined, accentuated by the conversion to Christianity of the ruling branch of the Shihab family. Druze jealousy of the Maronites, aggravated by the conflicting interests of the European powers, led in 1860 to Druze massacres of an estimated eleven thousand Christians, spreading from the Mountain to many parts of Syria, including the towns where Muslim hatred of the more prosperous and better educated Christians was most strongly felt. In 1861 France, Britain and Turkey negotiated the Organic Regulation, establishing an internationally guaranteed régime under a Christian administrator directly responsible to the sultan. The relative peace and quiet which this ensured lasted until the outbreak of World War I.

The nineteenth century also saw the arrival in Syria of American Presbyterian missionaries who established the first independent system of education in the Middle East. In their schools in the Lebanese mountains and at the American University of Beirut (founded in 1866) they taught and inspired the first generation of Christian Arabs, many of whom were at the forefront of the nationalist movement in its early days.

The nationalist movement was part of a general Arab renaissance which sought to meet the inroads of European ideas and politics; another aspect of this was the evolution of a purer Islam. By far the fiercest advocates of an Islamic revival were the Wahhabi reformers of central Arabia, adherents of a movement started in the Najd in the second half of the eighteenth century by Muhammad Ibn Abd al-Wahhab. The movement was directed primarily against innovations in Islam, such as the veneration of saints, and advocated a return to primitive Islam. This implicit attack on the authority of the Muslim establishment, and thence on the authority of the Ottoman sultanate, was put into effect when the Wahhabi cause was espoused by the Saudi amirate of central Arabia, which spread the revival throughout the peninsula in a *jihad* or holy war against resistance, notably Turkish, to Wahhabi ideals. Wahhabi armies showed the Turks to be vulnerable in Mesopotamia, which they invaded several times early in the nineteenth century to sack the sacred Shia shrines of Karbala and Najaf, and southern Syria where in 1810 they advanced nearly to Damascus. Egyptian armies sent at the direction of the Ottoman government eventually defeated the Saudi dynasty, restricting their activities to the Najd and the shaikhdoms of the Persian Gulf where they continued their proselytisation until their second rise to power at the beginning of this century.

Iraq never aroused the same interest in Europe as Syria apart from two periods at the beginning and end of the nineteenth century when it became the centre of discussions on quicker communications between Europe and India. Attempts by the Sultan to assert his authority and reintegrate the area into the Ottoman Empire foundered on tribal dissidence and anarchy which had been fostered by local governors for generations as their defence against Arab attack.

In Persia at the end of the eighteenth century the limited European contacts with the Safavids had been shattered by seventy years of invasion and civil war. In the 1770s, however, anarchy gave way to a semblance of order imposed by Aga Muhammad Khan, founder of the Qajar dynasty, who was crowned Shah in Tehran, the country's new capital, in 1796, having been effective ruler since 1779. A year after his coronation Aga Muhammad was assassinated and his nephew Fath Ali succeeded him. Fath Ali's uxoriousness reputedly left him with some three hundred sons; these excess offspring served the useful purpose of acting as provincial governors for the different regions of Persia to ensure Qajar dominion though not necessarily loyalty to the Shah. Throughout the nineteenth century, for instance, the Crown Prince governed Azerbaijan, one of the most prosperous parts of Persia and also the most vulnerable to Russian attack.

Under the tyranny of Aga Muhammad and the economies of Fath Ali the country recovered to some extent from the devastation of the silk-producing areas of the Caspian provinces and the loss of most foreign trade during the eighteenth century; but Qajar extravagance, from Fath Ali's successor Muhammad Shah onwards, gradually ran the treasury dry and gave foreign powers the excuse to intervene in Persian affairs.

British interest in Persia revived in 1800 when the East India Company sent Captain John Malcolm to Fath Ali principally to ascertain his views concerning an aggressive ruler of Afghanistan who was threatening India, but also to provide 'against the views which other powers may entertain of attacking the British possessions in India'. Two visits by Malcolm in the next ten years and one by an envoy of the British government, Sir Harford Jones Brydges, reaffirmed the friendship between Britain and Persia. By an agreement signed with the Shah in 1814 British officers were sent to Persia to help train the Persian army in Tabriz, under the authority of the Crown Prince, Abbas Mirza. Abbas died in 1833 and his father Fath Ali the following year, and the accession of Muhammad, even though with British help, saw an immediate decline in British influence. 'All means of access to the Royal ear, which through the women and eunuchs of the Harem enabled the British to maintain a salutary influence over the Shah are now cut off', wrote the historian James Baillie Fraser.

Russian and British rivalry for the dominant influence in Persia came into the open during the reign of Muhammad Shah. Russia's interest in Persia stemmed from her need for warm water ports which would enable her to compete in international trade. Britain broke off relations with Persia in 1837 when the Shah tried to counter Russian gains in the north by attacking Herat in Afghanistan. Although, under British pressure, he withdrew Persian troops shortly after, he attacked again in 1856 and this time occupied Herat. The Indian government retaliated in the Persian Gulf with a 'series of demonstrations'; in the three-month Anglo-Persian War of 1856–7 British troops landed in the Gulf, captured Bushire and several other towns, and routed the Persians with scarcely a life being lost in the process. The only contribution of the war to Anglo-Persian relations was the gift of *khaki* to the English vocabulary, meaning 'dust' in Persian and used to describe the colour of Persian uniforms which were invisible from a distance.

In 1848 Nasiru'd-Din Shah came to the throne to rule for a few days short of fifty years. Under the able rule of his first grand vezir, Mirza Taki Khan, severe repression of discontent was paralleled by the encouragement of trade and foreign travel. George Curzon later praised the security of the countryside, the regular exaction of revenue and the effective silencing of opposition. But the costs of these reforms were high. The suppression of the Babi movement is an example of the harsh injustice by which Nasiru'd-Din achieved a kind of peace. Babism, described by one modern authority* as a 'heterodox religious movement' to combat the materialist ambitions of foreign powers excited considerable sympathy among European Persophiles (notably the English scholar Edward Granville Browne) from the time of its appearance in the 1840s – largely for a vagueness

* Peter Avery, *Modern Iran*, pp. 53–9.

of theology which led to a remarkable tolerance of other religions. Its religious significance was soon outpaced by its attraction for political dissenters. The Bab himself, Sayyid Ali Muhammad, was executed in 1848 and in 1852, after an attempted assassination of the Shah by Babis, the movement was virtually massacred out of existence. The Bab's successor, Baha'ullah, was later exiled to Acre where he became yet another religious curiosity of the Holy Land, preaching a revised Babism. The descriptions of tortures inflicted on Babi prisoners in 1852 horrified European observers and European relations with Persia, already notably patronising, are marked from the middle of the century by a growing contempt and disregard for its politics and government.

Increasing foreign contact and the resultant expansion of trade had little effect on the poverty of the Shah's government, the new wealth being concentrated in the rising mercantile class in the cities at the expense of a debauched aristocracy and an impoverished rural population. Nasiru'd-Din first tried to alleviate the financial deficit, as well as popular discontent, by accepting loans from foreign governments; on discovering the dangerous strings attached to these he tried to raise money by selling concessions to foreign individuals. The most notorious of these was the seventy-year virtual monopoly of Persia's natural and financial resources awarded to Baron Julius de Reuter, a naturalised British subject. De Reuter was to construct a railway from the Caspian to the Gulf, develop the country's mineral resources and establish a national bank. Curzon described it as an 'oriental fantasy', politically impossible to realise. Popular opinion in Persia, implacable opposition from Russia and the indifference of the British government to what the Shah considered a gesture of friendship and the government merely a concession to a private individual, resulted in its withdrawal.

Even more outspoken opposition, however, was raised in Persia in 1890 to the Tobacco Monopoly — a concession awarded to a British company which gave it full control over the production, sale and export of all Persian tobacco. The power of the religious leaders was demonstrated when they forbade smoking throughout the country and imposed a ban on the sale of all tobacco – normally essential to any Persian gathering – with such success that even the Shah was unable to smoke. Disturbances broke out in the main towns and in the face of a remarkably united opposition the Shah was obliged to cancel the concession.

The effects of the French Revolution were more muted in Persia than in the Ottoman Empire. There were few signs of western influence – a few newspapers, schools, a printing press. The Shah continued to rule the country through his vezir in Tehran and the local governors. As early as 1859 he instituted a council of ministers but he was no more prepared to surrender any authority than his autocratic forebears. The discontent of the rural population began to combine with that of the new merchant class to form a dangerous body of opposition to the Shah. The inspired religious leadership of Jamal al-Din al-Afghani, who was largely responsible for waking Persian *mujtahids* (leaders of the Shia 'clergy') to their potential, as well as Persians who had travelled to Europe, studied and worked there, fed the growing agitation for change. The concessions highlighted the dependence of the Shah on his powerful so-called allies, Britain and Russia. As every aspect of Persian government and economy became mortgaged to more powerful neighbours, so popular opinion swung further in favour of the *anjuman* (secret societies) agitating for constitutional reform.

Nasiru'd-Din was assassinated in 1896. The financial straits of the new Shah, Muzaffaru'd-Din, who for reasons of health and prestige wanted to make a trip to Europe, led to the foundation of the Russian Bank and the advancement by Russia of two loans in 1900 and 1901. The same cause had been behind the appointment in 1898 of two Belgians to run the Persian customs. In 1905 a new customs tariff agreement with Russia was announced, heavily in Russia's favour. Popular discontent at these measures led to revolution in 1906.

There is no space here to go into the details of the revolution, the establishment of a constitution and its failure, due to lack of money, to keep out foreign interference, especially Russian. In 1907 the Anglo-Russian Convention divided Persia into three spheres of influence, a Russian zone in the north containing most of the main Persian cities, a neutral zone in the centre and a British zone in the south-east. The Persian government was not consulted. In 1911 the government engaged an American, Mr Morgan Shuster, to reorganise the country's finances but all efforts foundered on Anglo-Russian non-cooperation. Shuster's account of his efforts to right the economy, *The Strangling of Persia*, is a bitter attack on the policies of the two European powers. When war broke out in 1914 Russia had already 'temporarily' occupied northern Persia and the British, prevented from interfering by the Convention, lifted not a finger to help remove them.

This is only a brief outline of the political impact of Europe on Persia and the rest of the Middle East during the nineteenth century, forcing it out of its earlier position of disdainful isolation. In some ways this impact was beneficial and changed many outworn institutions. Contact between Muslim and Christian was easier and students travelling to Europe returned to open the windows of their countries on novel ideas of revolution, nationalism and socialism which were not easily reconciled with the rigid framework of the Islamic state. Europeans visiting the Middle East encouraged by their presence the tentative efforts of governments in Turkey, Egypt and Persia to modernise their countries.

Two attitudes are discernible among the British who came into contact with the Middle East in this period. The next three chapters describe that of the diplomats and administrators who, from a conviction in every way as firm as that of the sultans and shahs of previous centuries, of their own moral as well as political superiority, hoped to reform and mould the Middle East into a European shape. Subsequent chapters describe the attitude of those travellers, archaeologists, artists, missionaries and tourists who visited the Middle East in this period, influenced almost without exception by the political theories and deeds of their official countrymen, but whose own non-political activities gave some perspective to the picture painted by the reformers.

Britain's interest in the Middle East in the nineteenth century arose directly from her position as ruler of India, which she jealously guarded from the danger of invasion by France, Russia or Germany. Until the middle of the century, however, the nature of those Middle Eastern interests was still mainly trade and communications and it was to protect them that British statesmen drew up the policy of bolstering the Ottoman Empire. In the latter half of the century the obvious weaknesses of the Empire and the economic expansion of Europe led to a revision of earlier policies which were replaced by a more positive, but less tolerant, attitude towards the Middle East which by this time was feeling the full impact of the West. The efforts of the Ottoman Empire and Persia to cope with this impact met with little or no political sympathy in Britain, principally concerned as it was with the relation of the Middle East to its European or Indian policies.

8 The Red-Hot Horseshoe

British influence in the Ottoman Empire for the first half of the nineteenth century was largely the creation of one man, Stratford Canning. Until the 1870s, and less enthusiastically up to World War I, successive British governments maintained Canning's conviction that the danger of a hostile power controlling the eastern Mediterranean and thus communications with India – as Napoleon's Egyptian expedition had done – was best prevented by shoring up the crumbling ramparts of the Ottoman Empire and persuading the Sultan to reform its administration in order to ward off assaults by European powers.

The French expedition demonstrated – if any such demonstration was still needed – that the Empire could no longer defend its frontiers. The diplomatic activity which it stirred up led to the ambassador's commercial duties being firmly superseded by his political activities. In 1799 the Earl of Elgin was sent to Constantinople as ambassador and as long as his duties remained political he was paid by the Crown. Elgin's task was to deal with the Sultan while the Company's affairs were left in the hands of the secretary to the embassy, Spencer Smith (brother of Sir Sidney Smith). When by 1801 the diplomatic flurry had subsided the Company took over the payment of the ambassador. But on the appointment of a new ambassador in 1804 the Company was instructed to appoint a consul-general to take care of its interests* which were then separated from the embassy. The ambassador was now concerned exclusively with politics.

Canning first went to Constantinople in 1808, accompanying a new ambassador, Robert Adair, on a mission to wean Turkey from an alliance with France. After signing the Treaty of the Dardanelles Adair was sent to Vienna, leaving Canning in charge of the British mission, much to his distaste. Canning loathed the squalor and boredom of wartime Constantinople, 'not a fit place for a gentleman to live in,' he complained to his sister, 'and did not political circumstances make it at this moment more interesting than usual it would

* The first consul-general was Isaac Morier, father of James, the author of *Hajji Baba*.

be quite intolerable' – a remark he might have made at any moment of his association with the Ottoman capital. He disliked the Turks as much as their capital and told his friend Lord Wellesley that 'to reason with persons so totally regardless of justice, so insensible to the honour and interests of their sovereign, so ignorant of the law of nations, or rather so utterly indifferent to the consequences of their misconduct, was but a hopeless labour.'

Opinions may vary as to the justice of this remark but, more important in this context, it reflected contemporary opinion as much as it also helped to mould that opinion. Throughout the better part of the fifty years which he devoted to the preservation of the Ottoman Empire, Canning held to his conviction that the main

1. The cortege of the Turkish ambassador returning from St Petersburg meeting the British ambassador, Sir Robert Ainslie (the artist's employer) on his way to England in July, 1794, with an escort of 2,000 guards. Coloured aquatint from Luigi Mayer, *Views in the Ottoman Dominions in Europe and Asia* (1810)

2. Sultan Abdel-Mejid (1839–61), lithograph by Joseph Nash from a portrait by Sir David Wilkie. The Sultan rewarded Wilkie with a gold box at which Wilkie burst into tears, presumably of gratitude. From Wilkie's *Oriental Sketches* (1840)

danger to the Empire was internal: 'destruction will not come upon the Empire either from the north or from the south; it is rotten at the heart; the seat of corruption is in the government itself'. His devotion to the Empire was that of a father for an erring child.

Canning returned to England in 1812. In 1826 he was sent as ambassador to Constantinople to secure the pacification of Greece but left a year later after the Battle of Navarino. He was again appointed ambassador in 1842, to spend the next sixteen years administering the unpalatable medicine of reform by which he hoped to stave off the disintegration of the Empire. 'I am placed between Western energy and Eastern impassiveness,' he wrote to his wife, 'between British downrightness and local trickery, a red-hot horse-shoe between the anvil and half a dozen sledgehammers.'

Visitors to Constantinople in the middle of the century marvelled at the political power of the ambassador and told exaggerated tales of his influence over the Sultan and his ministers.* His appearance lent itself to this majestic image: 'his earnest grey eyes seemed to penetrate into one's very thoughts. His thin, compressed lips denoted a violent and passionate temper. His complexion was so trans-

* The fact that the Turks called him the Great Elchi was taken by the British to mean they considered him superior to the other ambassadors, disregarding the fact that all ambassadors were so called, *elchi* being the Turkish for envoy.

3. Sir Stratford Canning, ambassador in Constantinople 1824–8 and 1842–1858. Portrait by George Richmond, 1853

parent that the least emotion, whether of pleasure or anger, was at once shown by its varying tints. A broad and massive overhanging brow gave an air of profound wisdom and sagacity.' Altogether a very formidable person, whose actions his biographer described as embodying 'a doctrine of the divine rights of ambassadors', as many visitors bore witness – Henry Layard, David Urquhart and Lady Hester Stanhope among them.

Like so many of his contemporaries, reform to Canning meant the remodelling of state and society in a European mould. His immediate aim, however, which he gloomily recognised as limited, he once expressed to a colleague: 'if ever Easterns get imbued with liberal ideas of government their own doom is sealed; the most Englishmen can hope to do is to aid in the getting rid of corruption and in obtaining recognition of the principle that honesty is the best policy.' Disillusioned, he wrote that 'Turkish ministers have neither the capacity nor the knowledge to grapple with the difficulty of the time: they have not even the sagacity to recognise their real friends.'

For all the problems of the Eastern Question which haunted Canning and the corridors of European foreign ministries, life in the capital in the first half of the century was little changed from the less momentous days of the Levant Company. Constantinople's reputation for a beautiful exterior and a filthy interior was famous. Plague invaded its overcrowded alleys every spring, and the fragile links between the Europeans in Pera and the Ottoman Porte in Stambul would be severed for April, May and June except for the intrepid few, such as Alexander Kinglake, who disregarded all warnings of its contagion and pushed their way through the Galata crowds across the Golden Horn. Fires swept the Galata quayside with expensive regularity, often spreading up the hill to Pera, destroying embassies, palaces and slums with democratic impartiality.

Members of the embassy lived and worked in the same house (aptly described as 'the old barracks') as the ambassador in Pera, while the summer was spent in Therapia, a village on the Bosphorus near Constantinople. 'Our commonest mode of taking exercise', Canning wrote to his mother from the summer retreat, 'is either a walk on the garden terrace, where the air at this time of year is delightful, and where we enjoy one of the most charming views in the world, or a row to the opposite coast in one of the prettiest boats that eye ever beheld ... not our state barge ... but a smaller one in the bottom of which [we] have just room to sit, or rather to recline on our red morocco cushions, while our Armenian servant in his national dress squats on a round platform immediately behind us.'

Under Canning the embassy was ruled with military discipline. Every despatch was drafted by Canning, who wrote more than any other ambassador of the period, and was copied by overworked attachés who in later memoirs recalled with glowing hindsight a harrowing existence of sleeplessness, nervous strain and rigid etiquette. The embassy staff had changed considerably from the days of the Levant Company. During the first half of the century most of them were recruited personally in England by the ambassador, as Canning himself had been by Robert Adair. The ambassador's secretary acted as his deputy. John Alison served Canning in this capacity for most of the latter's last embassy; an expert in oriental languages and held in high esteem by the Turks, he later became minister in Tehran. Canning's dislike of personal negotiation ment that the bulk of this fell to Alison's lot. Young gentlemen who wanted to spend a year or so less expensively and more interestingly than on the grand tour tried to work their way on to an ambassador's party. Robert Curzon, author of *Monasteries of the Levant*, joined the embassy staff (travelling out in Canning's party in 1842) largely in order to pursue his hobby of collecting manuscripts.

Second only to the ambassador, in practice, was the chief dragoman. Until the establishment of the Student Interpreter Service in 1877, most of the embassy dragomans were members of two or three Italian or Greek families of which the Pisani family, Venetian in origin, was one of the most important. The first Pisani, Stefan, appears as secretary to the embassy in 1773; Bartholomew

Pisani was elected chancellor of the embassy in 1779, at the same time as his brother was chief dragoman; Count Frederick Pisani was chief dragoman for most of Canning's embassy and along with the embassy doctor, Dr MacGuffog, one of Canning's closest associates; Étienne Pisani was a courier from Constantinople to London for a while.

The Crimean War, which itself is hardly the concern of this book, acted as a catalyst for certain changes which became apparent around the middle of the century – in the life and society of the capital, in British policy towards the Ottoman Empire and, a little later, in the composition of the embassy. During the war Constantinople swarmed with elegant cavalry officers accompanied by wives and mistresses, and 'travelling gentlemen' visiting the front as tourists. Canning, aged sixty-seven and now Lord Stratford de Redcliffe, found the endless stream of visitors distracting and irritating: there were Lord Raglan and later the Duke of Cambridge to stay, Delane of *The Times* informing him on events at the front and keeping an eye on his correspondents, Florence Nightingale insisting on more supplies and money which Canning did not consider it his responsibility to supply, his old protégé Henry Layard writing colourful despatches on the Battle of the Alma, Dean Stanley commiserating and exchanging verses with him. To his wife in England he wrote of the hectic round of engagements: 'Another knock, what now? Brigadier Adams with General Sir de Lacy Evans. Show them into the drawing-room and I'll come. Anon, and I was smartened and appeared. Behold, not only a brace of generals, but their respective staffs too. . . . Squeezing of hands, rapid commonplaces and mutual "attendrissements" ensued. Tomorrow I am to dine fourteen of them, including the two generals – and then to Bruck's ball for the Emperor's marriage. . . . I mention all these particulars that you may have a notion of the life I lead.' For the duration of the war Constantinople donned all the gaiety and social urbanity of European capitals, a burden which it never wholly shed thereafter.

Lord and Lady Stratford de Redcliffe and the foreign community celebrated the ceasefire in 1856 with a magnificent fancy dress ball at the British embassy, attended by the Sultan – the first time an Ottoman sultan had been entertained in a Christian home. Everyone made a pilgrimage up the Bosphorus to the Crimea to marvel at the battlefields, the remains of the Sebastopol fortress* and the valley where the Light Brigade had charged. But the ball marked the end of an era. The last vestiges of Ottoman aloofness were destroyed by the apparent humiliation of a Muslim power having been rescued from a Christian enemy by Christian allies; the fact that the Sultan

---

* 'It is more like the crater of a volcano than a ruined city', wrote an appalled Lord Stratford.

sat and ate with infidels only demonstrated the extent of the humiliation.

Moreover European condescension no longer felt constrained to hide itself. Even before the war British loyalty to the preservation of the Ottoman Empire was waning. Delane was rebuking *The Times* correspondent in Constantinople as early as 1853: 'you seem to think that England can desire nothing better than to sacrifice all its greatest interest ... all to oblige the Turk. Pray undeceive yourself ... we were slow to fight for him when he had more vitality; we are less than ever inclined to do so when he is visibly fading away and when no amount of protection can preserve his boasted independence and integrity.' Canning returned to England on leave in 1857, a visit which coincided with the fall of Palmerston's government. Feeling that his policies were too tied up with Palmerston's he offered his resignation which, rather to his surprise, was accepted. He returned to Constantinople to take a ceremonial farewell of the Sultan but his successor, Sir Henry Bulwer, was already settled in the embassy. The day of the Great Elchi was over.

For the time being British interests remained linked with the Porte. The Sultan came to London in 1867 after a visit to the Great Exhibition in Paris, but, revealingly, the ambassador, Lord Lyon, was obliged to assure the Foreign Office that 'there will be nothing shocking to our notions or peculiar in the habits of the Sultan or his suite. The intention is to show the public in France and in England how far the Turks have advanced in civilisation.' The British government was determined to impress him with British power as 'the *richest* nation and the most *powerful at* sea'. Two years later the Prince and Princess of Wales returned the visit on their way home from Egypt. William Russell, *Times* correspondent during the Crimean War, who accompanied them, described the changes of the previous fifteen years: gas lights in the main streets, abundant water, the 'grand old turban' replaced by the fez; 'the "sick man" to the outward eye has shaken off all signs of the incurable disease from which he was supposed to be suffering so dreadfully.' There was a gala performance of the opera and the Sultan gave a state banquet. The large British community sent a deputation to the prince and princess, headed by Mr Hanson, head of the Ottoman Bank and of one of the oldest merchant families in the Levant: 'like most deputations they were bald-headed, immensely respectable and very tedious men', was Russell's snobbish verdict.

The mood of Turcophilism, characteristic of Canning's generation, died hard; its adherents, stimulated by the Crimean War, often confused their hatred of Russia with a romantic image of Turkey as the torchbearer of revolution against the bear of autocracy. The

Scots moralist, David Urquhart, was typical of those British admirers of a Turkey fighting against European onslaughts. Urquhart spent three years in and around Constantinople from 1831 to 1834, partly on the diplomatic staff, partly investigating on his own initiative how British trade might penetrate and benefit the Black Sea provinces of the Empire at Russia's expense. He was sent home in 1834 after over-needling the Russians and devoted the rest of his life to Turcophile polemics – in the pages of his periodical *The Portfolio* (rising to supremely imaginative heights during the Crimean War when he accused Palmerston of being a Russian spy), in prolonged visits to Lebanon and Druze shaikhs and in the House of Commons. Urquhart and his 'School of Orientalists' were convinced that the disarray of the Turkish Empire resulted not, as Canning maintained, from internal or inherent faults but from European interference. The noise of Urquhart's propaganda attracted considerable attention to his cause in the middle of the century; today he is only remembered as one of the more successful advocates of the Turkish bath in England ('just the thing I have fixed upon for wishing to have, and hoping to live to see, attached to every cleanly gentleman's establishment', he wrote after seeing the elegant baths at Beit ed-Din, palace of the Druze ruler, Bashir II) and as one of the designers of the baths in Jermyn Street.

Public opinion was already disenchanted with the Ottoman Empire and the Bulgarian massacres of 1876, upheld by Gladstone as an example of Ottoman barbarity, provided the pretext for the British government to moderate its hitherto close relations with the Porte. Layard, the last of the great Turcophile ambassadors to the Porte, found relations with the Sultan and his ministers made more difficult by the close telegraphic link with London which gave him less freedom of movement than his predecessors. 'Sir Henry has been very despondent about the future,' wrote his secretary Edward Malet in 1878; 'when these ardent Philo-Turks talk in this way it is a sign that affairs are pretty well past mending'. 1878 saw the signing of the Cyprus Convention, the first time Britain had joined in attempts to dismember the Empire. The victory of Gladstone's liberal and isolationist party in the same year led to a marked cooling off of British sympathy for the Ottoman Empire.

British interests throughout the Ottoman Empire were guarded by consular officials. In most cases they were responsible for commercial as well as political affairs, the exceptions to this being in Constantinople where the division of powers between the embassy and the consulate has already been noted, Alexandria* where the consul covered trade and the consul-general in Cairo attended to

* See below, p. 119.

politics, and Jerusalem* where there was virtually no British trade
to concern the consul. They were appointed by the ambassador or by
the Levant Company until the Company's demise in 1824; a few,
such as the Aleppo consul and, at the end of the eighteenth century,
the consul in Alexandria, were also paid by the East India Company in return for supervising mails between India and Britain.
After 1824 consular officials in the principal posts were appointed
by the Crown and lesser officials by the ambassador or the consul-
general in Constantinople.

The consul-general was responsible in the capital for the trade
and security of the British community, which was growing in numbers
and prosperity throughout the nineteenth century. The changing
attitude of this century to trade meant that it was no longer
necessarily regarded as a path to better things and generation after
generation of merchants were content to remain in Constantinople,
founding families that became as much a part of the capital as the
Sublime Porte itself. Russell's 'immensely respectable' merchants
played as important a part as the diplomats in introducing European
habits to the Turkish capital. Victorian evangelism inspired them to
endow schools and colleges for the redemption of Eastern Christians.
The English-language newspaper, the *Levant Herald*, provided both
reliable news and a useful forum for outbursts against the moral
turpitude of the Porte which occasionally obliged it temporarily to
cease publication. The resident community was also far less aloof
in its relations with the Turks than the diplomats. Mr Hanson and
his fellow directors of the Ottoman Bank for instance, 'proved most
helpful and understanding in tiding the profligate and inefficient
sultanate over repeated financial difficulties'.

Apart from Constantinople (and Egypt which became virtually
autonomous from the time of Muhammad Ali and will therefore be
described separately) the main consulates were at Smyrna, Aleppo,
Beirut and Damascus. Smyrna, 'the main point of commercial contact betwixt Europe and Asia' according to Kinglake, rivalled
Alexandria for being the most westernised town of the Middle East.
The British consul was usually a member of one of the wealthy Anglo-
Levantine families whose cool spacious palaces and impressive warehouses lined the waterfront. Visitors stayed at the Navy Hotel which
was designed like an English inn; at the Casino there were English
newspapers, billiards and cards, and there was a ball there for the
British community and its Levantine friends every Monday.

The unrest in Syria and Lebanon, one of the nagging irritants of
the Eastern Question, was reflected in the nature of the Beirut consulate. Social as well as religious rivalry between the Druzes and

* See below, p. 222.

4. Smyrna c. 1830–40; in the nineteenth century this became the principal trading post of the British Levantine community. Lithograph by L. Sabatier

Maronites was often agitated by Europeans and gave the European powers an excuse to intervene on a number of occasions. During the Egyptian occupation British and French agents were at work among the local population fomenting discontent against the Egyptians and trying to win the alliance of its different groups. Richard Wood, for instance, was sent in 1835 from the embassy in Constantinople to Beirut to wean the Druzes from their support of the Egyptians. Wood later became consul in Damascus and his knowledge and contacts with Druze leaders were invaluable in 1841 when the Anglo-Austrian expedition landed at Beirut – at that time a relatively insignificant port – to ensure the Egyptian withdrawal from Syria.

For the next few years the consul, Colonel Hugh Rose, who had landed with the expedition, was mainly concerned with the political problems of the area and was answerable directly to Palmerston, much to Canning's fury. In countering French activity among the Maronites he became quite a romantic hero, twice galloping at the last moment to Druze headquarters at Dair al-Khamr to prevent serious fighting between the two sects 'and the flames of civil war were extinguished ere they had time to gain head'. Later consuls in Beirut were not expected to lead such adventurous lives, and in the relative calm which succeeded the Organic Regulation of 1861

Beirut became a consulate-general, responsible for the more turbulent consulates of Damascus and Jerusalem as well as for a host of smaller places.

Damascus was for a long time hostile to non-Muslims and was one of the last cities in the Ottoman Empire outside Arabia to accept foreign consuls. This was due mainly to its sacred importance as the annual assembly point for thousands of pilgrims from the Balkans, Asia Minor and northern Asia to set out for the *hajj* to Mecca. Kinglake remarked that until about 1830 Damascus was so notorious for its fanaticism that no one would go near it dressed as a European. The greater tolerance towards western influences introduced into Syria by the Egyptians eventually permitted the appointment of European consuls. Even so, when the first British consul was appointed he entered the city with a sturdy escort of Egyptian soldiers and advisedly decided to live on the hill-slope above Damascus rather than risk the riots of the zealous Damascene mobs.

Thirty years later, when Richard and Isabel Burton came to Damascus, Jews and Christians were still regularly attacked by Muslims and Isabel Burton, partly from romantic inclination but also with an eye to her own safety, never ventured into the city except in Arab dress. Burton's two years as Damascus consul showed up the lack of British interest in the area after the construction of the Suez Canal. Diplomatic and political interest had switched from Asia Minor and the Levant to Egypt. Burton's own attempts to meddle in local affairs and battle against corruption merely resulted in his own recall and the Damascus consulate was reduced to a vice-consulate.

The other major consulate of the Levant was Aleppo, the channel through which the ambassador in Constantinople could feel 'the pulse of Asia'. One of the best-known consuls of the nineteenth-century Middle East was John Barker, who was consul in Aleppo from 1799 to 1825 when the consulate was temporarily closed after several years of increasing turbulence in the city. The Barker family had been merchants in the Levant trade for several generations. John was born in Smyrna, where his father was a merchant. He was sent to school in England but returned to Constantinople about 1797 as private secretary to the ambassador. In Aleppo, where he was sent in 1799, he was both consul for the Levant Company and agent for the East India Company, responsible for forwarding mails. He married the daughter of the previous consul and both of their two sons (one of whom was a godson of the traveller John Lewis Burckhardt, who stayed with the Barkers in Aleppo while studying Arabic) entered the consular service in the Levant.

Barker is notable for the depth of interest he took in developing the country and both during and after his years as consul he did all he could to foster trade, revive agriculture and reintroduce cottage industries which years of civil disturbances had driven out of business. He introduced smallpox vaccination into Syria in 1803. When he went to England on leave in 1818 he took with him several Arab horses to encourage the breeding of Arab stock. He returned to Syria with silk worm eggs to revive silk culture in Syria and later set up a silk reeling factory. In the 1830s he retired to Suwaidiyah on the Syrian coast where he tried to introduce a whole variety of fruit trees to the rich Syrian soil.* And he provided a haven for British travellers who regarded the consulates of the Middle East as convenient hotels in which to recover from their trials and travels. Undoubtedly the most difficult of such visitors for Barker was Lady Hester Stanhope, who even after her retirement to a convent near Saida kept up a voluminous correspondence with Barker whom she appointed her banker, mentor, father confessor and hotelier. Another traveller, Frederick Walpole, spoke for many of his travelling contemporaries when he described how delightful it was at Suwaidiyah 'to find oneself amidst English, more pleasant still amidst English ladies; and to complete the charm, fresh rosy, dear English children running about talking English as a household tongue.'

The importance of the Aleppo consulate dwindled after the development of the Egyptian route to India in the 1830s and 1840s. 'Society in Aleppo consisted of little more than the Levantine ladies and gentlemen', wrote Layard of his visit in 1839, 'who assembled on an evening and sat around on divans, speaking little and low everyone smoking the narguilé ... there was, of course, no conversation of an intellectual kind at such meetings.'

Consuls and consul-generals in Constantinople, Smyrna and Beirut (and Aleppo until the 1820s) were empowered to appoint lesser consuls, consular agents and vice-consuls, generally unpaid and most of them Jewish, Italian, Armenian or Greek, in towns within their jurisdiction. The consuls were responsible for the administration of British protection throughout the consular courts. By the 1880s there were reckoned to be about one million British subjects in the Levant, most of them from other parts of the Mediterranean, all entitled to British rather than to Turkish justice. Those convicted could appeal to the consul-general in Constantinople and beyond him to the ambassador, but there was no appeal to British courts. With little or no legal training for the consul, the courts were clearly open to every kind of abuse and few of the consuls were such models of Victorian rectitude as the Barkers. A Jaffa consul was tried for fraud, a Cyprus vice-consul for scuttling a ship to get its insurance;

---

* Among these was a nectorine with a sweet kernel: he sent one such tree to the Duke of Northumberland who sold it for £300 which he gave to the 'Fund for Decayed Gardeners'.

5. An Anglo-Turkish 'occasion' to mark the visit of the Prince and Princess of Wales to Constantinople in 1869. Watercolour by an unknown artist

Signor Damiani, another consul in Jaffa, was described by Buckingham as having 'nothing about him that seemed consistent with the notions of consular dignity'. In the 1860s, however, Sir Edmund Hornby's reform of the courts resulted in the separation of the legal and judicial powers of the consul from the commercial and the establishment of a new court in the capital with a competent lawyer and staff.

At the same time the establishment in 1877 of a dragomans' school in Constantinople indicated a belated attempt on the part of the British government to replace those exceedingly expert masters of intrigue – the Greek and Italian dragomans, on whom ambassadors had principally relied for their relations with the Porte and its provincial officials – with student interpreters, British officials who knew Turkish and Arabic. Officials who had attended the school formed the nucleus in 1903 of the Levant Consular Service. This resolved many of the shortcomings of the earlier consular system; except in very minor posts in the Ottoman Empire British officials were now appointed who could be relied on to execute government and ambassadorial directives. The LCS helped to balance the tendency of the British and Indian governments to regard the Middle East as a chess-board on which to play out their European and Asian policies against France and Russia. As the great Persian scholar, E. G. Browne, wrote, however, 'England, though more directly interested in the East than any other European country save Russia ... offers less encouragement to her sons to engage in Oriental languages than any other European nation.'

The reform of the consular service coincided with the dwindling of interest in the strategic value of the Levant after the opening of the Suez Canal in 1869. Sir Robert Morier, ambassador in St Petersburg,* voiced the prevalent opinion when he remarked in 1873 that 'as regards Russia and Constantinople, I shall be perfectly happy to see her there, if we secure an equivalent for ourselves in Egypt and Persia; this is quite as much part of our destiny as the possession of Constantinople is part of Russia's, and we shall not, in the long run, be able to hold India without these points d'appui.' For the sake of India, the reformers would turn elsewhere.

* Grandson of Isaac Morier (see above, p. 104).

6. Entrance to the Golden Horn, with Seraglio Point in the background. Watercolour by Count Amadeo Preziosi, 1853

9 *The Veiled Protectorate*

European interests were involved in nineteenth-century Egypt to a degree dreaded, as their own possible fate, by Persia and Turkey. Muhammad Ali and his descendants governed Egypt as a semi-autonomous province of the Ottoman Empire but their growing dependence on European finance replaced Ottoman rule with the far more onerous burden of British and French interference.

Trade with Egypt prior to the nineteenth century had generally been more dangerous than profitable; 'the intolerable Avarice and Insults of the Turkish Bashaws' discouraged the Levant Company from trading without diminishing its jealous monopoly of British interests there. In 1768 the traveller James Bruce was horrified to find no British merchants in Egypt and French merchants handling the small amount of British trade. In the Red Sea, however, traditionally a Muslim lake where no Christian shipping might venture, ships of the East India Company had occasionally been allowed to Jiddah and in 1773 Bruce was given permission for the British to trade as far as Suez; from 1775 to 1780 ships were sent annually from India to Suez. Towards the end of the century an ambitious and far-sighted British merchant, George Baldwin, came to Egypt determined to promote the use of Egypt as an economic and political bridge between Britain and India, thus firing the opening shots of a long battle against interests vested in the Levant which culminated nearly a century later in the concentration of British interests in Egypt. Although he had little success in promoting Anglo-Egyptian trade, his cause was publicised by his appointment both as consul for the Levant Company and as agent for the East India Company, a dual responsibility which remained incorporated in the title of the chief British representative in Egypt – consul-general and British agent – until Egypt was declared a British protectorate at the outbreak of World War I. Napoleon's invasion demonstrated at least the political accuracy of Baldwin's reasoning and Muhammad Ali's encouragement of European investment helped to fulfil his economic forecast.

The French occupation lasted only three years but its effects on Europe as well as on Egypt were more enduring. Napoleon's expedi-

1 The harbour of the European quarter in Alexandria, c. 1790, at the beginning of the European expansion in Egypt. Coloured aquatint by Luigi Mayer from his *Views in Egypt* (1801–4)

tion consisted of more than an army: the technicians who accompanied him were put to work setting up hospitals, a printing press, gunpowder factories, libraries and schools and many of them remained in Egypt after the French defeat, ultimately to work on similar projects for Muhammad Ali in his efforts to modernise Egypt. Among the European powers Britain, in particular, appreciated for the first time the strategic importance of Egypt, while scholars glimpsed a part of the greatness of ancient Egypt through the lavishly illustrated volumes of the *Déscription de l'Egypte*, produced by Napoleon's scholars.

From 1804 the British consul-general and agent supervised political affairs in Cairo, while British commercial interests were in the care of a vice-consul, later consul, in Alexandria. Europeans in Alexandria had always enjoyed a modicum of security, due to the large Levantine community of Greeks, Maltese, Syrians and Jews which bridged the gap between East and West, Christian and Muslim. As early as 1777 a visitor from India, Eyles Irwin, was impressed by the fact that European residents could walk around the city in European dress. During the eighteenth century the harbours of Rosetta and Damietta, Delta ports where Europeans had previously lived, had silted up; their traffic was inherited by Alexandria and they became instead quiet resorts where Europeans from Alexandria spent the summer. Alexandria soon became one of the most Europeanised cities of the eastern Mediterranean and most Europeans lived there rather than Cairo in the first part of the nine-

2. Commanders at the Battle of Alexandria, 1801, including Sir Ralph Abercromby, Sir Sidney Smith, General Menou the defeated French commander, and Lord Keith, the British admiral. Sketches by Sir Robert Ker Porter

teenth century. A Grand Square, centre of the European quarter, contained consulates, churches, the principal commercial offices and shops with European goods, demonstrating to one traveller that 'strangers from a once barbarous land were repaying the debt which the world owes to the mother of arts, and raising her from the ruin into which she had been plunged by years of misrule and anarchy'.

The commercial prosperity of this second capital of Egypt was based on corn and cotton, the cultivation of which, on the flat well-watered fields of the delta, had been developed by Muhammad Ali. Communications with Cairo and the Delta had been improved by the construction of the Mahmoudiyah Canal, linking Alexandria with the Nile; in the 1840s steamships appeared on the Nile and

3. In March 1811 Muhammad Ali invited the leading Mamluks to a celebration in the Cairo citadel in the course of which they were all massacred (one man escaped to Acre). Here Muhammad Ali is seen watching the massacre. Lithograph by Horace Vernet from Comte A. de Forbin, *Voyage du Levant* (1819)

shortly afterwards a railway connection was built between the two cities.

The Mahmoudiyah Canal was recommended to the viceroy by Samuel Briggs, merchant and banker, head of the oldest cotton broking firm in Alexandria and typical of the vigorous entrepreneurs who came to Egypt to take advantage of its new prosperity. Many of them founded commercial dynasties whose names crop up in the parish and consular records of Alexandria throughout the century. Briggs, 'the invariable and firm friend of English travellers', acted as proconsul when the Cairo or Alexandria consulates were unoccupied. He was considered to have more of Muhammad Ali's confidence than any foreigner in Egypt and was an invaluable go-between for

Boghos Youssouff Bey
The devoted Minister &
Confidential Adviser
of the Renowned Mohamed Ali
Viceroy of Egypt from 1817 to 1845

4. Boghos Youssef Bey, Muhammad Ali's principal minister, who be-friended many European visitors during his period of office, 1817–45. Pencil drawing by Edward Lear

travellers, archaeologists and engineers trying to attract the attention of the would-be moderniser of Egypt with their ideas. It was Briggs who in 1821 took a consignment of Muhammad Ali's long-staple Jumel cotton to Lancashire, thereby building a link between the Lancashire cotton mills and prosperous Greek and Syrian cotton planters in the Nile Delta which survived until the sequestration of their large estates after 1952.

Not all Europeans were as scrupulous in their relations with Egyptians as Briggs, however. The time-worn system of Capitulations, as little changed in Egypt as elsewhere in the Ottoman Empire, still served to protect Europeans ostensibly from oriental depredations but in fact as often from the legitimate course of justice. European communities were swelled by local Greeks, Maltese and other Mediterranean nationals who had somehow acquired consular protection. Capitulations were particularly liable to abuse in nineteenth-century Egypt because of the growing number of foreigners owning property in the country but still exempt from civil and fiscal law. Mixed courts, set up in 1875 to try civil cases involving litigants of different nationalities, removed some of the abuses without really affecting the 'great enclaves of privileges'*

* P. M. Holt, *Egypt and the Fertile Crescent*, p. 197.

that Capitulations had become and remained to some extent until their abolition in 1937.

Alexandria remained the commercial capital of Egypt throughout the century, in spite of scares in the 1860s that the Suez Canal and the new Port Said would destroy its trade. The growing of Egyptian cotton expanded rapidly during the American Civil War and many Europeans, especially British, bought large estates in the Delta to profit by the boom. Alexandria blossomed in the flood of wealth from cotton, enticing merchants and speculators from all over Europe. As much as a third of Alexandria's mid-century population of about one hundred and fifty thousand was European and of those about six thousand were British.

After the Arabi riots of 1882, in which a number of British were killed and much of the European quarter burned down, the centre of Alexandria was rebuilt, in a florid Riviera style in keeping with its character as the government's summer resort. A contemporary engraving shows the Place des Consuls, as the Central Square was now known, with gas lighting, pavements and fountains; a museum, largely financed by a Greek merchant, housed a respectable collection of antiquities; an opera house attracted itinerant Italian singers from time to time; there were good French restaurants; and an English public school, Victoria College, was founded towards the end of the century. Tourists glimpsing the East for the first time as they stepped on to the Alexandria quay from their Peninsular and Orient steamers might shudder at the noise and squalor of the dockside, but for the residents Alexandria had most of the pleasure and little of the pain of living in Egypt. British officials from Cairo, chaperoning their Egyptian ministers, descended on suburban Ramleh every summer, interrupting the gentle round of bridge and tea parties with their Cairo gossip; while their families were entertained on Sundays by a band playing in the park separating Ramleh from the town centre.

The completed Suez Canal was difficult to reconcile with an independent Egypt: no European power could afford to risk another controlling this vital passage to the East, least of all Britain with her vested interests in India. Disraeli's purchase of Canal shares in 1876 made it impossible even for Gladstone's government to ignore the financial problems of Egypt. A system of dual financial control by France and Britain was wrecked by the Arabi revolt in 1881 and in order to restore the order needed for the repayment of debts, as well as the protection of the British community, the British unwillingly and hesitatingly occupied Egypt in 1882. Alexandria was bombarded and a few weeks later a British force landed at Ismailia, about halfway along the Canal, defeating the Egyptian army at Tel el-Kebir. Arabi was exiled to Ceylon and Sir Evelyn Baring (later Lord

Cromer), who had already had some experience of Egyptian affairs as one of the Dual Controllers, was summoned from India to take up the post of British agent and consul-general in Cairo.

Cromer ruled Egypt from 1883 until 1907. During that period he drastically overhauled the country's finances, limiting public expenditure on all reforms except irrigation, which he selected as the one aspect of agriculture that with improvement would enable the country to pay its debts. Cromer had spent most of his earlier administrative career in India and came to Egypt imbued with a fervidly Christian belief in the inferiority of oriental peoples and in the divine superiority of European civilisation. This conviction was not unique to Cromer nor new to Egypt. Stephen Cave, author of the Cave Report on Egyptian finances of 1876, summed up his opinion of Egypt as suffering 'from the ignorance, dishonesty, waste and extravagance of the East', opinions reminiscent of Canning's on the Turks. George Curzon, visiting Egypt in the 1880s, wrote that 'civilisation is foiled by a country which refuses to be civilised, which cannot be civilised, which will remain uncivilised to the end,' a judgment more alliterative than accurate. One of the most influential books on the Egyptian question was Alfred Milner's *England in Egypt*, published in 1892, which is said to have persuaded Gladstone finally to abandon the idea of withdrawing from Egypt. 'Alike by the nature of our interests, by the nature of our power and by certain special qualities in our national character,' Milner declared, 'we seem marked out for the discharge of this particular duty' – the salvation of Egypt.

Cromer's enlightened despotism was as typical of the period as it was of the Anglo-Indian officials he brought to Egypt to help him execute his reforms. His own book, *Modern Egypt*, is a model of contemporary imperialism, painting a vivid and accurate picture of Egypt as seen by the British who lived, worked and amused themselves there and tried to recreate that inflexible European civilisation which Cromer believed implacably was the right one for everyone to live by. In words echoed all over the Middle East by would-be reformers, Cromer wrote: 'Let us, in Christian charity, make every possible allowance for the moral and intellectual shortcomings of the Egyptians, and do whatever can be done to rectify them.'

The business of government, of reforming the Egyptians, was in Cairo. Until the 1860s when the Khedive Ismail gave it a face-lift to welcome European dignataries for the opening of the Canal (adding thereby to the mounting Egyptian debt), Cairo had retained some of its medieval aloofness from European influence. In the early years of the century the Europeans still lived in one quarter of Cairo, the swampy area of Ezbekiyah with its own gates that were locked at night or on occasions of civil disturbance. Edward Lane commented how at night 'one might pass through the whole length of the metropolis and scarcely meet more than a dozen or twenty persons, excepting the watchmen and guards'. Society there was more informal than among the prosperous merchants of Alexandria: 'there are no ambassadors or great diplomats to attend to, and life is more free from ceremonial.' Scholars such as Edward Lane and artists such as J. F. Lewis could still disappear into the alleys of Cairo and live as native inhabitants, away from the inquisitive gossip of the small community of their compatriots.

In 1869 William Russell described Cairo 'with all its wealth of Eastern sights and Mahometan usages', as more civilised than Constantinople. 'The people are accustomed to the noisy, odd, capricious stream of tourists and travellers which runs for ever backwards and forwards through the alleys of their city.' By 1869 Russell would also have noticed the tide of European influence beginning to flow over the medieval exclusiveness. The Suez Canal celebrations of that year

5. Scene in Ezbekiyah Square showing Shepheard's 'British' Hotel, c. 1860, by which time Cairo was overtaking Alexandria as the centre of European activity. Lithograph by T. Picken from a drawing by Machereau, a French drawing master established in Cairo in the 1830's and 1840's.

were an admirable excuse for Ismail to beautify the capital. Muhammad Ali had set on foot the draining of the Ezbekiyah swamp, on which boats used to sail during the annual inundation of the Nile, but Ismail had grander schemes. Ezbekiyah became a formal garden with fountains, trees and cafés. A fencing club with a suave French manager was formed. Hotels sprang up around the square – Shepheard's and the Great Eastern were joined by others more modern. Greeks and other Europeans opened shops in the nearby streets, stocking them with European foods and comforts for tourists ascending the Nile. An opera house was built and Verdi commissioned to write an opera – *Aida* – for its opening. Thus the flocks of winter visitors could amuse themselves almost as pleasantly as on the Riviera and Ismail's extravagances countered some of the squalor and poverty which was glimpsed behind the scenes.

The number of British officials working in Egypt before the occupation had been growing along with the Egyptian debts – land settlement experts, financial experts and customs experts among them. Railway technicians were prominent among them, including Robert Stephenson who constructed the railway from Alexandria to Cairo. After 1882 the British community in the capital swelled with the influx of advisers assembled by Cromer, most of them from India, to help reorganise the economy. By 1894 every Egyptian ministry had a British adviser and a team of British assistants. The Khedive Tawfiq gave the British a site on the island of Gezirah which became the famous Sporting Club where, according to the hypercritical Ronald Storrs, who came to Egypt in 1904, most of the British spent between one and five hours of every day.* A race course, a polo ground and a golf course helped pass the leisure of the Anglo-Indian officials.

Some thirty-five years after Tel el-Kebir, Storrs commented sadly on the changes in Cairo – how the small informal British community had grown into an inflexible society dominated by the consul-general – known as Over-Baring before being awarded a peerage and then as The Lord – which, with a few exceptions, excluded 'orientals' from its gatherings. Storrs, who was one of the exceptions, blamed the Anglo-French Entente of 1904 for leaving the British in sole control in Egypt. One British official in the administration described the exclusive 'social circle' of Cairo as consisting of winter visitors, British advisers and 'the limited number of Egyptians who foregathered cordially with the foreign elements'; the most celebrated of these was probably Princess Nazli, much praised by the British in Cairo for 'liberating herself from the harem'. The number of British officials employed in the administration dramatically increased in

* The club was in fact for British officers; civilians could only become members 'by courtesy' of the military.

6. Evelyn Baring, Lord Cromer (1841–1917), Consul-General in Egypt.
Portrait by J. S. Sargent, 1902

the last ten years of Cromer's rule, when French diplomatic obstacles
were removed, exacerbating the social as well as administrative gulf
between British and Egyptians.

The most successful of Cromer's officials was Colin Scott Moncrieff,
an Anglo-Indian engineer in charge of irrigation works from
1883–92. 'Happy is the reformer', Moncrieff wrote, 'who finds things
so bad that he cannot make a move without making an improvement.' He and his band of engineers travelled indefatigably, clearing canals, rebuilding barrages (bringing the aged designer of
Muhammad Ali's barrage down river from Cairo to see it function-
ing again), teaching villagers new methods of irrigation perfected in
India. Later officials included Sir John Scott, an Anglo-Indian
judge who tried to impose on the national tribunals standards of
justice effectively tested in India; William Willcocks, a barrage

expert who built the Aswan Dam; Harold Hurst, one of the greatest experts on the Nile; and Thomas Russell who was instrumental in suppressing the hashish trade.

Of all the British officials brought to reform Egypt the army officers, under a British commander-in-chief known by the Indian title of Sirdar, produced some of the best results in training an efficient army in the fifteen years between the Arabi revolt, when the defeated Egyptian army was disbanded, and Kitchener's victory in the Sudan in 1898 achieved largely with Egyptian troops. The British officers acted as a focal point, however, for opposition to the whole British administration. Their favourite pastime of hunting led to some unfortunate incidents, of which the most serious occurred during a pigeon shoot at Dinshawai in the Delta in 1906. A party of British officers was menaced by Arab villagers while trying to arrange a shoot of the village's pigeons; they escaped unharmed but in running back to the camp one of them fell by the roadside and was later found dead. An Arab boy standing beside the body was kicked to death by soldiers, although it was later discovered that the officer had died of heat stroke.

The incident is interesting for the uproar it caused in Britain and among the British in Egypt, already on edge as the result of nationalist agitation in the local press. The village elders were arrested and four villagers sentenced to death by a special tribunal (and executed in Dinshawai the following day). A *Times* leader thundered that the authorities had to deal with a 'revolt upon a small scale on the part of the lowest and most fanatical of the Mussulman population. . . . The severe sentences passed upon the ringleaders are not only justified but imperatively demanded by the circumstances.' Cromer, who was away at the time, later admitted that the sentences, 'though just, were, I may now readily admit, unduly severe.'

A similar incident had occurred a few years earlier when British officers tried to hunt foxes sheltering on the estate outside Cairo of Cromer's most nagging opponent in Egypt and in England, Wilfrid Scawen Blunt. Cromer's cynical opinion of Blunt's romantic idealism – 'he appears to have believed in the possibility of a regeneration of Islam on Islamic principles', he mocked – was countered, ineffectively in that climate of opinion, by Blunt's view that 'the world would be a poor misshapen deformity were it planted from pole to pole with a single crop of wheat; and how valueless will it have become, according to any concern of beauty, when the Anglo-Saxon rule of law and order shall have overspread both hemispheres – which may God forbid – and established over them its debased industrialism, its crude cookery and its flavourless religious creed.'

7. Wilfred Blunt, whose romantic idealism towards the Islamic world was the antithesis of the attitude of Lord Cromer. Photograph by Bassano and Vandyke

Blunt began his career in the Foreign Office and first went to Egypt on holiday in 1873. Two years later he returned with his wife (a granddaughter of Byron), with whom he spent several winters travelling in the Najd and Mesopotamia, collecting Arab friends and Arab horses and taking the latter back to England, where they set up a stud in Sussex, in order to regenerate the Arab breed in England – with considerable success. 'If I can introduce a pure Arab breed of horses into England, and help to set Arabia free of the Turks, I shall not have lived in vain', he once wrote. In Egypt in 1880 he studied Arabic under a pupil of Muhammad Abdu, the great Islamic nationalist, 'one of the best and wisest and most interesting of men', and was strongly influenced by Abdu's ideas of an Islamic renaissance. Whereas Cromer wanted to lead Egypt towards western civilisation based on Christian morals, Blunt, influenced by what he had seen of Wahhabi Islam in Arabia, believed that therein lay the Middle East's survival. Although he agreed with Urquhart that the problems of the Middle East now stemmed from the importing of Europeans and their ways, he differed from him in

8. A British deputation to Muhammad Ali, 12 May 1839, which shows the British consul, Colonel Patrick Campbell, explaining to Muhammad Ali Thomas Waghorn's plans for improving the Overland Route via Suez. The artist, David Roberts, wearing civilian clothes is seated on the right, Waghorn is between Campbell and Roberts and Boghos Youssef is probably standing behind Muhammad Ali holding a fan. Lithograph by Louis Haghe from a drawing by David Roberts in his *Holy Land, Egypt and Nubia* (1842–9)

maintaining that the Ottoman sultanate had been corrupted by western influences ever since its conquest of Byzantium.

Blunt's fierce opposition to the British occupation (which he called a 'veiled protectorate'), publicised in his *Secret History of the British Occupation*, did not endear him to his compatriots in Cairo, but he was a popular figure with visitors. On his estate outside Cairo, named Sheykh Obeyd after a nearby tomb, visitors were received by Blunt and his wife in Arab dress and entertained with Arab food in the company of local village and beduin elders. All his pan-Islamic and Arabophile enthusiasm was mirrored in his delight in Sheykh Obeyd; returning there for the winter of 1893–4 Blunt described his feelings of 'perfect pleasure, perfect health and perfect power of enjoyment without the least shadow of annoyance'.

Blunt and Cromer were equally unrealistic about the Egyptian they were, in their very different ways, both trying to change. Cromer identified the Egyptians, or at least the 'blue-shirted fellah' for whom he professed to have so much sympathy, with the Indian *ryot*, regardless of the considerably superior standard of living of the former. In 1907, a year after the Dinshawai incident, Cromer retired and left Egypt after twenty-four years' service, an old and sick man embittered by the ingratitude of a people for whom he had done so much. 'It may be that at some future period the Egyptians may be rendered capable of governing themselves without the presence of a foreign army in their midst and without foreign guidance in civil and military affairs, but that period is far distant', he concluded in *Modern Egypt*.

Cromer's successor, Sir Eldon Gorst, was dogged by Cromer's detachment from public opinion and aloofness even from his own officials. In attempting to recover the support of the Khedive, alienated by Cromer, he failed to come to terms while it was still possible with the rising tide of nationalism; this was in spite of constitutional experiments, such as trying to replace some of the British officials in the administration by Egyptians. He was succeeded by Kitchener and the restoration of autocratic rule – once again it was Britain at the helm of Egypt. Kitchener and Cromer were alike in believing that their reforms were sufficient indication of the justice of British rule, whether or not the Egyptians themselves approved.

10 The Great Game

Threats to the security of India were the main factor in British policy towards Persia, southern Mesopotamia and the Persian Gulf during the nineteenth century. Commercial and political rivalry with Russia in particular left the British in Persia little time to think of reforming or modernising the country whose soul they were bargaining for. Throughout this period there was an interesting divergence of policy between the Anglo-Indian officials who staffed the consulates in Persia and often the embassy, who were more concerned with the survival of Persia, and their colleagues in the home government in London, whose Persian policy was influenced by European considerations. The comparative indifference of the latter to the plight of Persia is the only explanation for the apparent greediness of the Reuter Concession, the Tobacco Monopoly and the Anglo-Russian Convention of 1907. Only after the Persian Revolution appeared to have succeeded against all odds did the British government begin to recognise a genuine desire among the Persian Constitutionalists to modernise their country without the interference of either great power, by which time Britain was powerless to influence events.

British trade with Persia had almost come to a halt by the end of the eighteenth century, after the civil wars in which the Qajar dynasty established its authority throughout Persia. The isolation of Persia from outside contact is illustrated by the fact that when Captain John Malcolm visited Persia at the end of the century he was instructed on what to wear, when presented to the Shah, by a courtier who produced as a guide a painting of an English ambassador of two centuries earlier – probably Anthony Sherley – in the Elizabethan costume which Malcolm was supposed to copy.

Some visitors to Persia in the early nineteenth century, the romantic artist Sir Robert Ker Porter among them, were dazzled by the magnificence of Fath Ali's court, decorated with the loot of Nadir Shah's invasion of India. A more accurate impression of the mutual fascination and repugnance which British and Persians felt for each other was portrayed by James Morier, author of *Hajji Baba*, who accompanied three missions to Persia in the first quarter of the century and escorted the Persian ambassador Mirza Abul Hassan to

1. Nadir Quli Khan, Shah of Persia 1736–47, whom Hanway met in the course of his journey to seek trading concessions for the Muscovy Company. Engraving from Sir John Malcolm, *A History of Persia* (1818)

London. Morier describes how in Persia 'the philanthropic efforts' of the indecently dressed Englishmen – who showed their legs and their bared heads, much to the Persian's disgust – 'to force upon the reluctant Persians the triple boon of vaccination, post-mortem examination and potatoes' met with only limited success. In England, the Persian ambassador, accustomed to the exaggerated ceremony and lavish costumes of his sovereign and courtiers, was horrified when he was allowed to approach the Prince Regent, 'whom he took to be a *capigee* or porter', without taking off his shoes.

But England had its compensations, as the Mirza confessed, and one of his entourage was heard to declare on leaving England that he could not wish for a better paradise than Chelsea Hospital, where for the remainder of his days he would sit under the trees, do nothing and drink as much porter as he liked.

From about 1812 the British mission, when in Tehran, lived in a stately building designed by Sir Gore Ouseley, 'a commodious house, whose Italian portico and pillars were a perpetual record of Europe in Asia', blessed with a flat roof for spending the night and underground cellars, or sirdabs, for spending the day in the summer heat. Ouseley, who had spent several years in India, was responsible for the Persian ambassador, Abul Hassan, during the latter's visit to England in 1809, and was sent on a return visit to Persia the following year, accompanied by James Morier. He spent an exhausting

2. Mirza Abul Hassan who was sent on embassies to London in 1809–10 and 1819–20. On the first occasion he was accompanied by Morier who used him as a model in his books, *Hajji Baba of Isfahan* (1824) and *Hajji Baba in England* (1828). Watercolour by M. Gauci, 1810

three years in negotiations with the Shah and Russia, but spared more time than many subsequent diplomats in Persia for perfecting

3. Takht-i-Kajar, a summer palace built by Fath Ali a few miles north-east of Tehran, visited by Morier when he accompanied Sir Harford Jones Brydges in 1809. Engraving from Morier's *Journey*

his own knowledge of the language. In this he was helped by his erudite brother William, who acted as his secretary for much of the time. Gore Ouseley later helped to found the Royal Asiatic Society.

Another member of Ouseley's party was a doctor who was given the nearly impossible task of teaching the Persians to inoculate against smallpox. His efforts were beautifully satirised by the king's physician in Morier's hero, *Hajji Baba*. 'He makes no distinction between hot and cold diseases, and hot and cold remedies, as Galenus and Avicenna have ordained, but gives mercury by way of a cooling medicine, stabs the belly with a sharp instrument for wind in the stomach, and what is worse than all, pretends to do away with the smallpox altogether by infusing into our nature a certain extract of cow.... Now this will never do, Hajji. The smallpox has always been a comfortable source of income to me; I cannot afford to lose it, because an infidel chooses to come here and treat us like cattle.' On this and on many other occasions when European doctors were called to help where Persian methods had failed, the superstitions and suspicions of the invalids and their relations usually prevented any possible cure or prevention – a conservatism which was paralleled in politics. On the other hand, once they had established the effectiveness of their methods they were often given positions of great influence, and Dr Tholozan for instance, who was Nasiru'd-Din's French doctor, achieved more in the way of concessions for his compatriots than all the stealthy manoeuvring of the Russian and British legations.

4. Abbas Mirza, son and heir to Fath Ali Shah, drawn by Sir Robert Ker Porter when he was in Tehran in March 1818. Reproduced as frontispiece to Porter's *Travels*

The British officers sent to Persia under the 1814 agreement were based on Tabriz, capital of Azerbaijan and seat of the enlightened Crown Prince Abbas who had first set on foot the plans for modernising the army.* During his governorship the British and Russian diplomatic missions were also in Tabriz because of Abbas Mirza's power and influence with his father, Fath Ali, whom he pre-deceased in 1833. Tabriz at this time was enriched by its trading connections with the Black Sea, which made it in the first half of the century the leading transit market of Persia. It was one of the few Persian towns, apart from Tehran, to house British merchants who imported around a million pounds worth of goods annually. Although one jaded visitor, a Mr Armstrong, exhausted from crossing from Erivan, branded Tabriz as 'a confused assemblage of low mud edifices', its British residents found it the nearest approach to civilisation in Persia at that time, and the enthusiastic Ker Porter, one of several artistic admirers, compared its position, on the lower slopes of barren but majestic mountains surveying the well-irrigated fields and orchards

* It was one of the sergeants on the mission who was found growing his own potatoes in Tabriz, as well as other 'essential' vegetables, and brewing his own wine in spite of the general opinion that Persian wine was one of the country's few compensations.

5. Entry of Fath Ali Shah into Tehran 1816; the entry was at first delayed because of unpropitious omens but the execution of the cow in the left foreground seems to indicate that all is now well. Engraving from Morier, *A Second Journey through Persia* ... *etc*, (1818)

of the oasis, to that of 'a monarch looking down from the head of a vast amphitheatre'.

The foreign legations moved back to Tehran with the accession of Muhammad Shah in 1834. Although it had been the Persian capital for fifty years, Tehran still preserved some of its earlier provincial character, almost unaffected by the small foreign community until the latter half of the nineteenth century. Visitors (and artists such as Ker Porter) rhapsodised about the beauty of the city's position at the foot of the high-ranging Elborz Mountains, which formed a background to the north, and towering above them Mount Demavend, snow-capped for most of the year, of which George Curzon wrote that 'what Fujiyama is to the Japanese, Demavend is to the Persian language'. But grandeur of setting did little to alleviate the unromantic limitations of Tehran itself, once the traveller had passed through the imposing walls with their twelve massive gates into the narrow alleys and crowded bazaars of an overgrown market town; here merchants and pedlars from every diverse part of Persia were jostled by courtiers on horseback forcing their way to one or other of the splendid vulgar palaces of the Shah and his vast family, splashing their horses in and out of the streams which ran down the middle of the streets and so horrifying the British who regarded them as the prime source of the plague, cholera and other diseases which ransacked the city from time to time. But to the Persians water in whatever form was beautiful.

For the first half of the century the size of the foreign community in Tehran reflected the opinion of a Scottish traveller of the period who divided Persia into two portions – one being desert with salt, the other desert without salt. Merchants from India or Britain had to some extent been enticed back to the Persian trade, but they preferred to remain on the periphery, in the Persian Gulf or at Tabriz. Anglo-Indian officials, diplomats and occasional missionaries were in general the only British to live in Tehran at this time and as late as the 1840s Lady Sheil, the minister's wife, was obliged to wear Persian costume whenever she went outside the legation grounds in Tehran, one of the last Middle Eastern capitals to hold out against the onslaught of unveiled, indecently dressed European women.

Poor Lady Sheil was very depressed by 'the monotonous current of life in Persia', where the only other educated European woman in Tehran, the Russian minister's wife, lived on the other side of the city, while 'as to visiting, intimacy with Persian females has seldom

6. A view of Baghdad from the Tigris, from a series of *Lithographic Drawings from sketches by Robert Clive of subjects lying principally between the Persian Gulf and the Black Sea* (n.d.)

any attraction for a European'. While her husband fought a losing battle with the Russian minister for the confidence of the Shah, Lady Sheil spent her days gardening, appropriating the Shah's English gardener, Mr Burton, with whose help 'I astonished everyone with the fineness of my celery, cauliflowers, etc.', though even the garden was separated from the legation by a road across which she had to be escorted by servants.

If life was dull for the minister's wives, the ministers themselves had a frustrating and difficult task most of the time. There was little or no respect for such conventions as diplomatic immunity. In 1822 a British chargé d'affaires was threatened with decapitation by Fath Ali Shah. Muhammad Shah had a messenger of the minister, John McNeill, arrested and robbed of his papers at the outset of the 1837 Herat expedition. Persian designs on Herat were also behind the insulting behaviour of the Shah's chief adviser to another minister, Charles Murray, in 1854; Murray was accused of committing adultery with the wife of the British agent in Shiraz (the couple were both Persian and the wife, to make matters worse, a member of the royal family). Murray was deeply affronted, mainly by the infringement of the lady's diplomatic immunity when she was imprisoned, and withdrew to Baghdad until the Shah had apologised.

Most appointments in the first half of the century were held by officials from India dismayed as much by the indifference of the

7. The Mosque of Husain at Karbala, from Clive's *Sketches*

home government to the strategic importance of Persia as a gateway
to India as by the fickle attentions of the Shah and the corruption
of his ministers. The divergences between the Persian policies of the
British and the Indian governments was a chronic worry to British
officials on the spot, viewing 'the Great Game' played by the distant
Russian and British governments with as much apprehension as the
Shah himself. One British minister of the 1830s, John McNeill, who
had risen from being an assistant surgeon with the East India Company army, returned to England from Persia determined to rouse the
country to an awareness of Persia. His *Progress of Russia in the East*
sold thousands of copies, while 'the monthlies poured in a close
and galling fire, supported by the light artillery of leaders in the
daily journals and by charges of cavalry in the shape of pam-
phlets and reports', according to a later minister, Henry Rawlinson.
He failed, however, to make much impression on the government.

Rawlinson was one of the most outstanding of British officials in
nineteenth-century Persia, and this in spite of the brevity of his actual
service as minister; his career illustrates the nature of British involvement in Persia in the middle years of the century. Rawlinson first
went to Persia from India in 1833. He studied Persian, learning by
heart long passages of Persian poetry which later won him great
favour with the Shah and his court. In 1835 he was posted to
Kirmanshah, as military adviser to the Shah's brother who was
governor of Kurdistan (within easy reach of the already famous
cuneiform inscription of Bihistun which Rawlinson later de-
ciphered). In 1846 he went as consul to Baghdad for four years,
where he combined consular activities with deciphering cuneiform
lettering, collecting and domesticating wild animals and writing an
outline of the history of Assyria – drawn up, he wrote to his brother,
'in great haste, amid torrents of rain, in a little tent, upon the
mound of Nineveh, without any aids beyond a tolerably retentive
memory, a pocket bible and a notebook of inscriptions'.

In 1859 Rawlinson returned to Tehran as minister, appointed by
the India Office, which briefly administered the legation from
1858–9; but no sooner had he arrived than he heard that the
Foreign Office had taken over the responsibility for the appointment
and he resigned:* the Foreign Office he felt was less concerned than
the India Office with the maintenance of British influence in Persia
and the rescue of that country from a chaotic past and a dangerous
future, a cause very dear to Rawlinson's heart. Fifteen years later he

* Indian interests still dominated Anglo-Persian relations, however, and the
Indian government paid most of the cost of the British establishment in Persia.

8. Ruined fortress of Hoshab in Kurdistan, from Clive's *Sketches*

published an important collection of essays, *England and Russia in the East*, outlining what he called the 'triangular contest' between Britain, Russia and Persia. The enthusiastic reception given to the book when it was published in 1875 reflected a changing climate of opinion in Britain compared with the relative indifference with which the essays were received when originally published separately in the 1850s, at the height of Persian iniquities culminating in the Anglo-Persian War.

Meanwhile Tehran and its foreign community were changing with the growing political interest taken by European powers in Persia. The outward trappings of the Shah's court remained the same; the old tradition of putting on Persian slippers and throwing sand over the tracks of an infidel ambassador had been modernised only to the extent that ambassadors no longer needed to remove their shoes but were handed galoshes as they entered the Shah's presence. Upper-class Persians, like their Turkish counterparts, had discarded their picturesque traditional costumes for a particularly drab and shape-less adaptation of European dress which they wore on all but the most ceremonial occasions. George Curzon described Tehran court life as 'eloquently typical of the life of mingled splendour and frippery, and of the taste, half cultured and half debased of the Persian monarch and it may be said of the Persian aristocracy in general'. The frippery and half-culture which he so despised were largely the result of closer relations with Europe, titillating the appetites of the aristocracy with the flashier products of the industrial revolution. The Shah and his relatives built themselves innumerable palaces in Tehran and on the nearby mountain slopes, each one a bric-à-brac monument to the prevailing bad taste of contemporary Europe.

Three journeys to Europe had alarmed, confused and disappointed the Shah, who wrote long descriptions of his travels, published in Persian for the edification of his subjects and translated into English for the amusement of the Victorians. In Britain, as with the earlier visit of the Sultan of Turkey, every effort was made to impress the Shah with Britain's naval and military might. In 1873, his first visit, he was taken round dockyards, arsenals and on trips to the Midlands, as well as attending banquets galore. There were the usual problems of etiquette ('ask Mr Thompson to send as soon as possible a correct version of the Persian National Anthem if there is one', wrote an exasperated Lord Chamberlain). His second visit in 1889 lasted a month, giving his hosts scope for a still more energetic programme. The only result of the Shah's trips, however, which also included St Petersburg, was to convince him that his sole chance of survival at the hands of these powerful nations was to prevaricate as much as possible, a policy which commended itself neither to Britain nor to Russia.

As the Shah's indebtedness increased and with it the instability of the government, the rival European powers, principally Britain and Russia, increased their vigilance at the Persian court – each trying to prevent the other from gaining an advantage. The British and Russian legations in Tehran were rebuilt in the form of compounds for greater security; Valentine Chirol, arriving in Tehran in 1884 and noticing a building towering over the rest, assumed it was the Shah's palace and was most agreeably surprised to learn it was the British legation. Designed by the same architect who had designed the Victoria and Albert Museum in London, J. W. Wild, it was as symbolic of British imperialism as Gore Ouseley's earlier embassy had been of European culture. The British compound contained the offices and homes of members of the legation and gardens vast enough for twelve thousand Persians to camp there when seeking *bast*, or sanctuary, at the outbreak of the revolution in 1906. The legation had its own Indian consular guard, just as the Russians had a Cossack guard, both of which excited the envy and shame of Tehran's inhabitants and the Persian army, the latter being considered by the British and Russians as unfit to protect foreigners.

Sir Frederick Goldsmid, in Tehran in the 1870s to arrange details of the Indo-European Telegraph, described the leisurely social round of occasional dinners at other legations, persuading Persian guests to play party games, entertaining the constant trickle of Anglo-Indian visitors and travellers, hunting and other festivities. The summer months were spent in the mountains at Gulhak; in Lady Sheil's day the legation took its tents (a perpetuation of the nomadic character of the Qajar dynasty) – 'we have sleeping tents, nursery tents, and my private sitting room tent', she wrote; but a compound was at last built, on land given to the British by the Shah, which included a village whose revenues the legation could use to improve the approaches.

For the impoverished Shah to raise money from individuals was far less politically risky than from governments, and by the 1870s Tehran's foreign community was already swollen by European entrepreneurs, or 'chevaliers d'industrie' as Curzon called them. Commercial speculation reached a peak during the last thirty years of the century. Popular opinion found its voice over such issues as the Reuter Concession and the Tobacco Monopoly, but in Britain Rawlinson spoke for the majority when he denounced Persia as 'effete' and attempts to rejuvenate her as visionary. 'It is even more incapable than Turkey of adopting European habits of vigorous thought or of moral sense.' Henry Drummond Wolff went to Tehran as minister in 1888 ('the Wolff from the mountains will be down upon us very soon', wrote a facetious attaché), staunchly believing that 'every encouragement should be given to European capitalists to establish themselves in Persia and to develop its resources', but the businessmen who flocked to the parlours of Tehran were not all endowed with the same moral scrupulousness as Wolff envisaged and their activities only agitated existing discontent.

After the Anglo-Russian Convention British commercial activity was restricted to the south and south-east. The majority of those few British who lived outside Tehran or the British 'zone' were employees of the Indo-European Telegraph Company, sometimes acting as British consular agents, or missionaries. Outside the Gulf area there were by the end of the century British consuls or consular agents in several of the main towns of Persia – Kirman, Kirmanshah, Isfahan, Shiraz and Tabriz among them. 'They are really news-writers, but act as consuls and look after British interests', wrote one recipient of their hospitality.*

The missionaries were to be found wherever there was a large enough non-Muslim community to justify their presence – as for

---

* Few consuls were as energetic as the young Percy Sykes who was given the unenviable task of founding the Kirman consulate. 'I soon organised a weekly gymkhana', he wrote, 'with tent-pegging and lemon-cutting etc. which ... finally culminated in an organised race meeting.'

instance among the Nestorians in the north or among the Armenians in Isfahan. The Isfahan mission was industrious enough, much to the rage of the Armenian Church; they translated the Bible into Persian and the Common Prayer Book into Julfa Armenian and they ran a large boy's school and a dispensary for their exclusively Christian converts. But Curzon for one felt the results did not justify the large expenditure of money and labour. The British lived in the Armenian suburb of Julfa and had little or no reason to venture across the river to the city which had so dazzled their seventeenth-century predecessors. Ker Porter bemoaned its lost glories, 'its palaces solitary and forlorn', with all his romantic enthusiasm: 'the nocturnal laugh and song which used to echo from every part of the gardens [are] now succeeded by yells of jackalls and the howls of famishing dogs.' To a certain extent, however, the atmosphere of past splendour depended on the visitor and Isfahan remained one of the most important of Persian cities. James Silk Buckingham, who was there in 1815 only a few years before Ker Porter, remarked on the luxuries of the city: 'my whole time was spent in one unbroken succession of pleasures, during which I was highly honoured, so constantly delighted and in short, so completely surrounded by gratification of every kind, that I neither had, nor wished to have, a moment of leisure or seclusion, to note the impressions to which all this train of pleasures naturally gave rise.' He bathed in the ancient bath of Shah Abbas, he was welcomed with every honour by the governor, he was shown the sights by the chief of artillery, feasted in the palace and entertained in the gardens – the Hasht Bihasht or Eight Paradises, where 'all that Muhammad, or the Christian authors of the Apocalypse had painted of a sensual heaven seems to have been anticipated'.

In the Persian Gulf, still the focal point of British interest in Persia, the British lived in a very different world from that of their compatriots in Tehran. The Gulf was considered vital for the defence of India and gave rise to such vehemence as Lord Lansdowne's in 1903 – 'I say it without hesitation,' he thundered in the House of Lords, 'we should regard the establishment of a naval base or of a fortified place in the Persian Gulf by any other power as a very grave menace to British interests.' British officials in the Gulf made up for the absence of any other effective overall authority and the fact that their hegemony of the Gulf was virtually unchallenged for most of the nineteenth century gave them the freedom to meet the stern obligations of the white man's burden. Britain was in the Gulf, not only to protect an approach to India, but also 'in obedience to the calls that have been made upon her in the past to enforce peace between warring tribes, to give a free course to trade, to hold back the arm of the marauder and the oppressor and to stand between the slave dealer and his victim'. The role of reformer could be played to the full.

There is little mention of the Persians in the story of the British in the Gulf. This was a naval-based power and as John Malcolm wrote, the Persians have always 'abhorred and dreaded the sea'. British authority in the Gulf was based on Bushire but directed from India. All British officials in the Gulf were appointed by the Indian government. The extent to which the Gulf was virtually a part of the Indian Empire is illustrated by the fact that anyone wishing to travel by sea from the Gulf to Britain had to go via India.

The major challenge facing the establishment of British authority in the Gulf at the beginning of the nineteenth century was Arab piracy. Organised to a large extent on the lines of a *jihad* by the Jawasmi tribesmen of Ras al-Khaima, inspired by the Wahhabis, it was at first studiously ignored and ultimately ruthlessly destroyed. Buckingham was with the British expedition which attacked and burned Ras al-Khaima in 1816 and he described the bloodless battle in which only one European died – from the shock of hearing the first shot fired. By the General Treaty of Peace of 1820 and the Maritime Truce of 1835 the Trucial Shaikhs, as the signatories were known, were bound to cease fighting by sea and a Treaty of Peace in Perpetuity, signed by the dutiful shaikhs in 1853, included a clause of reinforcement by British vessels.

The worst abuses of the slave trade were also removed by a treaty with the Gulf Arabs and the Persians. Gun-running was harder to eradicate. In the early part of the century the arms were mostly British. Even as late as 1903 Curzon's patronising remark, made in Muscat, that he was satisfied that 'the predominance of Great Britain in the mercantile interests of this state is supreme and incontestable', hardly took account of the fact that many of these mercantile interests still revolved round fire-arms. Not until it was discovered that the guns landed at Muscat were being smuggled into south-east Persia and Afghanistan and used against the British on the north-west frontier of India did the policemen of the Gulf effectively suppress a traffic which by 1900 was worth well over £100,000.

Considering the patronising tone of the period, British residents in the Gulf during the nineteenth century are noticeable for their comparative toleration and humility. The authority of the British was such that their representatives were able to travel widely in the Gulf area and they acquired an extraordinarily detailed knowledge of its tribes, its dialects, its flora and fauna, which they described in erudite articles in the current periodicals of the flourishing 'Asian' societies in London. One of the most knowledgeable and most

9. The castle of the Sultan of Aden at Lahaj, c. 1809, engraving from an original drawing by Henry Salt, published in Salt's *Voyage to Abyssinia ... in the years 1809–10 etc.* (1814)

energetic, Lewis Pelly, who was British Resident at Bushire in the middle of the century, voiced the fascination of the Gulf, in spite of its physical drawbacks. 'Here before you is society in the making,' he told the Royal Geographical Society; 'meeting these Arabs you readily comprehend how they once stormed across the world; and you leave them persuaded that they still possess qualities which may again render them renowned, should outward circumstances favour.'

Bushire, the British headquarters in the Gulf, was one of those gruesome towns about which even the most dedicated servant of the empire could find little to say in its favour – 'particularly uninviting and even fatiguing to the view', was Buckingham's verdict. The climate was much the same as that of Bandar Abbas and the comments on the great heat – which drove British and Persians alike to sleep on their roofs in wet sheets in the height of the summer – have a familiar ring. It did not even have the advantage of a good port; ships had to anchor four miles off and passengers and cargoes were rowed across the sand bar in local boats.

Muscat was the other Gulf base of British activities. For the first thirty years of the century the climate, which even Curzon described as an 'exceptional horror', drove the British to direct their interests

10. Bushire, the British political and commercial headquarters in the Persian Gulf during the nineteenth century. Engraving from J. S. Buckingham, *Travels in Assyria ...* (1829)

there from Bushire until the 1870s, through a local agent. The town of Muscat, built round a small bay guarded by two Portuguese forts, 'an ill-built, crowded, not over-clean place', was hemmed in by a high wall of mountains from the deserts of the interior of Arabia. British ships from India called there regularly after the first treaty – to prevent the French winning a foothold in the Gulf – was signed with the Sultan of Muscat in 1799, by an 'English gentleman of respectability' – John Malcolm. The preliminary of the treaty hoped that 'the friendship of the two states may remain unshook to the end of time and till the sun and moon have finished their revolving career', which, with occasional interruptions, has so far been the case.

The Sultan of Muscat, by the end of the nineteenth century, was little more than a British vassal who, after the suppression of the slave trade and the subsequent loss to Muscat of most of its revenue, was paid a handsome annual subsidy. Curzon, who never minced words, described Muscat's independence as grotesque and with the reappearance of a French menace in the Gulf in the 1890s would dearly have liked to annex Muscat to the Indian Empire. British fears of a French intrusion were considered justified when in 1894 the French opened a consulate in Muscat. Their first consul, M. Ottavi, spoke Arabic so superior to that of his British colleagues that he was able to conclude an agreement with the Sultan for the lease

11. View of Muscat from the harbour, drawn by Lieutenant Temple of the Bombay Marine in 1809 and subsequently published as a coloured aquatint in his *Views in the Persian Gulph* (1813)

to the French of a coaling station without the British hearing about it until it appeared in the French press.

The subsequent friction between the Sultan and his British paymasters included not only the temporary withdrawal of the Sultan's subsidy but also minor but significant insults from the Sultan, such as his refusal in 1898 to fire a salute on Queen Victoria's birthday until the resident explained 'the breach of courtesy'. On the whole, however, these incidents were exaggerated by their isolation in the calm passage of time in Muscat, where the arrival of a British warship was an occasion for a week of celebrations – 'dinners and parties in fancy dress at the Agency and the India Office thoughtfully supplied a billiard table' – and the Shaikh of Abu Dhabi, west of Muscat, could write to Percy Cox, the resident, that 'the news of our part is good, and the movements are tranquil and nothing has transpired except what is pleasant to the mind'.

Curzon's state visit must have upset the routine, however. As the responsibility of the Indian government, the Persian Gulf was not the least of the viceroy's commitments and he included it in his triumphal tour of 1903. Curzon, like Canning and Cromer, was remarkable, even in the context of Victorian evangelism, for his righteous conviction of Britain's mission to improve the peoples of the areas with which he was concerned. He has been ill-treated by history: more people remember the aphorism, 'My name is George Nathaniel Curzon, I am a most superior person', than that he was the author of one of the best books ever written on Persia.

12. Arab dhow being repaired at Yembo, on the Arabian littoral, water-colour by Captain Robert Moresby. Moresby was with the Bombay Marine and as a pioneer of the Overland Route surveyed the Red Sea and adjacent areas. He was later employed by the P. & O. to captain one of their largest steamships on the route

Persia and the Persian Question, written after a year's travel in Persia in 1889–90, was the first full-length and life-size portrait of Persia and Curzon showed a far greater understanding of the problems facing countries like Persia in the face of European encroachments than many of his contemporaries, in spite of his conviction that the British were the best people to solve those problems.

Ten years after his original visit Curzon found himself in the Gulf in a very different position from that of the anonymous traveller of 1889. His tour of three weeks was designed to impress Gulf rulers with British might and the French and Russian governments with the futility of trying to assault Britain's hegemony of the Gulf. A durbah for all the Trucial Shaikhs was held on board ship at Sharjah on the Arabian littoral. Here, in spite of a heaving sea, Curzon delivered a memorable speech. 'We found strife, and we have created order,' he told the sea-sick shaikhs; 'we saved you from extinction at the hands of your neighbours.... We are not now going to throw away this century of costly and triumphant enterprise; we shall not wipe out the most unselfish page in history.... The influence of the British government must remain supreme.'

If Curzon's words echoed the convictions of several generations of well-meaning reformers, the words of John Masefield evoke those of David Urquhart in his calmer youth, and of Wilfrid Blunt. 'Shall we and this great ally make sand of All a nation's budding green, and wreak Our winter will on that unhappy land?' asked Masefield.

The reforming instinct was very pronounced in the Victorians, and
the diplomats and administrators working in the Middle East to
protect British interests were by no means averse to describing their
political activities as labour for the good of the country concerned,
which indeed they often were. The drawback was that British
interests were not always compatible with those of the Middle East
peoples as they roused themselves from the torpor induced by
centuries of despotism. Fortunately the presence of British officials
in the Middle East encouraged an increasing number of their
countrymen to visit the area for less strategic reasons, be it archaeology, exploration or merely tourism. This helped to rebuild among
the peoples of the Middle East a pride in their history and culture,
which the official policies of Britain as of other European powers
often tended to denigrate. It is essential, however, to remember that
none of these visitors was free from the influence of officialdom, in
particular of Canning, Cromer and Curzon who quite apart from
their policies possessed an outstanding fund of knowledge for their
contemporaries to draw upon often to the exclusion of opposing,
pro-nationalist views.

13. Fath Ali receiving Sir Harford Jones Brydges in audience in 1809, by
Robert Smirke R.A., probably from a sketch by James Morier who is
standing behind the ambassador. The figure in the centre, with his back
turned, is probably Mirza Abul Hassan who went as the Shah's ambassador
to London later that year.

11 *The Road to India*

Communications with India assumed considerable importance in this period; several generations of travellers, merchants and technicians were occupied with their development and successive British governments with their protection from the intrusion of other European powers. Not everyone had the time to spare for the sea journey round the Cape of Good Hope, which took five to eight months under sail and often as much as three months in the early days of steam. All the faster routes to India passed through the Middle East; through Egypt and via the Red Sea to Bombay; through Syria to the Euphrates and on either to Basra and down the Persian Gulf or to Baghdad and across to Persia; and finally through the Black Sea to Tiflis or Trebizond and overland to Tabriz. There were as many different methods of travelling as there were routes. The perennial discussion of communications with India in the industrial age was concerned almost as much with the development of steam (by river as well as by sea), railways and telegraph – that whip for curbing recalcitrant ambassadors and Indian governments – as with the direction.

The early years of the debate on the best road to India centred round the Overland Route, via Egypt and the Red Sea, so-called in contrast with the Cape route. George Baldwin was among the first to realise the vital position of Egypt for communications, as well as trade, between Europe and India, proving his case in 1778 when he was able to forward to India the news of the outbreak of war with France in time for the British to capture Pondicherry. James Bruce acquired permission in 1773 for the British to trade to Suez and as a result a number of East India Company officials chose this route to return to Europe, its brevity compensating to some extent for its hazards.

The Red Sea was virtually closed to shipping for nine months of the year by contrary winds; it was inadequately charted and notorious for its fickle currents. Europeans landing anywhere on the Arabian shore were in constant danger from the fanatical Muslim population. Ships sometimes went to Suez, leaving only a three-day journey to Cairo, but Qusair, to the south, was more popular

1. Godfrey Vigne and escort crossing from Turkey to Persia on his way to India, in March snow. Watercolour by Vigne

at the beginning of the century in spite of its reputation for flies, lack of water and a thieving population which did away with several European travellers. From Qusair the traveller faced a nightmarish journey across the desert to the Nile at Qeneh; Buckingham, travelling in the opposite direction on the regular caravan route in 1816, 'was stripped naked, among the mountains, plundered of money, paper, arms and instruments and abandoned to my fate. I had to trace the rocky path naked and barefoot, scorched by day and frozen by night . . . I continued for two days without food or water, and the first nourishment of which I partook was some raw wheat from a sack, which, swelling in the stomach, had nearly proved fatal to me.' Buckingham was lucky to survive; many of his countrymen did not after similar mishaps and one, Eyles Irwin, gave thanks for his survival in 1777 with a picturesque if unpoetical ode to the desert:

> Dread Cause! too subtle to define,
> Where horror! danger! ruin join! –
> Stop, stop its pestilential breath,
> That 'whelms a caravan in death!

Baldwin continued his efforts to develop the Suez route after his appointment as consul-general in 1785, though the hostility of the Turks and the instability of the Egyptian government, which was unable to provide security for the desert crossing, prevented any immediate success. Napoleon's occupation vindicated many of his arguments, however, and the fact that a force was sent from India to block the entrance to the Red Sea at Perim illustrated the value of the passage.

The invention of the steam engine put a new emphasis on the route. In the early days of steam navigation, engines were of little avail against the winds and high seas of the open water but their development was only a matter of time. The great advocate of the use of steam in combination with the Overland Route was Thomas Waghorn, an enthusiastic and imaginative lieutenant with the Bombay Marine. By the 1820s when Waghorn first began to consider the possibilities of steam it was already being used for domestic river transport and cross-channel packets. In 1829 Waghorn set out from London to prove his arguments in favour of the route, carrying despatches for Sir John Malcolm, now governor of Bombay. He posted to Trieste and found a ship going to Alexandria, sailed up river from Rosetta to Cairo and rode by camel for three days from Cairo to Suez. At this point his journey began to run less smoothly: he was robbed, he fell ill and the journey from Suez to Bombay took him far longer than he had anticipated. Nevertheless he completed the whole journey in forty days, even without the still dubious advantage of steam, proving the value of travelling via Egypt to himself and the more adventurous of his supporters.

At the same time as Waghorn was setting out on his momentous voyage, a similar effort was being made to understand, if not to reduce, the hazards of Red Sea navigation by other members of the Bombay Marine, Captain Moresby of the *Palinurus* and Captain Elwon of the *Benares*, whose meticulous surveys of every island, reef, current and harbour of the waterway are a memorial to their skill, endurance and, incidentally, remarkable proficiency as artists.* 'There is *no* respite and no change', ran one desciption of the Red Sea, 'Glowing morning rushes on to fiery noon. Fiery noon fades to blood-red evening and blood-red evening to black and sultry night. But scorching, roasting heat, never leaves us nor forsakes us!'

The coaling problems of steam navigation were enormous. In 1830 the *Hugh Lindsay* steamed from Bombay to Aden in eleven days, so stuffed with coal that the single passenger on board was turned out of the passenger salon to make room for more coal. Waghorn recommended that Mokha and Suez should be used as coaling stations; in the event Perim and then Aden were substituted for Mokha, Aden supplied with coal sent by the Cape route and Suez

* See below, p. 251.

2. Title of a portfolio of engravings after original drawings by Robert Moresby and Thomas Grieve, *Route of the Overland Mail to India* (1842). Moresby played an important part in surveying the Red Sea ports that lay on the new route to India

supplied by camel caravan from Alexandria.*

By the 1840s the Overland Route was being used by passengers as well as mails. Travel on early steamships and through Egypt was far from luxurious, so that those travelling to India only chose the Overland Route because they were in a hurry or because they were prepared to suffer its discomforts for the sake of a chance to see the newly-vaunted wonders of the Nile – 'there, where the deities of the earlier world keep their colossal state in the silence of the Desert – where the mysterious Nile pours forth exhaustless abundance – it would be impossible to sojourn without pleasure, or to depart without instruction', enthused one advertisement for steam travel.

Waghorn's imagination and perseverance set on foot the development of the route by larger concerns, in particular the Peninsular and Orient. After his appointment as the East India Company's deputy agent in Egypt in 1837, Waghorn developed his own pas-

* Captain Haines of the Bombay Marine attacked and captured Aden in 1839 with a small force after an Indian ship with a British flag had been wrecked and its crew and cargo held to ransom by the Sultan of Lahaj. Aden was annexed to the Bombay Presidency and became a Crown Colony in 1937.

3. Joseph's Hall outside Cairo showing the Cairo heliograph in the left background, part of a communications system set up by Muhammad Ali between Cairo and Alexandria. Lithograph by J. C. Bourne from a drawing by Robert Hay, published in Hay's *Illustrations of Cairo* (1840)

senger traffic but he was soon overtaken by another British firm, Messrs Hill and Raven, who were themselves bought up by the Viceroy Abbas I in the 1840s as part of his policy to ward off foreign enterprise. Waghorn's travel brochures still recall some of the excitement which has been drowned by the efficiency of later tours. Travellers landed at Alexandria, for many of them their first glimpse – generally an unfavourable one – of the east,* and from there travelled by barge and later steamboat up the Mahmoudiyah Canal and the Nile to Bulak, two miles down river from Cairo. Outside the towns travellers were dependent on their own portable resources. A recommended list of travelling essentials reads like the children's game of 'My-Aunt-Went-To-India': one interpreter-servant, four hundred and fifty Spanish dollars, a supply of tea, coffee, sugar, pepper and mustard, two dozen bottles each of sherry, brandy and water, also water for cooking, candles, powder and shot, camping equipment (including a camp bed with posts and curtains), and a milch goat with a cradle so that it could be carried on a camel.

The steamship for India would be waiting at Suez. Signal towers along the desert route sent semaphore messages to Cairo announcing

---

* 'You might as well be impressed with Wapping as with your first step on Egyptian soil', complained Thackeray.

4. Conveyances used on the Overland Route. Travel in covered carts was considered quite comfortable by Samuel Bevan, 'drawn by good horses and being well balanced on their enormously large wheels, their motion was both easy and agreeable'. Lithograph by V. Adam from a drawing by Count Andrassi, c. 1845

its arrival, so that passengers could wait till the last minute in the relative comfort of their Cairo hotels and complete their sight-seeing. All sorts of conveyances linked Cairo with Suez: coaches with four or six horses, two-wheeled vans, donkey chairs, horses and donkeys. Post-houses had been built at intervals along the route, but passengers were seldom allowed more than half an hour's pause at any of them except the half-way house, a desert haven described by one visitor as having 'tolerable cuisine for the locality' in spite of the insect life which made the dishes 'look to be full of heaps of flies'. Abbas I, relishing the serenity of Waghorn's desert route, built himself a palace opposite the half-way house to share its solitude. Waghorn's own enthusiasm and impatience provided the best publicity for the route. 'He left Bombay yesterday morning,' wrote Thackeray after a breathless meeting with him in Cairo, 'was seen in the Red Sea on Thursday, is engaged to dine this afternoon in Regent's Park and (as it is about two minutes since I saw him in the courtyard) I make no doubt he is by this time at Alexandria or Malta, or perhaps both.' He added, 'Waghorn conquered the Pyramids themselves, dragged the unwieldy structures a month nearer England than they were and brought the country with them.' Waghorn himself was carried away by the vision of the 'fanatic population of Egypt and India' coming to Britain to learn the bene-

5. The rival project to the Overland Route to India was to travel by steam-ship down the Euphrates to Basra. Colonel Francis Chesney undertook to pioneer this route. The boiler of one of his ships is seen here being transported to the Euphrates in 1835. Engraving from Chesney's *Narrative of the Euphrates Expedition* (1868)

fits of civilisation; fortunately perhaps for the survival of the Overland Route the East India Company saw its value in more practical terms as facilitating the defence of India.

The completion of the Suez Canal in 1869 hardly concerns this book, since virtually the only part placed by the British was the somewhat ignoble one of obstructing the original project as far as was politically possible. The new French-designed towns of Port Said and Ismailia, with their Parisian boulevards, the smell of French coffee in the cafés and the comforting rattle of the *tric-trac* boards and billiard cues were welcomed by connoisseurs of the Overland Route which for the most part now lay deserted, the post-houses ignored and Abbas' palace left to crumble away in the desert isolation its original owner had prized so highly.

The success of the Egyptian route was determined by the failure of a far more popular project which was debated for many years – the Euphrates Valley route. This seemed a far more logical route to India: it was shorter by some thousand miles, the contemporary steam ship was more suited to river than sea navigation and the Persian Gulf was far safer than the Red Sea. Thomas Love Peacock, working for the East India Company, drew up the original project to survey the Euphrates as a possible way to speed up mails between Britain and India. In 1829 Francis Chesney, an artillery officer, was sent on a remarkable journey throughout the Middle East to compare the Euphrates route with the Egyptian Overland Route.* Chesney

* Before setting off on his first journey Chesney had been with the Turkish army during the Russo-Turkish war of 1828–30, accompanying 'rockets' ordered by the sultan and instructed to set up a rocket corps.

6. Top-hatted British passengers arriving at Bulak, the Nile port of Cairo, on the first stage of the journey to Alexandria. Engraving from Moresby and Grieve's *Overland Mail*

favoured the former and in 1834 the Steam Committee of the House of Commons voted twenty thousand pounds for a Euphrates expedition to steam down the great river. Messrs Laird of Liverpool built two small flat-bottomed river steamers, while Chesney assembled the members of the expedition – 'officers and men of the highest calibre', insisted William IV, an enthusiastic sponsor of the project – all of them experts in one field or another.

The expedition left England with great aplomb in the spring of 1835, landing on the Syrian coast at Suwaidiyah. From there the boats, appropriately named *s.s. Tigris* and *Euphrates*, had to be carried over the mountains to Antioch and thence by land and water to be assembled beside the Euphrates near Bir, on a site named Port William after the expedition's patron. The problems of transport were enormous and were aggravated by obstructions from the Egyptians occupying Syria, since any successful development of the Euphrates route would be at Egypt's expense. Special carriages were built to carry the ponderous boilers over the mountains, each one pulled by forty oxen and a hundred men. The keels of the boats

7. A station on the Overland Route, one of seven between Cairo and Suez.
Engraving from Moresby and Grieve's *Overland Mail*

were too long to turn the bends of the mountain road; the bell
anchor sank into several feet of mud; eight hundred and forty-one
camels had to be hired. Chesney himself was so near death's door
at one time that his second-in-command, Henry Lynch, ordered the
hammering on the boats to be stopped until it was discovered that
the ensuing silence only aggravated Chesney's feverish agitation.

By the time the boats reached Port William it was winter and too
late to start down the river. Chesney, William Ainsworth and several
other members of the expedition spent the interval exploring the
relatively unknown parts of eastern Anatolia. By March all was set;
the steamers were gingerly lowered down a twenty-five foot bank
into the river – 'they actually *leapt* into the water', Chesney recalled
– and the wondering inhabitants of Bir watched the iron monsters
steam away into the distance.

Their problems were by no means over. Fuel was always scarce.
Both boats were loaded with coal and an erratic supply, attacked
by riverain Arabs, was kept up through Bir, but when all else had
failed the crews were put to cutting down the sparse undergrowth.
At Hit, with its smoking bitumen pits, Chesney experimented with
using a mixture of bitumen and earth as fuel. Navigation was
difficult; in spite of their shallow draught the boats went aground
very easily and nothing could move them except a squall of rain in
the vicinity. Arabs on either bank were generally hostile and those
on the Mesopotamian bank were often at war with those on the
Syrian bank, catching the passengers on the *Tigris* and *Euphrates* in

8. Lake Timsah on the Suez Canal, showing de Lesseps' private steamer *Mathilde.* Watercolour by William Simpson

9. A ride to a picnic at the Pyramids, a welcome respite from the Overland Route. From *The Illustrated London News,* 9 January 1858

10. View of Port William and the town of Bir, the assembly and starting point of the expedition, on the Euphrates. Frontispiece engraving to Chesney's *Narrative*

an unpleasant cross-fire. The rules for the day were strict: breakfast at daybreak, dinner at half-past five and tea soon after 'in order to afford time for noting down the events of the day, and that all may retire early'; lights out at half-past nine and no smoking below decks. Members of the expedition landed most days to collect specimens, take measurements and enjoy the local game, while the boats steamed on slowly.

Disaster struck near Al-Ghaim. Even forty years later Ainsworth, the surgeon and geologist of the expedition who wrote one of the better accounts of it,* was able to describe the full horror. 'The sky assumed an appearance such as we had never before witnessed, and which was awful and terrible in the extreme. A dense black arch enveloped the whole of the horizon, and the space beneath the arch

* Chesney's official history of the expedition was never completed, the author being ordered to China before he had managed to write more than two volumes of the intended four; he lost the manuscript of the latter half of the account on his return to England, 'by an accident which is unnecessary to dwell on' and by this time had used up the £1,500 which the Treasury had promised towards publication. The two published volumes contain minutely detailed surveys of Middle Eastern history (from the most ancient times), geography, geology, ethnology and many other subjects, but unfortunately did not get as far as describing the actual expedition.

11. Chesney's steamships, *Tigris* and *Euphrates*, passing Hamman near Rakka, on the Euphrates. Engraving from Chesney's *Narrative*

was filled up with a body of dust . . . whirling round and at the same time advancing towards us with fearful rapidity. . . . The crash broke upon us like heaven's own artillery, and the hurricane seemed as if bent upon hurling both steamers at once to the bottom of the river.' Both ships tried to tie up at the bank in the face of the oncoming cyclone but the *Tigris* was caught too soon: in no time at all the wind had wrenched off the paddles, the waves washed overboard, pouring in through the cabin windows which in dead calm were only just above the waterline, and before the eyes of the horrified passengers watching from the *Euphrates* the *Tigris* stood up on her bows and sank. Nineteen people were drowned.

Although Chesney tried to minimise the seriousness of the loss, it cast a cloud over the expedition which was never quite dispelled. The rest of the journey down river was relatively uneventful. At Fellujah several of the party landed and travelled overland to Baghdad. Further south the *Euphrates* was nearly stuck in the Lemlun marshes where the river channel narrowed and became almost indistinguishable from the flooded land on either side. At Basra plague prevented them from landing, so they paused only to stock up on provisions and fuel before steaming into the open waters of the Gulf to refit at Bushire.

The next six months were spent trying to prove the value of steam navigation on nearby rivers. The expedition steamed up the Karun River to Ahwaz, up the Tigris to Baghdad and finally up the Euphrates again, hoping to reach Bir and so complete the round trip. But the marshes effectively blocked their way, the engine broke down and a disappointed Chesney was forced to return to

12. Monument to Lieutenant Waghorn, pioneer of the Overland Route, at Suez. From *The Illustrated London News*, c. 1870

Bushire and thence to Bombay, calling off the expedition for lack of funds.

In the eyes of the expedition the feasibility of the route had been proved, but to a parsimonious government and the East India Company the expense was not justified by the returns. Waghorn and his colleagues had been working hard on the Red Sea route, where the field of political danger was far smaller than the Euphrates route, an area of virtual anarchy, where strategic alliances were of little value. The scientific value of the expedition was immense but it had only momentarily distracted attention from the Red Sea.

However, the demand for some form of efficient river transport in Mesopotamia was evident, where travel by land was impractical because of the terrain and the hostility of local tribes. The exploration of the lower Tigris and Euphrates was developed by Henry Lynch, Chesney's second-in-command (his brother had been drowned aboard the *Tigris*). Lynch remained in Iraq after the expedition had been disbanded, navigating the Tigris in the old

13. On 21 May 1836, the ships were struck by a very heavy squall in which the *Tigris* foundered with the loss of all but fifteen of her complement. Engraving from Chesney's *Narrative*

Euphrates and three other river steamers, which he had sent round the Cape and assembled in the Shatt al-Arab. His brothers Thomas and Stephen later set up the Euphrates Steam Navigation Company to operate between the Tigris and India, carrying the Indian mails, exporting the precious cargoes of Arab horses for the Indian army and ferrying Anglo-Indian officials and British agents to and from their posts. Thomas' son, another Henry, built up the firm to become one of the main trading companies in the Middle East. Their offices on the waterfronts of Basra and Baghdad were one of the most welcome havens in that part of the Middle East.

Although Anglo-Indian traffic was now switching to the Egyptian route, the Indian government was sufficiently aware of the strategic and commercial possibilities of southern Iraq, or Mesopotamia, to consider it an outpost of its jealous guardianship of the Gulf. In Baghdad and Basra, from the 1830s onwards, the authority of the

14. Basra from the Euphrates, from a sketch by Captain Robert Mignan of the East India Company, published in his *Travels in Chaldea . . . 1827* (1829)

British Resident, appointed by the Indian government, far exceeded that of any other foreign envoy, though the latter were few and far between.* To most foreigners Baghdad and Basra seemed to rival each other for the distinction of being the most unpleasant city in the Middle East. Baghdad, from a distance, excited a certain admiration in visitors, probably because of their arduous journeys to get there, but even before the plague of 1831 it took a Buckingham, exploring it from the hospitable residency of Claudius and Mary Rich, to see anything interesting about Baghdad from close quarters. In 1831 Baghdad suffered one of the most devastating plagues of its disease-ridden history. The story of its two-months' destruction, at the height of which five thousand people were dying each day, was most movingly told in the diary of the Reverend A. N. Groves, a missionary in Baghdad dedicated to the thankless task of converting Armenian Christians. The river burst its banks, drowning many hundreds, and the city was attacked and ransacked by beduin. Later travellers described Baghdad as a run-down, half-ruined city, whose past splendour could only be conjured up at a considerable distance from its crumbling walls and palaces, in the middle of which the stately British residency with its Indian sepoy guards was a sturdy landmark.†

* The British Resident was responsible, among other duties, for Indian Muslims coming to visit Karbala and Najaf.

† The residency was later known as the consulate-general, to meet Turkish objections that 'residency' implied a degree of sovereignty.

Basra was hardly more impressive, though it suffered less than Baghdad from the general anarchy which accompanied the slackening of Ottoman authority in the country between Basra and Baghdad and benefited in the latter half of the century from the development of steam navigation and telegraph. Percy Sykes, approaching Basra by river at the end of the century, spoke with evident pride of the right bank of the river 'lined almost entirely by the substantial houses of the British firms and the Consulate' (though he later decided that Basra was 'not an ideal place of residence, as riding is almost impossible').

In spite of the failure of the Euphrates expedition Chesney never lacked support among Anglo-Indians for the Euphrates Valley route by which the dying cities of Iraq could be opened to the advantages of British commerce. A few years after the expedition Chesney formed a company with an Indian railways official, William Andrew, for a Euphrates Valley railway, described by its detractors as 'a parade ground for imperialists and a pawn for statesmen'. The railway was planned to follow a similar route by land to that of the river expedition. Andrew was one of the many enthusiasts (the younger Henry Lynch was another) to speak impressively of the civilising advantages, as well as the commercial and political gains, to be won from such a project, but the main drawback throughout the century (the project was revived on several occasions) was the uncertainty of being able to restrict its use to the British. The reaction of cautious governments in London, when asked for financial support, was always to fear a French, Russian or German intrusion, via a British line, into Britain's monopoly of the Persian Gulf. Towards the end of the century Germany began to canvass the idea of a Baghdad railway following a similar route, an idea which horrified Indian and home officials with its political presumption. However, the sheer physical difficulties of laying such a line over the Taurus together with the prolonged negotiations in Constantinople, prevented the completion of the line before World War I broke out.

Thomas Lynch's son, Henry, developed a project close to his uncle's heart, the opening of the Karun River in south-west Persia to steam navigation, by which British merchants hoped to be able to penetrate to the centre of Persia. Both Lynches kept the issue before the public in the pages of the Royal Geographical Society journal, in the House of Commons and through their supporters in Tehran. The most forceful of these, Sir Henry Drummond Wolff, at last persuaded the Shah in 1888 to give the Lynches a concession to navigate on the lower Karun as far as Ahwaz. Curzon went up the Karun on the Lynches' steamer the following year, from Muhammarah – 'a small and exceptionally filthy place' – to Ahwaz, coping with the obstructive Persian officials who seemed to Curzon determined to ensure the failure of Lynch's efforts, and the hostility of the Arabs, who found that the opening of the river was being used as an excuse for the Persian government to impose officials on an area which had been virtually independent for many years. At Ahwaz passengers disembarked to cross the rapids and continued their journey by a boat, run by a Persian company, as far as Shuster if they were lucky. Curzon was not; after steaming half way in double the time he had been assured the whole journey would take, he completed it by land.

The lower Karun route came into its own with the discovery of oil in the first decade of this century. Surface oil, in the form of bituminous pools, had been exploited for centuries all over Persia by the local inhabitants for lamp oil; Geoffrey Duckett, one of the Muscovy Company agents to visit Persia in the sixteenth century, found at Baku, then part of Persia, 'a strange thing to behold; for there issueth out of the ground a marvellous quantitie of oile, which oile they fetch from the uttermost bounds of all Persia; it serveth all the countrey to burn in their houses'. By the late nineteenth century, however, the 'commercially apathetic' Persians were content to use imported American oil in their lamps and interest in the development of any oil resources came as usual from outside.*

A French archaeologist, Jacques de Morgan, drew attention to oil seepages in south-west Persia in 1892, but not until 1901 was there any attempt to exploit them. William d'Arcy, an Englishman who had made a fortune in Australian gold mining, was persuaded by de Morgan and others to press the Shah for a concession, which was finally awarded that year; it was for sixty years and covered the whole of Persia except the five northern provinces. The Anglo-Persian Oil Company was set up with its operations in south-western Persia directed by a remarkably persevering engineer, G. B. Reynolds. Reynolds' persistence outwitted the company's parsimony; oil was struck in January 1908 at the site of an ancient fire temple at Masjid-i-Sulaiman, just as the company was ordering Reynolds to give up.

Reynolds had to overcome appalling obstacles in his battle for the oil, not the least of which was the hostility of local Bakhtiari tribesmen to anything which implied the intrusion of an outside authority. With the help of his colleague, Dr Young, he immeasurably increased the local prestige of the company by a hospital he had built and Bakhtiari predations were effectively prevented by

* It is interesting to note the curiosity of Muhammad Ibn Rashid about petroleum, when Doughty met him as early as 1876 (*Arabia Deserta*, I, p. 600).

enrolling members of the tribe in a guard for the company's operations. All tools and machinery had to come from abroad and were
transhipped across the Ahwaz rapids to the same stern-wheeler on
which Curzon had travelled nearly twenty years earlier, off-loaded
at Waiss and carried the last stage by mules, nine hundred of which
were used in a single year. Arnold Wilson, who as assistant to the
British vice-consul at Ahwaz acted as unofficial adviser to the company on local affairs, was full of admiration and sympathy for
Reynolds and Young: 'the position of a company which is working
under a concession from one government (Persian) but depends on
the goodwill of a provincial administration (Arab and Bakhtiari)
and the military and moral support of a third (British and Indian)
with a head office in Glasgow dealing with the Foreign Office in
London and a Foreign Department (Simla) through local officers
(in Persia) is not easy.'

The speed with which the British and Indian governments were
able to meet the potential threat to oil supplies in Persia in 1914
was entirely due to yet another means of communication from which
Persia, as the half-way house between India and Europe, benefited
in more than one respect – the telegraph. The Anglo-Persian War
and the Indian Mutiny, both in 1857, showed up the need for swift
communications between India and Britain. The same arguments,
comparing the Gulf with the Red Sea, were used over the route of
the telegraph cable. However, an attempt to lay a submarine cable
in the Red Sea failed for various technical reasons, the most disastrous of which was the unsuspected predilection of a sea worm,
teredo navalis, for the rubber with which the line was covered.

In 1862 therefore it was decided to take advantage of Turkish
telegraph lines from Constantinople to Baghdad, to link India with
Europe via Basra and the Gulf. Fourteen hundred miles of cable
were loaded in Bombay on to five sailing vessels, accompanied by
a small steamer to tow them when laying the cable. Eminent telegraph officials and engineers joined the expedition from England –
among them Sir Charles Bright who had been responsible for laying
the Atlantic cable and Frederick Goldsmid (whose account of the
operation must be one of the earliest examples of how technical
jargon can warp the English language).

The headquarters of the Gulf cable were at Karachi and four other
stations were set up – at Gwader, Masandam (where the enmity of
local Arabs was overcome by a free-masonry wink from Sir Charles
which the Arabs apparently understood), Bushire and Fao at the
mouth of the Shatt al-Arab. 'Swamps, flats, ditches, here and there
a dwarf tree or shrub; men and things disturbed and exaggerated',
was one officer's graphic impression of Fao. Laying the cable over

the shallow estuary of the Shatt al-Arab presented considerable problems, as it was clear that neither the steamer nor the sailing ships would be able to cross the mud flats off Fao, so Sir Charles Bright leapt overboard to stand waist high in mud, 'an example which was followed by all the officers and men who were soon all wallowing in the soft yielding slush up to their chests'.

The telegraphic link through Iraq was unfortunately soon rendered virtually unworkable by Turkish inefficiencies on the Constantinople-Baghdad stretch and by the Muntafiq Arabs over the Baghdad-Basra stretch, who had few qualms about removing the odd telegraph pole, cutting the line or attacking telegraph officials when they tried to patrol it. An alternative was essential. In 1864 Frederick Goldsmid was sent to Tehran to negotiate a settlement with the Persians for a line to be laid from the Persian frontier near Baghdad to Kirmanshah, Hamadan, Tehran and thence south to Bushire to join up with the Gulf cable. Eight years later the Indo-

15. Erecting a telegraph pole in Persia, title page vignette from Sir Frederick Goldsmid, *Telegraph and Travel* (1874)

European Telegraph Company, set up by Siemens, succeeded in linking India with Europe across the Black Sea to Tiflis, Tabriz and Tehran. Finally the British laid an overland cable through southern Persia from Bushire to Karachi.

The telegraph system scattered throughout Persia the British who manned its fourteen stations, an unprecedented and painless way of opening Persia to outside influences. The Persian belief that all telegraph lines ended at the foot of the Shah's throne was extended in the provinces to the convention that the neat bungalows of the telegraph officials and their wives were *bast*, or sanctuary, and during the revolution they were crowded out by political refugees. The telegraph line was also used in territorial disputes. Many of the first telegraph officials were army officers and certain strategically sited stations remained in the army's employ until after World War 1; at Fao, for instance, effectively guarding the mouth of the Shatt al-Arab, the Turks were furious to discover that the telegraph officer had sketched the full layout of their fort – a plan that proved useful when the British expeditionary force landed there in 1914.

Most of the stations were staffed by a superintendent, his deputy and six clerks, who were responsible for maintaining the line, replacing stolen poles and dealing with unfortunate criminals who had been punished by being nailed to the poles by the ear. Some stations were lucky enough to have a doctor on the staff and became rudimentary hospitals for the surrounding district. British travellers were entertained with all the pomp of the old East India Company days, the superintendent and his staff riding out of the town to welcome or speed on the infrequent guest.

'Verily we live in stirring and marvellous times', wrote the *Calcutta Review* at the end of the century, seeing hopefully into the future, 'when ere many years are over, we are borne along the Euphrates Valley Railway to England in twenty days, or along the "World's Highway"* in ten, while our thoughts are flashed along the telegraph wires in so many minutes, we shall begin to feel ourselves so close to home that we shall cease to consider our separation from our mother country as "an honourable exile"'.

---

*The French won the internal combustion race when Claude Anet travelled through Persia by car in 1906, publishing his description of the journey the following year.

12 *Luminous Vapours*

'A quibble is to Shakespeare what luminous vapours are to the traveller; he follows it at all adventures; it is sure to lead him out of his way and sure to engulf him in the mire.' So wrote the worldly-wise Johnson. Acknowledging the danger, most travellers of this period kept to the old caravan routes in the Middle East. They followed Arab slave traders up the Nile through Nubia into what is now the Sudan, to Dongola and Shendy and to Suakin on the coast. They followed the great *hajj* caravans to Mecca and Medina and returned with them across the Syrian Desert and sailed down the Euphrates on rafts, or followed the Tigris by land to Baghdad and the Gulf, as merchants had for centuries before them. In Persia they followed well-worn paths from town to town. Richard Burton, one of the greatest of Middle Eastern travellers, complained of what he called a lack of initiative among travellers who all assumed (more justifiably than Burton would allow) that anywhere unexplored was difficult and dangerous to reach. It was easy enough, however, to fall into Johnson's mire, waylaid from the path by archaeological or scientific curiosity. Few people dared to travel alone – a guide was indispensable for his knowledge as much of local shaikhs or villagers as of the route; those who did travel on their own, such as Layard in south-west Persia, discovered that there was no limit to the number of times they could be robbed, right down to their last garment. In eastern Anatolia and Kurdistan, and in Arabia, the two largest blanks on the map, the traveller had a hard enough time surviving on the recognised routes without wandering off into the wilds; Burton himself found the Arabs were often the ones who were afraid and communicated their fear to their companions, as when he tried to find a guide to take him across the Empty Quarter from Mecca.

Travellers' books gradually filled in the remarkably dim outline of the Middle East inherited from their mercantile predecessors. Every traveller was intent upon committing to paper his impressions, opinions and endless criticisms of what he saw, not all of it always accurate: 'certainly I have heard fables worthy of the Arabs from the lips of excellent Europeans too long remaining in the East,' wrote

Charles Doughty in his curious style. No one expected literature in a book of travel, said Mary Kingsley, and more bad books of travel were written in the nineteenth century than ever before or since. The Victorians had an insatiable appetite for reading about unfamiliar parts of the world. The literature of the Middle East is particularly rich, however, in accounts as revealing of the writers and their companions as of the countryside through which they travelled; a handful out of the hundreds who published their impressions evoke in the reader an affinity and comprehension as important as their contribution to scientific knowledge of the area.

The handsome quarto volumes of James Silk Buckingham bridge the gap between the earlier travelogues, heavily laced with classical references, and the fresher, more personal accounts of the middle of the nineteenth century which described the contemporary scene in a way that their carefully exclusive predecessors generally did more by accident than by design. Buckingham caught the excitement of travel when he went to sea at the early age of ten. Some ten years later he abandoned the restrictions of ship life for the freedom to wander throughout Egypt, Palestine, Syria, Mesopotamia and Persia. In 1817 he reached India where he began publishing the *Calcutta Journal*; it was brazenly critical of the government which exiled him in 1823. Back in England he published his travels to cover the expenses of his long suit for damages against the East India Company, which he eventually won in 1834.

Buckingham reckoned he had all the necessary qualities for the good traveller – 'ardour in the present enquiry and research', good health, tolerance of foreigners and some knowledge of Arabs and Arabic. Buckingham's companions catch the reader's attention on page after page: the Abyssinian Prince Moussa and Muhammad the renegade Italian, both of whom he met in Jerusalem, Lady Hester Stanhope, with whom he stayed while recovering from fever, the rich Hajji Abd al-Rahman, whose caravan Buckingham joined to cross from Aleppo to Mardin, and the fanatical dervish on the way to Baghdad, who goaded Buckingham's ass so that it threw him and his baggage and left him sitting in the scorching desert for hours. Another dervish, Hajji Ismail, who accompanied Buckingham from Baghdad to Persia, is one of the most sympathetic characters of Middle Eastern travel. Buckingham, 'a man of great kindness of heart and liberality of opinion', holds the interest of his reader not

1. (*opposite*) Richard Burton in Cairo, after his return from Arabia. Lithograph from a portrait by Thomas Seddon, published in Burton's *A Personal Narrative of a Pilgrimage to Al-Medinah and Meccah*

2. Alexander William Kinglake, (1809–91). Portrait by Harriet M. Haviland, c. 1863

by his pages of antiquarian statistics but for his own interest in the people around him.

The most successful and entertaining account of the Middle East is *Eothen* whose author, Alexander Kinglake, toured the Levant and Egypt in 1834 and 1835. *Eothen* excels all previous and most later books of travel. Kinglake addressed it to his friend Elliott Warburton who followed a similar route a year later and generously described *Eothen* as 'entertaining more truth and vividness of description, deeper thought, and more delicate and subtle humour than any book upon the East I have ever seen'. There was nothing particularly adventurous about Kinglake's journey and he took little or no interest in ruins and antiquarian comment: he confessed to a 'jarring discord between the associations properly belonging to interesting sites and the tone in which I speak of them'. Rather he viewed his travels egotistically; 'the people and the things that most concern him personally, however mean and insignificant, take large proportions in his picture, because they stand so near to him' wrote one critic. Buckingham began this tendency towards the subjective travelogue; Kinglake carried it to perfection.

Kinglake took nine years to write *Eothen*, in spite of its unfashion-
able brevity, taking pains to reproduce as accurately as possible his
own emotions and impressions of scenes rendered over-familiar by
his predecessors in Egypt and the Levant. The Bosphorus is 'the
stormy bride of the Doge', 'the knowing slave of the sultan [who]
comes to his feet with the treasures of the world . . . by some unfailing
witchcraft she entices the breezes to follow her and fan the pale cheek
of her Lord'. At the pyramids, 'when I came, and trod, and touched
with my hands, and climbed, in order that by climbing I might come
to the top of one single stone, then, and almost suddenly, a cold sense
and understanding of the Pyramid's enormity came down over-
casting my brain'. Of Damascus he wrote, 'she is a city of hidden
palaces, of copses, and gardens, and fountains, and bubbling streams.
. . . Close along on the river's edge, through seven sweet miles of
rustling boughs and deepest shade, the city spreads out her whole
length: as a man falls flat, face forward on the brook, that he may
drink, and drink again; so Damascus, thirsting for ever, lies down
with her lips to the stream and clings to its rushing waters.'

Nor will Kinglake countenance unreliable myths: in Cairo during
one of the worst plagues in its history, he disregarded European
fears in order to go sightseeing, disproving at least to his own
satisfaction the belief that the disease was contagious by having his
throat examined by a doctor sick with the plague. And as for the
desert, 'practically I think Childe Harold would have found it a
dreadful bore to make "the desert his dwelling place"'. *Eothen* comes
as a breath of exhilarating life upon a field that can be as dreary as
Kinglake found the desert.

The conquest of Syria by the Egyptians introduced a period of
relative peace in the countryside which was more conducive to
foreign travel. Robert Curzon, who must have been one of the most
agreeable of travelling companions, visited the Levant and Egypt
between 1834 and 1837 to collect ancient manuscripts. Those he
found now form one of the chief treasures of the British Museum,
but his account of his experiences, *Monasteries of the Levant*, is equally
valuable and entertaining in its field. His descriptions of the semi-
literate, impoverished monks of the Greek Church are touching as
well as amusing and show the same devotion to subjective impressions as *Eothen*.

Robert Curzon and Kinglake were rare in keeping their accounts
to a manageable size. Elliott Warburton's *The Crescent and the Cross* is
good reading and it enjoyed an even greater success than *Eothen* with
the Victorian public, which appreciated his occasional strictures
against Islam and its adherents, but it is four times the length of the
two earlier books. The prolixity of so many travel accounts of this

period is their great drawback, particularly as the bulk of it is mere padding. Frederick Walpole is another culprit. His account – of his visit to Layard at Nimrud, his desperation, in looking at the map of the Middle East to find an area where no one else had been, to find it had 'all' been visited before and his decision to explore the Ansayria Mountains in Syria – contains much interesting material but it is so needlessly long. Indeed both Warburton and Walpole could have taken a lesson in brevity, if nothing else, from one of the first 'professional' travellers of the period, John MacGregor, who went round the rivers of the world, including those of the Levant, with his canoe Rob Roy producing a series of travelogues each one as bad in its style and mock humour as Mary Kingsley allowed.

Edward Lane's *Manners and Customs of the Modern Egyptians* is hardly about travel except insofar as the author clearly roamed throughout the country in his researches. These researches resulted in the most complete picture of Egypt and its people ever published. As David Urquhart wrote, *Modern Egyptians* was 'eminently qualified

3. Edward William Lane (1801–76), one of the leading Arabic scholars of his day as well as being a competent amateur artist who left many sketch-books of Egypt. Sculpture by his brother R. J. Lane A.R.A.

to improve our position in the east because it is now impossible for a traveller to proceed thither without knowing that there exists there a distinct code of manners and politeness'. Urquhart was perhaps too optimistic; not many of the diplomats and administrators who tried to unravel Egyptian affairs in the latter half of the nineteenth century were so concerned with local customs. Lane first went to Egypt in 1825. As Mansur Effendi he rented a house away from the European quarter, studying from the inside not only the literature but every other aspect of Egyptian life; 'in order to make as much progress as possible in the study of their literature, it was my intention to associate almost exclusively with the Muslim inhabitants.' The fact that at that time little had changed in Cairo since the Middle Ages makes Lane's classic the best commentary on both medieval Arab descriptions and contemporary travellers' accounts. He returned to England in 1828, his initial study, *A Description of Egypt*, in hand but too expensive to publish because of the number of drawings he had included. He continued his studies in Egypt in 1833, working towards *Modern Egyptians*, in which the Society for the Diffusion of Useful Knowledge had expressed an interest and which it eventually published in 1836 as a companion volume to John Gardiner Wilkinson's *Ancient Egyptians*. Lane covered an immense range of subjects: religion, government, domestic life, superstitions, magic, industry, recreations, story-telling, death and even a whole chapter on Egyptian female ornaments. This is not an entertainment like Morier's *Hajji Baba* but a serious explanation of Muslim society; it provides a background for oriental fantasies such as Lane's own translation of the *Thousand and One Nights* and a social commentary to his later lexicon which is perhaps the greatest monument to Arabic scholarship of the nineteenth century.

At the end of half a century of long-winded, fulsome and moralising accounts come the magnificent writings of Gertrude Bell to cheer the reader. Gertrude Bell first visited the Middle East when her uncle was ambassador in Persia in the 1890s. Her finest descriptions, however, are of Syria and Mesopotamia. 'To those bred under an elaborate social world,' she wrote, 'few such moments of exhilaration come as that which stands at the threshold of wild travel.' There is an unexpected combination of learning and poetry in her two best known accounts, *The Desert and the Sown* and *Amurath to Amurath*, and in her extraordinarily evocative letters. She desribes, in a detailed archaeological account of the Sassanid palace of Ukhaidir, how 'it reared its mighty walls out of the sand, almost untouched by time, breaking the long lines of the waste with its huge towers, steadfast and massive as though it were... the work of nature, not of man'. An unabashed romantic, she refutes Kinglake's distaste for the desert and its inhabitants: 'to wake in that desert was like waking in the heart of an opal, the mists lifting their heads out of the hollows, the dews floating in ghostly wreaths from the black tents...'. Her books are lavishly illustrated with hundreds of photographs – portraits of

4. John Lewis Burckhardt, 'Sheikh Ibrahim', a lithograph from an original portrait drawing by Henry Salt in 1817 shortly before Burckhardt's death. It forms the frontispiece to Burckhardt's *Travels to Syria and the Holy Land* (1822)

her guides, companions, chance acquaintances, who speak for themselves in the text in that curious English conventionally supposed to represent Arabic. The photographs are small, scattered haphazardly about the pages, an integral part of the vivid impression of the text.

Gertrude Bell best described the empty stony wastes which to many people comprise the Middle East. These great deserts have from time immemorial exercised an inexplicable fascination for the civilised world, though it generally preferred to be fascinated from a distance. Many, when they came closer, found their illusion spoiled; the desert Arab could be as uncharitable as his town brethren and the harsh severity of desert life seemed ill-suited to any but the most world-weary traveller.

Until the eighteenth century what little was known of the peninsular of Arabia came mostly from Arab sources; the trade routes avoided it and Europeans were warded off by Muslim fanaticism. At the end of the eighteenth century, interest in so exclusive a land was stimulated by the religious revival of the Wahhabis as they extended their influence over the pirates of the Gulf coast and were with difficulty defeated by the Egyptians. Muhammad Ali's victory left two-thirds of the peninsula in the hands of a semi-western power.

John Lewis Burckhardt was probably the first European to demonstrate the greater accessibility which this occupation implied. A Swiss by birth, Burckhardt had studied in England and was engaged by the newly founded Africa Society to equip himself to explore the Sahara by a thorough study of Arabic and Islam. Burckhardt took the Society at its word and spent eight years so doing, basing himself on Aleppo and Consul Barker, and as Shaikh Ibrahim adopting both the personality and the religion of an Arab. During his extensive exploration of Syria he discovered the ruined Nabataean city of Petra, an event he described with characteristic nonchalance in contrast to the 'rose-red' hyperbole of later visitors (except Layard who thought 'the architecture debased and wanting both in elegance and grandeur'). He also met Lady Hester Stanhope and criticised her to her face for her stately progress round the Syrian countryside, affronting the 'Queen of Palmyra' as few people dared.

Reaching Cairo in 1812 he decided to prepare himself still further for his great trek east by going up the Nile through Nubia (where he found the temple of Abu Simbel three-quarters buried in sand) to Dongola and later as far south as Shendy; from Shendy he crossed to the coast at Suakin and sailed to Jiddah. He then set out for Mecca, in the disguise of a 'reduced Egyptian gentleman' to make the *hajj*. Penniless and recovering from fever induced by indulging in too much over-ripe fruit after the abstinence of his months of travel, he applied for money to Muhammad Ali, who was resting at

Tayf, east of Mecca, after his campaign against the Wahhabis. Burckhardt was summoned to Tayf to defend himself against the pasha's doubts of his conversion to Islam; Burckhardt thought the pasha was more worried that he was being fooled than that anyone was trespassing on Muslim holy places. He was examined by the *Qadi* of Mecca: what Arabic books had he read, what commentaries on the Quran, all of which Burckhardt knew rather better than the *Qadi*. Later they supped and performed the evening prayers together, 'when I took great care to chaunt as long a chapter of the Koran as my memory furnished at the moment'. Eventually he was allowed to return to Mecca, which he had had to bypass on his way to Tayf.

Burckhardt's account of the *hajj* and of Mecca was the first complete description of the intricacies of Islam to have reached Europe and it has hardly been bettered since. Some forty years later Burton found Burckhardt's account of Mecca impossible to improve upon and quoted it entire. Burckhardt found himself peculiarly at home in Mecca, a city of strangers like himself, where he was never an object of curiosity or hostility – 'I never enjoyed such perfect ease as at Mekka', he later confessed. Mecca, the holy places and the *hajj* itself are described minutely, though of all the great writers on Arabia Burckhardt's style is the most economical.

Burckhardt has been described as being 'of that small company of profoundly wise and foreseeing travellers who go with ease where others may not go even with pain and know no stirring moments in a land wherein some every hour brings peril'. Not all his travelling was pleasurable, however: 'the Bedouin mode of life may have some charms even for civilised men; the frankness and uncorrupted manners of the Bedouins most powerfully attract every stranger... but after a few days' residence in their tents the novelty subsides. ... I have passed among Bedouins some of the happiest days of my life; but I have likewise passed among them some of the most irksome and tedious.' Even keeping a record of his journeys was a problem; he would write sometimes on his camel, his cloak pulled over his head as if protecting him from the sun, or lying on the ground pretending to sleep, again with his cloak pulled up; 'at other times I feigned to go aside to answer a call of nature and then crouched down, in the Arab manner, hidden under my cloak.' It was on one of these last occasions that his guide spotted him; Burckhardt persuaded him, only half successfully, that he was writing down prayers for their safety.

Burckhardt continued to plan for his journey across the Sahara after his return to Cairo in 1816. Meanwhile he visited Sinai, his account of which is one of his most sympathetic, and wrote up his copious journals, but his health was slowly sapped by repeated

5. An Egyptian bey. Coloured aquatint from a drawing by Luigi Mayer in his *Views in Egypt*.

attacks of dysentery which he had contracted in Medina. He died in 1818 and was buried by the Turks in a Muslim cemetery outside Cairo. 'What shall I say of the late Shaikh Burckhardt?' wrote Giovanni Belzoni, the Italian archaeologist, who was not normally given to praise of others, 'who was so well acquainted with the language and manners of these people that none of them suspected him to be a European.'

Remarkably little exploration resulted from Burckhardt's journey. Between his trip and that of Richard Burton in 1853 the only Englishmen to venture into the interior of Arabia were officials of the East India Company. Captain Sadlier was sent in 1819 to try to contact Ibrahim Pasha whose recent defeat of the Wahhabis in the Najd encouraged the Company to look for an alliance with him to help control the Jawasmi pirates. Poor Sadlier and his companions travelled right across the peninsula to catch up with Ibrahim, who was heading as fast as possible for Egypt and was not the least interested in the Company's offers. Sadlier's account, one of the dullest descriptions of Arabia to be published at this time, unsparingly relives the monotony of its author's desert crossing.

James Wellsted, a lieutenant with the Bombay Marine, travelled extensively in Oman in 1835–6. A second journey in 1837 was thwarted by his collapsing with fever and returning to Muscat in such delirium that 'he discharged both barrels of his gun into his mouth, but the balls passing upwards only inflicted two ghastly wounds in the upper jaw'. Considering his 'shattered health and impaired mental powers', Wellsted's account of Oman was a substantial contribution to the scientific knowledge of that corner of Arabia.

On his way to Jiddah after performing the *hajj*, Richard Burton composed a long (and rather bad) poem, the *Kasidah*, later published as by one Hajji Abdu al-Yazdi and translated by Frank Baker, a *nom de plume* used by Burton.* In it Burton describes Hajji Abdu: 'He had travelled far and wide with his eyes open ... to a natural facility, a knack for language-learning, he added a store of desultory reading; nor was he ignorant of the "-ologies" and the triumphs of modern scientific discovery – briefly his memory was well stored.' This was far nearer the true Burton than the melodramatic picture treasured by most of his admirers and detractors. His contributions to the knowledge of Arab literature and poetry are as great as that of his journeys to the knowledge of Arabian geography; and of the journeys, those east of the Gulf of Aqaba and 'unexplored Syria' (the western edge of the Syrian Desert) added far more to the scientific

---

* It has been argued that in fact Burton wrote it much later; see Fawn M. Brodie, *The Devil Drives*, pp. 276–7.

6. Head of a *hajji*, by Sir Edwin Landseer R.A.

7. Shaytan al-Kabir, the ceremony of stoning the Great Devil which is part of the Mecca pilgrimage. Lithograph from Burton's *Pilgrimage*

and archaeological knowledge of the Middle East than the work by which he is better known, his *Pilgrimage to Makka and Madinah*.

The *Pilgrimage* is written in three volumes, in the first of which Burton explains why he went – ostensibly to investigate the *Rub al-Khali*, the Empty Quarter, and the hydrography of the Hijaz and to see the famous horses of Najd. But another explanation, pandering more to his own excitable nature, lies in his description of what he calls the Arabs' *kayf*: 'the savouring of animal existence, the passive enjoyment of mere sense; the pleasant languor, the dreamy tranquillity, the airy castle-building, which in Asia stand in lieu of the vigorous intensive passionate life of Europe.' This much quoted passage explains the melancholy and sensuality which Burton felt he had in common with the Arabs. The same characteristics shocked and titillated his Victorian public, personified in his long-suffering and suffocating wife Isabel; and a popular portrait of Burton by Frederick Leighton, showing a Tartar-like face of high cheek bones and flowing moustaches, did nothing to dispel this fascination.

Burton went to Mecca disguised as an Indian merchant. He first visited Medina, where he was able to improve upon the invalid Burckhardt's earlier description, and then went to Mecca with the Damascus caravan, the greatest *hajj* of all, a huge moving mass of many hundreds of camels and pilgrims heading for the Holy City, restlessly camping during the hot days and marching at night (much to Burton's rage because it prevented him from seeing the country-side); he describes 'the huge and doubtful forms of spongy-footed camels with silent tread, looking like phantoms in the midnight air', the quarrels among the exhausted pilgrims, the Meccans badgering for lodgers, the fierce desert wind which 'moaned and whirled from the torches sheets of flame and fiery smoke', and the sight of the caravans converging on Mecca, filling the plain a day away from the city with scurrying white-robed figures. His enthusiasm is like that of the Elizabethan pilgrims to Jerusalem, their scepticism falling away under the sway of more credulous pilgrims. Burton, whose disguise as a Muslim was certainly no more than a disguise, describes with gratified pride his entrance to the great mosque of Mecca, the *Bait Allah*: 'there at last it lay, the bourn of my long and weary pilgrimage, realising the plans and hopes of many and many a long year.'

Burton returned to the coast after the *hajj*, planning to come back to investigate the interior, but bad health kept him in Cairo and he never achieved it. There is a note of melancholy in the closing sentence of his account which is more characteristic of Burton than the modesty which is sometimes attributed to him: 'I have been exposed to perils, and I have escaped from them; I have traversed the sea, and have not succumbed under the severest fatigues; and my heart is moved with emotions of gratitude, that I have been permitted to effect the objects which I had in view.'

Arabia in the nineteenth century was in a violent state of turmoil induced mainly by the Wahhabi Saudi dynasty and their opponents, first the Egyptians and later the Ibn Rashidi dynasty, which was dominant in central Arabia for the last thirty years of the century. The greatest of the Rashidis, Muhammad Ibn Rashid, attracted a remarkable amount of attention among Europeans, partly because of his almost undisputed authority, recognised and accepted by the Turks, over a vast area of Arabia, and partly because of his magnificent stud of some three hundred mares. Even Doughty, who had no reason to be grateful to the Rashidis and who condemned Muhammad Ibn Rashid for committing 'crimes which before were not known in the world', conceded that 'never was the government in more sufficient handling'.

An English ex-Jesuit from the French mission at Zahleh in Syria,

William Palgrave, went to Arabia in 1862–3 in the disguise of a Syrian doctor, visiting the Rashidi capital of Hayil and that of the Saudis at Riyadh. His bombastic style, and the many inaccuracies and exaggerations of his book, later led to accusations that he had never been there, but many of his facts are supported by the accounts of the Blunts and Doughty. The Blunts came to Hayil to inspect the stud and buy some mares for their own stud in Sussex. But the real ferocity of Wahhabi Arabia was shown up by Charles Doughty, to whom the British consul and Turkish authorities in Damascus refused to give any promises of protection because his proposals of Arabian travel seemed so reckless.* Doughty refused to disguise himself as a Muslim, even making a point of advertising his Christianity, and consequently suffered almost to the point of losing his life at the hands of the fanatical Najdis. No other traveller in the Middle East tried so hard to follow Johnson's luminous vapours.

Doughty went to the Middle East in 1874, spent two years travelling in the Levant, Syria and Sinai and learning Arabic. In 1876 he decided to join the Damascus caravan as far as the Nabataean ruin of Madain Salih in north-west Arabia, which no European had previously visited. Doughty condescended to take an Arab name, Khalil, only because it resembled Charles: 'the Sun made me an Arab but never warped me to Orientalism', he wrote, no doubt with Burton and Burckhardt in mind. At Madain Salih, Doughty and the caravan parted company; when it passed by on its return to Damascus he had already decided he would explore the interior of Arabia. ' "This," said Zaid [his companion], showing me the wild earth with his swarthy hand, "is the land of the Beduw" ' as they left the caravan to spend the next eighteen months in and around the Najd. After surviving the appalling vicissitudes of Arabian travel, in his case heightened by his religion which made him an object of hostile and often violent curiosity in the towns he visited, he eventually came to Tayf and under Turkish protection bypassed Mecca, reached Jiddah and sailed to Bombay half dead with the miseries of his travels. Back in England he immediately published his data on Madain Salih in order to establish his claim to have been the first European to visit it and spent the next ten years writing *Travels in Arabia Deserta*. The first edition cost him £700 and many of the thousand copies printed remained unsold. Not until an abridged edition was published in 1908 did his great work achieve the wide recognition it deserved.

Doughty was a product of the same enthusiasm for the rigid

---

* The consul told him 'it was his duty to take no cognizance of my Arabian travels lest he might hear any word of blame, if I miscarried.'

8. Charles Montagu Doughty (1843–1926). Portrait by E. Kennington (1921)

discipline of medieval culture as the Pre-Raphaelite Brotherhood. Among the first to acclaim *Arabia Deserta* were William Morris and Burne-Jones, to whom the book had been recommended by Wilfrid Blunt. Some critics suggested that Doughty should write it in decent English; and Richard Burton was enraged, 'more for his sake than for my own', that Doughty admitted to not having read Burton's own books on Arabia. But T. E. Lawrence, who edited the second edition, described it as the 'first and indispensable work upon the Arabs of the desert' and no other Arabian traveller has re-created the ugliness and beauty of the desert as effectively as Doughty.

Doughty apologised for his book in his introduction; 'we set but a name upon the ship, that our hands have built (with incessant labour) in a decennium,' adding very rightly that 'the book is not milk for babes'. Accompanied on his travels by Chaucer's *Canterbury Tales* and already a fervid admirer of Spenser's English, he uses an archaic style with dramatic effectiveness to describe the desert Arabs, themselves speakers of the purest and oldest Arabic. 'If the words were rehearsed to them in Arabic, there might everyone whose life is remembered therein, hear, as it were, his proper voice', Doughty explained.

But the most enthusiastic of Doughty's admirers must wonder with his Damascus friend who greeted him on his return: ' "Tell me, since thou art here again in the peace and assurance of Ullah, and whilst we walk, as in the former years, towards the new blossoming orchards, full of the sweet spring as the garden of God, what moved thee, or how couldst thou take such journeys into the fanatic Arabia?" ' The reader is spared none of Doughty's agonising progress: 'the loud, confused rumour of a great caravan', the comfortless deaths every day among its members, that 'wayworn suffering multitude', the summer 'when the sun entering as a tyrant upon the waste landscape darts upon us a torment of fiery beams' as he crossed the volcanic wastes of the Harra, 'a direful country'. He loathed Islam, 'with a secret horror at the fiendlike malice of these fanatical Beduins with whom no keeping touch nor truth of honourable life, no performance of good offices might win the least favour from the dreary inhuman and ... inveterate dotage of their bloodthirsty religion'. As to why he endured such hardship he claimed a lofty surpassing interest in the 'Story of the Earth, Her manifold living creatures, the human generations and Her ancient Rocks'; in 'those vast waterless marches of the nomad Arabs, tent dwellers, inhabiting, from the beginning, as it were beyond the world.' 'It is an art to examine the Beduins, of these countries; pains which I took the more willingly, that my passing life add somewhat of lasting worth to the European geography.'

It has been said of Arabia that no quarter of the globe has been better served by writers. Certainly they added greatly to European knowledge of the peninsula, a fact which is often obscured by literary controversy. By the end of the nineteenth century the only part of Arabia still unexplored was the *Rub al-Khali*, the Empty Quarter, occupying nearly half the peninsula, 'void of the breath of life', of which Burton, enquiring for guides to take him across, found that even the *beduin* avoided its relentless wastes. Even the impenetrable and savage mountains of south-western Arabia had been exhaustively travelled by an intrepid couple, Theodore Bent and his wife.

Further east, however, Mesopotamia and Persia were far less well served by literate travellers. Henry Layard, E. G. Browne and George Curzon compensate to some extent for the deficiencies of the countless descriptions of journeys to and from India and England, outstanding for their incomprehension of the complex problems of the different regions through which their authors travelled, but presumably meeting the demands of a public stimulated by Russophobia to learn a little about the area. James Morier's accounts of his two journeys in Persia are interesting, particularly the second where he paid special attention to the 'local scenery and manners' of the country, but his accounts lack the curiosity, noticed above in Buckingham, Kinglake, Gertrude Bell and the better writers on Arabia, in the individuals he met during his travels; it is all too apparent that Morier was riding around with an armed escort and English companions. A contemporary of Morier's, James Baillie Fraser, described his extensive travels in northern Persia, which were useful because of Europe's almost total ignorance of that part of the country, but spoiled by Fraser's own unfamiliarity with Persian. John MacDonald Kinnier was an Anglo-Indian officer and a remarkably fearless traveller, whose valuable account of his travels in Iraq, Persia and Anatolia set an unfortunate precedent for the 'soldier's plain unvarnished account', which Indian army officers felt obliged to write, rolling Persia out like a map with 'commanding' passes, good or bad gun positions and 'quartering' themselves on Persian villages.

Robert Ker Porter, his pen as lavish as his pencil, filled his *Travels*, published in 1820, with picturesque scenes of Persia and Persian society in keeping with contemporary taste for the exotic. Whether relating how he met the Crown Prince Abbas Mirza in Tabriz, or joined his glittering procession for the journey through savage mountain scenery, or sketched the magnificent Fath Ali Shah, Ker Porter captured some of the glamour still attached to the land of the Great Sophy. His portrait of the Shah, dressed in a blaze of jewels – 'I never before had beheld any thing like such perfect majesty' – was written for a generation which revelled in such splendour as much as had the wondering Elizabethans.

Henry Layard left England in 1839 to travel with a friend overland to Ceylon, but on reaching Persia he decided to explore the southwest corner of the country for antiquities. Layard's greatest archaeological contributions, the excavations of Nineveh and Nimrud, will be discussed later;* his travels in south-west Persia were less important archaeologically than they were in exploring the mountain strongholds of the virtually autonomous Bakhtiari tribe. His description of his travels, *Early Adventures*, was not published until 1887 and is a remarkable account of a violent people jealously guarding their independence against outsiders. Layard lived with them for several months, sharing their hardships and dangers and accompanying the great Bakhtiari leader, Mehmet Taki Khan, when he and his family were driven out of their mountains in mid-winter by the governor of Isfahan.

It is interesting to compare Layard with Curzon; the one informal, accepted by the Bakhtiaris, speaking their language, living their life, suffering their unhappiness and achieving an unprecedented familiarity with a wary and often hostile people; and the other, 'the most untiring and most vigilant of explorers', immensely painstaking and energetic, whose extensive travels in Persia were planned to give him an insight into all the political problems confronting Britain in Persia. Curzon visited the Bakhtiari mountains during his travels in Persia in 1889, but his account is altogether too reminiscent of politics. Between Layard and Curzon lay a generation of imperial commitment. Curzon's travels are interesting to follow for their scope – only the great central desert, the Dasht-i-Kavir, deterred him – and for political historians of Persia his account is more valuable than Layard's. But his overpowering embrace daunts the reader of *Persia and the Persian Question*. There is something to be said for the critic who wrote that 'Mr Curzon seems to be under the impression that he has discovered Persia and that having discovered it he now in some mysterious way owns it.'

Edward Granville Browne was the most at home in Persia, standing with Kinglake and Doughty among the great discoverers of the Middle East. His account of Persia, *A Year Among the Persians*, was written as a record of travel, but is more in the nature of a guide to the society of nineteenth-century Persia in all its diversity – its language, literature and people – than to its monuments. No other writer of the period 'discovered the soul of the people' nor absorbed it to quite the same extent as Browne; throughout his journey he steeped himself in Persian culture and studied its exponents wherever he happened to be. When he quotes an ancient authority it will be a Persian authority; when he visits Persepolis he draws the reader's attention to the Muslim names carved on the monuments instead of the European names noted by Browne's European contemporaries.

'The most striking thing about the Persians is their passion for

* See below, p. 210.

metaphysical speculation', Browne wrote – also perhaps the most striking characteristic he had in common with them. In Isfahan a pedlar of antiquities approached him to whisper in his ear that he could introduce him to members of the outlawed Babi sect – the moment Browne had been waiting for since he had entered the country at Tabriz, where the Bab had been executed in 1848. On meeting the Babis in Kirman he wrote: 'my whole being was permeated with that glow of tranquil beatitude, conscious of itself, nay almost exultant in its own peaceful serenity, which constitutes the fatal charm of what the Persians call par excellence "The Antidote".' Their conversation began quietly enough, but rose to an enthusiasm and vehemence which half-frightened, half-disgusted the fascinated Browne, who was nevertheless 'spellbound by their eloquence'. 'The memory of these assemblies [with the Babis] can never fade from my mind; the recollection of faces and those tones – no time can efface. I have gazed with awe on the workings of a mighty spirit and I marvel whereunto it tends.' The degree of Browne's commitment to the Persian and above all to the Babi cause follows naturally from the idiosyncratic accounts of Buckingham, Kinglake, Layard and the Arabian writers, whose facts and figures are far outweighed by their sympathy. It is a measure of Browne's whole-hearted identification with the Persians that the day of his death in 1926 was declared a day of public mourning in Persia.

13   Old Desolate Places

Most people in Britain still thought of the Middle East as the land of the Bible and the development of archaeology in the nineteenth century from antiquarian trophy-hunting was particularly suited to the elucidation of the Bible, an aspect emphasised by archaeologists to encourage financial as well as academic interest. Curiosity about the sites of Asia Minor survived the fashion for Graeco-Roman sculpture and the greater excitement over Egypt, and in the middle of the century led to some dramatic discoveries of hitherto undetected sites. Egypt was the scene of the most spectacular discoveries and also of the development of the science of excavation, in which preservation took precedence over removal. Excavations in Iraq revealed the remains of ancient civilisations whose existence was hardly suspected before the nineteenth century, though their elucidation, particularly of those in lower Mesopotamia, falls mainly outside this period. Archaeology in Palestine was hampered by centuries of religious suspicion and superstition, but by the outbreak of war the country was as well explored as anywhere else in the Middle East, if less extensively excavated. By that time interest in biblical study was matched, if not overshadowed, by the study of earlier and grander civilisations which had contributed at least as much to European civilisation as Christianity.

At the end of the eighteenth century no landscaped garden was complete without a tasteful sprinkling of busts, torsos, vases and capitals conducive to the fashionable mood of melancholy. No one had any scruples about removing objects from their sites; the Elgin Marbles are only the most famous of many collections assembled on the theory that the natives were showing no interest in their preservation. The rapacity of those who held the purse-strings was unlimited and only the enormous quantity of material, and often its colossal size, prevented every site from being ransacked. 'Antiquity is a garden which belongs by natural right to those who cultivate and harvest it', a Frenchman wrote on behalf of his antiquarian colleagues. To the wealthy patrons of the eighteenth century were added in the nineteenth century the jealously patriotic trustees of national collections in the British Museum, the Louvre and in Berlin.

1. Pompey's Pillar in Alexandria being measured in July 1798, a week after the French landings, by scholars using a kite attached to two strings. Napoleon and the artist, Dominique Vivant Denon, are seen watching in the right foreground. Watercolour.

Dr Johnson remarked how 'an antiquary is a rugged being', and we have already noticed Graeco-Roman enthusiasts braving the considerable dangers of Levantine travel in the eighteenth century to collect their antiques. Good relations with the Porte eased the

removal of abundant supplies of these from the more accessible sites
near the coast, avoiding the complications of hauling over land.
Charles Fellows (later knighted for his services to the British
Museum) was among the most persistent explorers of the immediate
hinterland, which he first visited in 1838, and an extensive search
among the rugged hills and inaccessible valleys of Lydia and Lycia
led him to the sites of some thirteen vanished cities. The journal of
his discoveries which he published a year after his return aroused
tremendous excitement in London and the British Museum was
persuaded to finance his return to Asia Minor, where he collected
no less than eighty-two cases of sculpture, marble fragments and
inscriptions, the most famous of which were the Xanthus marbles.
The expedition which he organised in 1844 was one of the most
efficient of the century, as indeed it needed to be to overcome the
physical obstacles between his treasures and the sea; with the help
of sailors from the British fleet, stone cutters brought specially from
Malta and plaster casters from Rome, Fellows was able to load
another twenty-seven cases of antiquities on to naval vessels waiting
offshore.

Depredation on such a scale as this alarmed the Ottoman authorities (alerted by rival archaeologists) and Canning had some difficulty
the following year in obtaining permission to remove from Bodrum
in south-west Turkey the great marble frieze which had decorated
the tomb of Mausolus at Halicarnassus, once among the seven
wonders of the world. Slabs of the frieze had been built by the
Knights of St John into the walls of their castle at Bodrum. But in
1846 Canning was writing to his wife that he had at last surmounted
his difficulties over the marbles and John Alison had been despatched
to Bodrum to organise their removal and to ship them to England.
'Oh! if they should stick in the wall!' Canning agonised. 'Oh! if they
should break in coming out of it! Oh! if they should founder on the
way to England! Think of my venturing all at my own expense!...
Indeed, my own Artemisia,* I shall be much surprised if the new
Ministry and the Corn Laws shall not be thrown into the shade by
these celebrated marbles, which it has cost me nearly three years of
patient perseverance to obtain.'

In London the Bodrum marbles and Fellows' treasures were
checked, verified and arranged by Charles Newton with such success
that in 1852 he was appointed vice-consul at Mytilene, with freedom
to roam around outside his area, in order to rescue further fragments
from destruction by the local populace. It was also unofficially

* Canning was alluding to the temple of Artemis, or Diana, at Ephesus, the
object of several expeditions in the nineteenth century, the site of which was
first excavated by Mr Wood in 1866.

2. One of the Luxor obelisks packed for transport to the Place de la Concorde in Paris. Originally granted to the British consul in Alexandria, John Barker, they were later, in 1831, re-allocated to a naturalised Frenchman, Baron Taylor – an example of Anglo-French rivalry over antiquities. Lithograph from a drawing by Sir John Gardiner Wilkinson from his *General View of Egypt* (1835)

recognised that consuls in Asia Minor and the Levant, who had previously compensated for their meagre or non-existent salaries by private trading, now supplemented their incomes by trading in antiquities.

Egypt was a relatively unknown country before Napoleon's expedition in 1798. Most Europeans stayed in and around Cairo and Alexandria and only a few travellers, among them Richard Pococke, Charles Perry, James Bruce and the Danish traveller Frederick Norden, had preceded the expedition up the Nile. Charles Perry's enthusiasm for Egyptian art was unprecedented when he described Egyptian temples in 1743 and the 'Quantity and Quality of their Sculpture, their Painting, and other Ornaments, that ravish and astonish the Beholder', but even the more adventurous who saw the abundance of remains in upper Egypt, well schooled as they were in the classical tradition, described every Egyptian temple as a facsimile of the Parthenon. As late as 1817 Charles Barry, commenting on the 'forcible impressions' made on him by the temple of Denderah, attributed this to its novelty rather than to its beauty.

Among the members of Napoleon's expedition was Dominique Vivant Denon, a man of extraordinary courage and perseverance, a considerable scholar and an even better artist. Denon accompanied part of Napoleon's army to the Upper Nile and in 1801 published his illustrated description of the unsuspected wealth of pharaohnic remains which he had seen.* Denon described these magnificent ruins with unqualified admiration, exclaiming of Hermopolis, most unfashionably, that 'the Greeks have never devised or executed anything in a grander style', while Esnah was 'the most perfect monument of ancient architecture'.† There was clearly infinite scope here for the collector and the French did indeed amass a vast hoard of antiquities during the three years of their occupation. Most of this, including the Rosetta Stone, fell into the hands of the British after the French defeat in 1801, thanks to the perspicacity of Elgin's secretary, William Hamilton. Hamilton arrived in Egypt at the moment of the French evacuation and captured several antiquities, among them the celebrated hiero-glyphic stone, from the ship which was surreptitiously about to carry them away.‡

After 1800 every visitor to Egypt took some memento back to England. A more ambitious collector than most was Henry Salt, a friend of Hamilton's who arrived in Egypt in 1816 as consul-general, hoping to collect enough to augment his salary; he had already visited Egypt briefly on his return from a mission to Abyssinia in 1811. Salt employed one of the most colourful figures in Egyptology to do much of his collecting, Giovanni Belzoni, an Italian, who after several years on the English stage impersonating Samson and other similarly muscular characters came to Egypt to sell Muhammad Ali an hydraulic device for hauling water from the Nile. His project foundered on conservative opposition, but he and his wife Sarah were saved from destitution by John Lewis Burckhardt, who introduced Belzoni to Salt. Salt immediately despatched him to Thebes to remove certain large antiquities admired by earlier travellers. Battling in Thebes against sun-stroke, ophthalmia and recalcitrant Arabs, Belzoni managed to move the head of a sixty-foot colossus from the Ramasseum to the edge of the Nile. A seven-ton block of granite, known as the Young Memnon, this was Shelley's 'shattered

---

* An English edition was published in 1803 and a second much improved edition was published, in French, in London in 1809.

† Even Denon, it is interesting to note, most admired the later, Ptolemaic, temples which had been influenced by Greek styles.

‡ Hamilton the following year supervised the removal from Athens of Elgin's marbles.

3. William Bankes M.P. (1786–1855), traveller, scholar and collector; while working with Henry Salt, then consul-general in Egypt, he acquired and had shipped to England a bilingual obelisk, discovered at Philae in 1815, which he re-erected in the grounds of his house at Kingston Lacey, Dorset. Drawing attributed to M. Gauci

visage';* it had been coveted by several antiquarians after James Bruce had described it in great detail in 1776, since when it had been broken up by the French. Over the next three years, travelling up and down the Nile, Belzoni opened up the temple of Abu Simbel, which Burckhardt had discovered a few years earlier, unearthed the entrance to the second pyramid at Gizah and excavated the magnificent tomb of the Pharaoh Seti I in the Theban Valley of the

* The achievement created a sufficient stir in England – even before the arrival of the head – for Shelley to write his famous sonnet *Ozymandias*. See below, p. 258.

Kings. He also helped the traveller William Bankes to remove an obelisk from Philae, which Bankes later erected in the grounds of Kingston Lacey, his Dorset home. Belzoni's greatest problem in all his excavations was labour; archaeology throughout the century was dogged by the fact that local inhabitants were convinced the foreigners could be digging only for treasure and would cheat them of their right to it. At Abu Simbel Belzoni became so exasperated

4. Giovanni Battista Belzoni (1778–1823), an Italian explorer, adventurer and circus 'strong man' who worked for Henry Salt in Egypt 1817–20. Lithograph and original drawing by M. Gauci: frontispiece of Belzoni's *Narrative of Operations and Recent Discoveries* (1820)

with his Nubian labourers that he sacked them all and with the help
of the two naval captains, Irby and Mangles,* excavated the
entrance to the temple with his own bare hands, much to the rage
of the Nubians.

Belzoni has been described as 'an extraordinary farrago of vanity,
ignorance and self-seeking pomposity' (which ultimately led to a
bitter quarrel with the inoffensive Salt), but 'also of patience and
endurance and a certain inborn instinct for what was either beautiful
or valuable'. His methods of excavating were drastic and probably

5. Wall painting from the tomb of Seti I which Belzoni discovered in the
Valley of the Kings at Thebes in 1818. Seti's sarcophagus was later brought
to London and is now in the Soane Museum. Engraving from a drawing
by Belzoni illustrating his *Narrative*

destroyed more than they preserved; fighting his way through one
tomb he described how, to regain his breath, he sat on a pile of
mummies which 'crushed like a bandbox' beneath his weight and in
another 'every step I took I crushed a mummy in some part or
another'. Nevertheless through Belzoni and Salt the British Museum
acquired some of its finest monuments.

Belzoni's discoveries aroused considerable interest in London and
his colossal vanity, offended by what he considered jealous intrusions on his own achievements by Salt and others in Egypt, was
recompensed to some extent by society's lionisation on his return to
London in 1820. The following year he had an exhibition, in the

* Irby and Mangles went on to the Red Sea from Abu Simbel to visit Palestine
and Syria, including Palmyra (above, p. 73). The account of their travels (published
as letters in 1823 and 1844) was one of the more popular travel books of the period.

6. Gerf Husein, a Nubian ruin visited by the artist, Frederick Catherwood, in the course of a trip to Upper Egypt in 1825. Watercolour

Egyptian Hall in Piccadilly (one of the most fanciful of Regency buildings) of a model of Seti's tomb.* Egypt and things Egyptian were all the rage, parodied in the *Morning Chronicle* by 'Priscilla Plainstitch' (Charles Lamb): 'My eldest boy rides on a sphinx instead of a rocking horse, and my youngest has a pap-boat in the shape of a crocodile. My husband has built a water-closet in the form of a pyramid, and has his shirts marked with a lotus. He talks in his sleep of Ibis, Apis and *Sir* Apis ...'. But in 1823, restless again and bored by his quarrels with Salt (who had already sold one collection of antiquities to the British Museum at considerable profit), Belzoni set off on his travels again, financed by his sale of Seti's sarcophagus to Sir John Soane for two thousand pounds, to find the source of the Niger. He died of dysentery at Benin a few months later.

The hungry antiquarian was gradually giving way to the archaeologist. One of the most remarkable of early Egyptologists – John Gardiner Wilkinson – came to Egypt as early as 1821. He was acting on the advice of a noted classical architect, Sir William Gell, an indication of the growing appreciation of these ancient builders. Wilkinson spent the next twelve years in Egypt, based on Cairo and travelling extensively – twice up the Nile to the second cataract above Abu Simbel, to the eastern desert of Upper Nubia and many times to Thebes. The year after his arrival, Champollion's decipher-

* This was mainly the work of Alessandro Ricci, an Italian doctor working in Egypt who was employed by Belzoni one summer for this purpose.

7. A view of Bulak from which Nile port travellers set out for Upper Egypt;
later Thomas Cook set up his dockyard and workshop here. From Robert
Hay, *Illustrations of Cairo*

ment of the hieroglyphs on the Rosetta Stone gave a much needed
impetus to the development of a more serious approach to Egyptology than the quest for loot, and this was encouraged by Wilkinson's
own researches.

Wilkinson's long experience of excavation in Egypt, particularly
in Thebes where he opened up several of the most beautiful tombs,
made him foremost among pioneering archaeologists, among them
the prosperous Scotsman Robert Hay, who financed many early excavations. Hay himself spent several winters between 1828 and 1836
living in a tomb in Thebes, excavating more tombs, drawing,
cataloguing and recording finds and employing a group of draughts-
men and artists (including briefly Edward Lane) on similar ploys.
Wilkinson and one of Hay's artists, Joseph Bonomi, became the
greatest publicists of the new science of Egyptology. In 1834 Wilkinson published his *Topography of Thebes and General Survey of Egypt,*
the first improvement on the *Description de l'Egypte,* though also
intended as a guide for the increasing number of tourists to Egypt.
Three years later, Wilkinson's *Manners and Customs of the Ancient
Egyptians* revealed in a remarkable entirety the history and art of a
civilisation long buried beneath the deserts and which had preserved
its great monuments so perfectly. Many of the superb illustrations
to Wilkinson's text were done by Bonomi, who had originally come
to Egypt in 1824 at Hay's suggestion; as one of the most skilled

8. The tenth-century aqueduct in Cairo (into which Nile water was raised by oxen via the seventy-foot tower in the distance). From Hay's *Illustrations of Cairo*

9. Cleopatra's Needle. Under an agreement made in 1801 the half-buried obelisk lying on its side was taken to London in 1878 where it stands upon the Embankment. The upright one, supposedly in poorer condition, was acquired by William H. Vanderbilt and re-erected for $75,000 in Central Park, New York. Watercolour by Dominique Vivant Denon hieroglyphic draughtsmen of the century, Bonomi did almost as much as Wilkinson in publicising the discoveries of ancient Egypt.

Wilkinson's ill health and Bonomi's quarrels with Hay obliged them eventually to return to England, where they inspired a new generation of scholars to develop the practical and theoretical study of Egyptology – not only along the banks of the Nile but also in the dusty corners of the British Museum under the aegis of the energetic keeper of oriental antiquities, Samuel Birch. Europeans in Cairo and scholars in Europe founded learned societies to publish the latest finds and deductions. In Cairo a Literary Association was founded by Henry Abbott, once a medical orderly in the British Navy; the Association, and the kindred Egyptian Society in Alexandria, provided a meeting ground in Egypt for scholars and travellers of all nationalities. In England John Lee, antiquarian and scientist, was the great patron of Egyptology. At his home at Hartwell, packed with antiquities from all over the Middle East, his 'unbounded benevolence' entertained a continuous round of scientific meetings which developed into the Meteorological, the Syro-Egyptian, the Anglo-Biblical Societies, the Palestine Archaeological Association and the Chronological Society. The last four were dissolved in 1872 and replaced by the Society for Biblical Archaeology, founded in Bonomi's rooms at the Sir John Soane Museum where he was now curator.

Another wealthy sponsor of Egyptology was Erasmus Wilson who in 1877 offered to pay for the removal to London of Cleopatra's Needle. The great obelisk, which had been given to Britain by the Turks at the instigation of Abercromby who wanted it as a memorial to the Anglo-Turkish defeat of the French, was described with monotonous regularity by every visitor to Alexandria. As knowledge of the ancient Egyptians and their art developed, however, and more exciting and less cumbersome objects were found, the British government became more and more unwilling to pay for shifting an obelisk which was neither beautiful nor rare. Thackeray, viewing it with considerable distaste in 1845, wished the British government 'would offer the Trafalgar Square pillar to the Egyptians; and that both of the huge, ugly monsters were lying in the dirt there, side by side.' Thanks to Erasmus Wilson the obelisk was brought to London where, after an extremely hazardous voyage, it was erected on the banks of the Thames above an archaeologist's cache of contemporary treasures.*

---

* These included a Bible, toys, cigars, a razor, the dress and toiletries of a fashionable woman, photographs of the most beautiful women of Victorian England and a complete set of current English coinage. The companion obelisk to Cleopatra's Needle was set up in New York's Central Park.

10. Interior of the tomb of Rameses IX. The French archaeologist Champollion lived in this tomb in 1829 and the picture shows Owen Jones and his companion, Jules Goury relaxing with a pipe at the entrance. Lithograph from a drawing by Owen Jones, published in his *Views of the Nile* (1843)

The scientific excavation of ancient Egypt owed most to Flinders Petrie who in 1882 founded the Egyptian Exploration Society with

11. Excavation of the Great Temple of Rameses II at Abu Simbel, February 1819. Watercolour by Linant de Bellefonds (1799–1883). Linant accompanied Henry Salt to Abu Simbel in 1818–19. The painting shows Salt and his party directing the clearing of the facade and entrance and preventing loose sand pouring back by a palisade of palm trunks and river mud

Amelia Edwards, a tourist converted to archaeology after a winter spent at Luxor in 1873–4. Petrie provided answers to several problems which had eluded Egyptologists for many years: his survey of the pyramids, for instance, finally established their purpose as tombs and his excavations at Abydos revealed some of the earliest chapters of ancient Egyptian history. One of his most interesting discoveries was the cuneiform-inscribed tablets at Tel al-Amarna, former capital of the heretic Pharaoh Akhnaton, thereby linking Egyptology with the more unfamiliar archaeology of Mesopotamia and south-west Persia.*

* A colleague of Petrie's was Francis Griffiths, the founder of the Griffith Institute at the Ashmolean in Oxford, which has contributed greatly to modern Egyptology.

12. Persepolis: uncoloured aquatint from an original drawing by Morier, from his *Journey through Persia to Constantinople* (1818)

13. Gateway to the King's Palace at Persepolis; imaginary figures in ancient costume are shown to indicate the scale of the monument. From a drawing by Ker Porter, published in his *Travels*

Here the archaeologist was an explorer with nothing except his own wits to protect his excavations and often his life. With the exception of Median and Sassanian ruins in south-west Persia, none of the sites was as spectacular as those of Egypt and the Levant; most of the cities had been built of sun-dried bricks which over the centuries had disintegrated, like giant candles, into confused shapeless mounds. Antiquarians found these 'rude heaps of earth' harder to ransack – particularly in lower Mesopotamia, home of the Sumerian, Akkadian and Babylonian civilisations – and popular interest was therefore harder to arouse and wealthy patrons harder to attract.

Persepolis in south-west Persia, not far from the Shiraz-Isfahan road, was regularly visited by English, French and Dutch merchants from the seventeenth century onwards. Its relative inaccessibility and perhaps also the confusion of accounts, which Ker Porter attacked in his detailed description of the ruins, had to a certain extent protected Persepolis from the predatory inclinations of foreigners to which Egypt and the Levant were so exposed. Sir Gore Ouseley stopped on his way to Tehran in 1810 and used his artillery escort to clear out one of the tombs, collecting a few choice fragments which he later gave to the British Museum, but anything larger would have been impossible to transport. Other memorials to the great Median and later Persian empires – at Taksh-i-Bestan, Bihistun, Pasargadae, Shapur and Shuster were described by most visitors from a distance and with considerable assistance from ancient authorities.

The great featureless mounds of Assyria and Babylonia never attracted the same attention and it was only gradually realised that the inscriptions so laboriously copied from Persepolis resembled the curious wedge-shaped 'decoration' on bricks which the more perceptive visitors to Babylon were beginning to pick up. Claudius Rich, appointed the East India Company's Resident in Baghdad in 1808, was the first man really to explore the ruins of Babylon, along the banks of the Euphrates near Hillah. He and his wife Mary visited the site for the first time in 1811 accompanied by 'my own troop of Hussars, with a galloper gun, a Havildar and twelve sepoys, about 70 baggage mules, a mehmander from the Pasha and a man from the Shaikh of the Jirbah Arabs'. Rich's account of the great mounds round Hillah – Birs Nimrud, Mujalibah and others – was as meticulous as could be expected, but his deductions were little more than conjectures. Excavating was clearly impossible with the country as unsettled as it was then and for many years to come. Ker Porter, for instance, when sketching the mounds in 1818, was protected by a hundred Turkish soldiers.

Mounds similar to those of Babylon had been noticed near Mosul

14. The Rev. S. C. Malan sketching Layard's excavations at Nineveh. Malan took over as expedition artist from F. C. Cooper who had been sent by the British Museum but had to return to England after a breakdown. Lithograph from a drawing by Malan from Sir Henry Layard, *Nineveh and Babylon* (1853)

as being the possible site of the great Assyrian capital of Nineveh. Here again Rich was the first to throw any light on them, visiting them in 1816 and again in 1820, collecting more inscribed bricks and coins.* The main interest of Rich's collection of antiquities centred round the coins and also his Syriac manuscripts, for no one could yet decipher the inscriptions. But scholars were already at work on the cuneiform writing, as it came to be called, in particular on a tri-lingual inscription at Bihistun near Kirmanshah in Persia – written in what were later known as Old Persian, Elamite and Babylonian. A German, Grotefend, first worked out the names of kings in the text, and Henry Rawlinson's decipherment of the Old Persian text gave the same impetus to Assyriology as Champollion had given to Egyptology.

Bihistun is a huge mass of crags rising steeply from the plain for some two thousand feet; three hundred feet off the ground smooth-faced ledges are inscribed with the tri-lingual record of Darius' reign. Rawlinson first examined the inscription in 1834, while on his way to Tehran as a member of the British military mission; after he had been posted to Kirmanshah in 1835 he copied down the Persian and Elamite inscriptions (with the greatest difficulty) and translated two paragraphs of the Persian. The Afghan War interrupted his researches but in 1843 he was sent to Baghdad as a British Resident. Here he spent the long hot summer puzzling out the rest of the secret, building himself a small summer house that jutted out over the Tigris from the Residency garden and was cooled by a water wheel pouring a continuous stream of water over the roof. In 1847 Rawlinson returned to Bihistun to copy down the inaccessible Babylonian inscription, accompanied by 'an entourage of muscular attendants and small wiry boys', one of whom suspended himself from a cradle and copied it out for Rawlinson, who worked on it back in Baghdad, in between lessons in Arabic, Zend and Sanskrit.

By this time Henry Layard was sending fresh material from Nimrud, near Mosul, and himself had spent Christmas 1845 with Rawlinson to see how his work was progressing. Layard had been attracted by the great mounds of Kuyunjik and Nimrud on his return journey from south-west Persia to Constantinople in 1842; after spending several days with the French archaeologist, Paul Botta, on the site of Kuyunjik (which Botta failed to prove was Nineveh),

* He and Mary carved their names near a sacred spring and Rich afterwards mused how later travellers would wonder at their intrepidity, as indeed they did: 'he will not be aware that had [Mary's] name been inscribed at every spot she had visited in the course of her weary pilgrimage it would be found in places compared with which Mosul is the centre of civilisation.' Rich died a few years later at Shiraz, after visiting Persepolis ('the celebrated ruin I had come so far to see') and was buried near the tomb of the poet Hafiz.

Layard wrote that they had 'made a deeper impression on me, gave rise to more serious thought and more earnest reflection, than the temples of Baalbek and the theatres of Ionia'. During the three years Layard worked for Canning in and around Constantinople, Botta abandoned Kuyunjik for the nearby mound of Khorsabad, excavating some magnificent sculptures and bas-reliefs and provoking an enthusiastic missionary, G. P. Badger, who was working among the Nestorian Christians of Mosul, into writing to Canning urging the British government to investigate Assyrian remains before everything was removed by the French. Canning, already interested in Bodrum, replied by sending Layard in 1845 to see what he could salvage.

Mosul, on which Layard's activities were based, was dilapidated by the same plague and floods that had devastated Baghdad fifteen years earlier; the pasha, a Turk yearning for the greater comforts of Constantinople, was only concerned with getting rich and haunted Layard's excavations at the slightest rumour of a new discovery in case it led to treasure. Realising the danger of treasure-seekers interfering, Layard informed the pasha that he was going to hunt boar and set off for the mound of Nimrud, about twenty miles southeast of Mosul, which at that time he assumed to be Nineveh; of his attempts to puzzle out the buried city he wrote that he was at a loss 'to give any form to the rude heaps of earth...desolation meets desolation, a feeling of awe succeeds to wonder: for there is nothing to relieve the mind, to lead to hope or to tell what has gone by.'

Here Layard spent the first winter in half a ruined house; in summer he tried to imitate Rawlinson's summer house by building a mud hut over the river, only to find the mud walls alive with insects and the river bank a haunt of snakes. Fortunately the very first day of digging brought immediate results, revealing the remains of two palaces at opposite ends of the mound. From then on every day produced some new discovery. From dawn to dusk Layard was 'drawing sculptures, copying and moulding the inscriptions and superintending the excavations and the removals and packing of the bas-reliefs', in spite of the constant heckling of the pasha and his messengers, who at one point thought Layard had found inscriptions proving that the Franks had once held the country and would come to reclaim it. Layard's account of the excavations and discoveries of exquisite bas-reliefs are written with unimpassioned hindsight until one morning – and his enthusiasm is still there in the printed page – the Arab diggers came running to his house: 'Hasten O Bey, hasten to the diggers, for they have found Nimrud himself.' This was the great winged bull which now stands in the gloomy gallery of the British Museum.

15. Winged lion excavated from Nineveh by Layard being installed in the Assyrian room at the British Museum in 1852. Frontispiece to Joseph Bonomi, *Nineveh and its Palaces* (1869)

A delighted Canning, who had financed the excavation, wrote to his wife: 'I am quite proud of my public spirit in the cause of antiquity and fine art', though adding, with Lord Elgin in mind, that he would not carry it to the point of impoverishing his family. He told the Prime Minister, Sir Robert Peel, that the British Museum 'will beat the Louvre hollow'. Acting on Peel's recommendation, the Museum sent Layard two thousand pounds, part of which he used to float the massive sculptures down-river to Basra, on an enlarged version of the *kelek*, a raft balanced on inflated skins. Bas-reliefs were removed from the excavating trenches, packed in felt and matting and screwed down in rough cases to be taken down the river. Although a similar consignment from Khorsabad came to grief when a raft capsized in the river, sending its precious cargo to the bottom, Layard's consignments suffered most when sitting on the quay at Bombay, where eager sight-seers, who had already heard of his discoveries, insisted on breaking open the crates to explore their fragile contents, many of which broke under the onslaught.

Layard spent the rest of the British Museum money on excavating the mounds of Qalaat Sharqat and Kuyunjik. Rivalry with the French was now so heated that while Layard was digging at one end of the Kuyunjik mound the French, continuing Botta's excavations, were digging at the other, a situation which led to acrimonious exchanges when the trenches ran into each other. It was Layard, however, who found the famous palace of Sennacherib and proved at last that the mound was the site of Nineveh.

Back in England, Layard found himself a popular hero; his packages of Assyrian sculptures and the publication of his impressive account, *Nineveh and Its Remains*, stimulated public interest and persuaded the British Museum to send him off to see what more he could find. The great success of his second expedition was his discovery of the King's Library at Kuyunjik, containing some twenty-four thousand tablets describing the Assyrian state, tablets 'resembling cakes of Windsor soap', commented Frederick Walpole, who visited him about this time. Layard left Mosul in 1850 to explore some of the Babylonian mounds, with less success, and returned to England a year later to abandon archaeology for politics, leaving his excavations in Rawlinson's hands.*

Archaeology in lower Mesopotamia was more hampered by the unsettled state of the country and the greatest discoveries of the Sumerian and Akkadian civilisations based on that area in the third and second millennia occurred after World War I. William Loftus was the first to investigate some of the mounds at Warka (later proved to have been the site of Ur) and Tal al-Muqayyar, when making his way to Basra as member of the Turco-Persian Frontier Commission of 1842, and he later returned to Warka. Colonel Taylor, Rawlinson's successor as resident, continued the archaeological duties of the post and investigated Tal al-Muqayyar; neither Loftus nor Taylor, however, realised the antiquity of the civilisations they were excavating.

As in Egypt so in Mesopotamia the haphazard methods of early archaeologists, anxious to add to the glories of national collections, were gradually superseded by more cautious exploration, encouraged by the scholars' demands for documents. Layard's methods were fairly drastic and those of his successor, Hormuzd Rassam, even more so. As far as the public was concerned they produced results – friezes of bas-reliefs from Kuyunjik, bronze gates from Tal Balawat and important stelae – but at an immense cost to other antiquities. Layard gave his friends presents of cuneiform tablets and his wife an Assyrian necklace, to the frustration of later archaeologists, but if he had left them where he found them they would certainly have been pilfered by the local inhabitants and clearly the British Museum could not buy everything. A winged bull left at Kuyunjik, for instance, was sold by the pasha of Mosul for 'three and sixpence . . . and burnt into lime by its purchaser'. European archaeologists

* 'The public in England look upon [Layard] as an oracle on all political questions in Asia, because he was an energetic excavator of antiquities at Nineveh', wrote *Punch*.

realised something had to be done to preserve their discoveries, just as the inhabitants of Mesopotamia and Egypt realised the nature and extent of the 'treasure' the foreigners had been digging up and began trying to corner the market in antiquities. There might not be gold in the holes but at least the objects could be converted to gold.

Wallis Budge was sent by the British Museum to Baghdad in 1888 to see why the London market was being flooded by cuneiform tablets which clearly came from sites excavated by Layard's successor, Hormuzd Rassam, for the British Museum.* Budge discovered that many of the Baghdad dealers exporting the antiquities were the same men Rassam had carelessly appointed as guards for the sites. With a little sharp practice Budge was able to buy up the tablets remaining on the market and get them out of the country.

Luxor and Cairo were as busy as the Baghdad market, feeding tourists with real and faked mementos of their visits. 'Forgers, diggers and dealers play into one another's hands, and drive a roaring trade', wrote Amelia Edwards of Luxor; 'every man, woman and child about the place is bent on selling a bargain; and the bargain, in ninety-nine cases out of a hundred, is valuable in so far as it represents the industry of Luxor but no further.' The most successful forger, on a rather larger scale than the inhabitants of Luxor, was Constantine Simonides, who specialised in forged manuscripts, ranging from cuneiform and hieroglyphic papyri to poems by Aristotle:

> O ye who patiently explore
> The wreck of Herculanean lore,
>   What rapture! could you seize
> Some Theban fragment, or unroll
> One precious tender-hearted scroll
>   Of pure Simonides!

All these discoveries in Egypt and Mesopotamia – as well as ones in Asia Minor and Syria not mentioned here – excited the greatest interest in England principally for the light they threw on the Bible. Documentary evidence helped to verify biblical events, while tomb paintings and sculptured reliefs depicted the life of biblical times. In the history of the ancient empires, which scholars were gradually unfolding, the small kingdom of Israel played a relatively small part and was seldom mentioned in Assyrian, Babylonian or Egyptian

---

* Rassam, a Nestorian Christian from Mosul, was the brother of Christian Rassam who had acted as interpreter for Chesney's expedition and who later became British consul in Mosul; Hormuzd Rassam was notorious for his violent excavating methods which, however, produced some of the finest Mesopotamian objects in the British Museum collection.

documents. Time and again the country was over-run by more powerful neighbours, the last invasion – by the Muslims – obliterating remains of the most celebrated Jewish monument, the Temple, with their sacred Dome of the Rock. The lack of obvious ruins to excavate combined with local superstition and local political and religious disorder discouraged all but the most dedicated scholar. The Holy Places attracted more than their fair share of Anglican divines who lamented their deplorable condition and longed for a chance to excavate the Bible, but they were discouraged by local consuls from what would have been inevitable conflict with the Turkish authorities.

Archaeological exploration in Palestine during the nineteenth century was therefore mainly topographical. The Palestine Exploration Society was founded in 1865 to repel 'the onslaught which contemporary scientists were making upon the foundations of orthodox religion'. Captain Warren was despatched in 1865 to survey underground Jerusalem, inspired by the Sanitary Commission of Jerusalem which wanted to know how the sewers ran. In the 1870s began the great topographical survey of Palestine, under the auspices of which many celebrated scholars were able to indulge their enthusiasm for Middle Eastern wandering. The most effective survey was that of an expedition staffed and partly financed by the War Office, which had its own reasons for wanting precise details of the area; Herbert Kitchener was one of the members. This official survey was published in 1881 in three volumes; the leader of the expedition, Lieutenant Conder, published his own account, *Tent Work in Palestine*, and Kitchener, who was handier with the camera than the pen, produced *Lieutenant Kitchener's Guinea Book of Biblical Photographs*. Richard Burton's and Charles Tyrwhitt Drake's *Unexplored Syria* was another account of topographical exploration, dry as dust, but one can imagine the journey giving Burton a welcome break from the irritations of the Damascus consulate.

Tyrwhitt Drake also explored in Sinai with a remarkable scholar, linguist and traveller, Edward Palmer. Palmer was known to his contemporaries as a language collector, who knew Romany, innumerable Italian and Mediterranean dialects and the more conventional oriental languages, which made him particularly suited to the task of collecting correct place names for the Palestine survey. Not content with the rigours of extensive travel in Sinai, they wound up by walking back to Jerusalem without an escort or dragoman, almost unheard of in those days. Later, in 1882, Palmer tried the same tactic when he was sent by Gladstone to detach Arab tribes of Sinai from support of Arabi and was tragically robbed and killed on the way to securing the allegiance of the last stubborn shaikhs.

14 *The Noisy, Odd, Capricious Stream*

It is hardly surprising, given the development of travel to India, the archaeological discoveries described in the last chapter and the devotion to the Middle East of such public figures as Canning, Cromer and Curzon, that the more accessible parts began to attract increasing numbers of tourists in the nineteenth century – Russell's 'noisy, odd, capricious stream'. The mass tours of the twentieth century are nothing compared to the elaborate arrangements and temptations for the nineteenth-century excursions. Their leisurely pace and infinite scope, the guide books, the vocabularies which included hieroglyphs and cuneiform lettering, the lists of essentials, which left nothing to chance or local initiative, were all calculated to ensnare the prosperous sightseer. In theory and sometimes in practice oriental excursions were all part of the great Victorian desire for improvement, though the American historian Henry Prescott was partly justified when he said of British travellers that 'the body travels, not the mind'. Most of them believed the very fact of their presence in the area might lift it out of the degenerate state into which they were all agreed it had fallen. Nineteenth-century tourists to the Middle East included those searching for peace of mind, among them Lady Hester Stanhope, pilgrims to Jerusalem, missionaries and mystics, would-be antiquarians such as the Belmores and Amelia Edwards, the sick seeking health, such as Lucy Duff Gordon, as well as the devotees of Thomas Cook from Kaiser Wilhelm down.

Lady Hester Stanhope was one of the most self-centred tourists to visit the Middle East during this period and it is a measure of her success in perpetrating, among her own countrymen, an image of herself as queen and goddess of wild Arabs, that even today some will associate the Middle East more with Lady Hester than with any other of her more deserving contemporaries. The fact that Richard Burton and Lord Byron are close runners-up in this assessment indicates the prevailing appeal of the Middle East as something wild and unfamiliar; all three (Byron particularly since to him much of the area was indeed wild and unfamiliar) were suited by nature to bring out all that was remote or unpredictable about the Middle

1. European visitors at Karnak, 1847, from a sketch by F. Broughton. Broughton was a typical tourist of the period, an official of the East India Company who probably visited Karnak during a journey between India and Europe

East. There is no denying, in Lady Hester's case, that she enjoyed remarkable respect and prestige for several years among the Druzes of Mount Lebanon where she lived for more than twenty years, nor that she was given a royal welcome by Arabs at Palmyra, but it should be remembered that both were largely the result of extravagant spending and the prestige disappeared with the pennies.

Hester Stanhope left England in 1810, after the death of her uncle, William Pitt, to visit the eastern Mediterranean, inspired (according to Kinglake, who is as responsible as anyone for the aura surrounding her) by a 'longing for the East very commonly felt by proud people when goaded by sorrow', in this case for her uncle to whom she had been very close. Canning, yearning for London society in Constantinople, confessed the strong attraction of her conversation. 'notwithstanding its measureless exuberance and the not infrequent singularities it displayed', and though they quarrelled over Lady Hester's meetings with the French chargé d'affaires with whom she was trying to arrange a visa to France (England being at war with France Canning was obliged to disapprove such

2. John Cartwright, British consul-general in Constantinople for many years, depicted with his 'Albanian' who acted as guide to British travellers. Lithograph from Wilkie's *Oriental Sketches*

fraternisation with the enemy), they maintained a regular correspondence over the years.

Lady Hester's party (which included a young man, Michael Bruce, as lover, escort and, through his father, banker; Dr Meryon, the faithful physician who looked after her for most of her years in the Middle East; and her equally faithful maid) reached Cairo from Constantinople in 1811. Her triumphal course through the Levant over the next three years, accompanied during most of it by a large and expensive retinue, is best described in her own words in a letter to Canning. In Cairo Muhammad Ali 'admitted me to the Divan and when at Acre I rode Soliman Pasha's parade horse, having the use of his own sword and khangar, all over jewels. My visit to the Pasha of Damascus [where European consuls were still excluded] in the night during Ramadan was the finest thing possible. I was

3. View of Jouni, the Lebanese village where Lady Hester Stanhope lived and where the artist of this watercolour, W. H. Bartlett, visited her in 1835

mounted on an Arab horse he had given me, my people on foot and he surrounded with two thousand servants and picked guards. . . . You see the Turks are not quite such brutes as you once thought them, or they would never have treated me with the degree of friendship and hospitality they have done.' Without spending vast sums (for which Burckhardt sternly rebuked her) it is unlikely that she would have achieved her greatest triumph – the revival of Zenobia's splendour at Palmyra, where 'I carried everything before me, and was crowned under the triumphal arch . . . pitched my tent amidst thousands of Arabs and spent a month with these very interesting people', who were themselves convinced that no one but a queen could be so rich.

The expense, however, was more than Bruce's father could afford and in 1813 he persuaded his son to return to earn a respectable livelihood in England, depriving Lady Hester of a considerable part of her income. After Bruce's departure she went to live near Saida in the convent of Mar Elias, later moving to another convent on a hilltop near the village of Jouni, again not far from Saida, where she lived until her death in 1839. For a while her own finances enabled her to keep up sufficient state; again to Canning she described her continuing friendship with the Amir Bashir II of the Druzes, whose palace at Beit ed-Din was no distance from her convent at Saida: 'I am quite at home all over the country; the common people pay me the same sort of respect as they do a great Turk, and the great men treat me as if I was one of them.' John Barker bore the brunt of her complaints that her countrymen did not appreciate the good work she had done in their cause in the Levant and that it was their duty to recompense her for her own achievements as well as to avoid the disgrace of seeing a niece of Pitt's reduced to indigence. 'Their imagination is as miserable as their humanity is bounded', she told Canning.

The strangeness of her later way of life as described by European visitors was at least partly due to her chronic lack of money. Her crumbling grey-walled convent ('one of the most striking and interesting spots ever visited', wrote Warburton, 'its silence and beauty, its richness and desolation, lent to it a touching and mysterious character that well suited the memory of that strange hermit lady') became a goal more sought after by British tourists than any ruin. Buckingham spent several weeks with her recuperating from fever, 'breathing the pure and bracing morning air of the hills, basking in the sunny noon of the vales, inhaling the evening breeze', inspired, like so many of his countrymen by 'the danger and enterprise of a life passed amid deserts and mountains surrounded by wandering tribes and fierce and hostile nations'. Kinglake visited her three years before her lonely and penniless death in 1839 – already 'the victim of fallen greatness, false hopes and super-human efforts to effect vast projects of philanthropy and political combinations on small means and ruined resources'. For Kinglake she kept up her pose of mystic, prophetess and seer, only receiving him at night and then dressed in flowing white robes, striving for spiritual power now that her earthly kingdom had vanished. Dr Meryon painted the other side of the picture, of a hypochondriac old lady dying under a leaking roof. A few years after her death Warburton related how she was robbed on her deathbed, but this is only the last of many similar occasions in her life when fact and fiction are inextricably woven into legend.

Of all the qualities attributed to Lady Hester Stanhope, the most justified was courage, for travel, at least in the first half of the century, was still hazardous and the paraphernalia of guides and dragomans was still essential. Buckingham attempted to travel from Nazareth to Damascus without a guide and was turned back three times by brigands. Consuls played a large part in the tourist's life. They invited tourists to their houses, protected them as far as was possible on their journeys (unless they were as reckless as Doughty) and acted as their bankers. John Barker describes how he had to listen to the disputes of eccentric and avaricious travellers, 'who

4. Lady Hester Stanhope, frontispiece from Dr Meryon, *Memoir of Lady Hester Stanhope*, 1845. The doctor was a loyal companion of Lady Hester's for many years

give an immense deal of trouble and sometimes waste the consul's precious time in some very extravagant whim'; in Egypt, after he had been posted to Alexandria his house was always 'full of gentlemen and lady travellers going up the Nile, and many going to Mt Sinai and Palestine'. Barker even employed a special dragoman to procure permits for travellers from the viceroy. Signor Antonio Damiani, 'with his dirty pelisse, his greasy cocked hat and mock-heroic dignity of deportment', was another consul who appears regularly in accounts for the reason that he was consul at Jaffa where many tourists landed to visit the Holy Land. His flea-ridden house was put at the disposal of each boat-load of tourists, Damiani and his wife sleeping (in far greater comfort, one suspects) on the roof. Meryon, who stayed there with Lady Hester and described Damiani as a venerable old man, yet suspected he had amassed a vast fortune from the so-called presents left by English tourists.

Palestine, or the Holy Land as most visitors preferred to call it, was particularly popular with Victorian tourists who relished the element of danger which heightened the atmosphere of pilgrim's progress. Their accounts run into the hundreds and one begins to dread the introductory sentence apologising for adding one more literary pilgrimage to the existing list but assuring the reader that this will

5. The Wailing Wall, Jerusalem, 1869, sketch by William Simpson. Simpson visited Jerusalem to see the excavation of Captain Charles Warren, the first serious archaeological survey of the city carried out with a view to improving the sewage

be different.* 'Pilgrims see everything through a peculiar medium', the cynical Burton told Frederick Leighton, referring to the cloud of devotion which surrounded the impressions of most of these visitors, many of whom were clergymen or missionaries.

Jerusalem, the obvious goal of all Holy Land journeys, was still in the early part of the century the disappointing mixture of squalor, poverty and decay that had so shocked earlier pilgrims. 'O my nose! O my eyes! O my feet! How you suffered in that vile place! For let me tell you, physically Jerusalem is the foulest and odiousest place on earth. A bitter doleful soul-ague comes over you in its streets, and your memories of its interior are nothing but horrid dreams of squalor and filth, clamour and uneasiness, hatred and malice and all uncharitableness', wrote Edward Lear after a visit in 1858. What trade there was revolved round the commercialisation of the Holy Places, as vigorous then as it is now. The atmosphere of intolerance which still prevailed was scathingly denounced by Laurence

* A pleasant account of one of the more comfortable visits is that of Mrs Harvey who sailed to the Holy Land with a party of friends aboard a private yacht in 1860 and travelled to Jerusalem in considerable style – sleeping in camp beds with muslin curtains, the floor of the tent covered with Persian rugs and dining on apricot ices among other delicacies.

6. Mount Tabor in the Holy Land, watercolour from Spilsbury's *Picturesque Scenery*

Oliphant: 'the crowds of pilgrims and devotees calling themselves Christian who were only kept from flying at each other's throats over the tomb of the founder of their religion by a strong guard of Muslim soldiers, evidently inspired the latter with a contempt and disgust which one felt compelled to share.'

From 1839 – after lengthy negotiations in Constantinople – the presence of a British consul in Jerusalem ensured a measure of protection for visitors as well as for the missionaries who were flocking to the Holy City. Missionary activity was mainly directed to the conversion of the Jews, since proselytisation among Muslims was expressly forbidden and among oriental Christians politically dangerous. The London Society for Promoting Christianity among the Jews sent its first mission to Jerusalem in 1820 and the first bishop, Michael Alexander, of the joint Anglo-Prussian see* was a

---

* The idea of founding a Protestant see was first mooted by the King of Prussia who advocated a united see as presenting the best image of Protestantism; the existing English mission was made the headquarters of the see, the King of Prussia endowed it and British appointments to the bishopric alternated with Prussia. It became purely Anglican in 1886.

7. The chapel of St Helena in the Church of the Holy Sepulchre. Water-colour by David Roberts, 1839

converted Jew. Alexander was remarkable for his lack of tact in a position which demanded extreme delicacy, referring in his first sermon to the 'usurped government' of the Ottomans and starting to build the Anglican cathedral (under the auspices of the London Society) before Canning had wheedled permission to do so from the Sultan. Relations between the Anglican mission and the Jewish communities were always acrimonious; one member of the mission who was tactless enough to try preaching in the open street in the Jewish quarter was driven out by rabbis with stones and dead cats. Edward Lear wrote that 'the idea of converting [the Jews] to Christianity in Jerusalem is to the sober observer fully as absurd as that you should institute a society to convert all the cabbages and strawberries in Covent Garden into pigeon pies and Turkey carpets'.

Alexander's successor, Samuel Gobalt, found the rate of conversion among the Jews so discouraging that he turned to the oriental Christians – with as little success, in spite of the courage of his missionaries in withstanding the hostility of the religious leaders of those communities into which they ventured. It is interesting to compare the animosity of oriental Christians in Palestine to the intrusions of other denominations with the success of American and British missionaries and teachers among the Maronite and Greek Orthodox Christians of Lebanon. At Bhawwara, for instance, a village not far from Beirut owned by Colonel Charles Churchill (who had settled in Lebanon after the 1841 expedition), an Englishman, John Lowthian, opened the first of a series of schools which evoked remarkably little opposition, in spite of their secondary task of converting to Protestantism.

Notwithstanding the failure to achieve a mass conversion of Jews, Jerusalem was to some extent resuscitated from the lifelessness of which early nineteenth-century tourists complained by the revival of religious interest displayed by visitors, missionaries and consuls. William Bartlett, author of two mid-century books on Jerusalem – by far the best contemporary accounts of the city – remarked on the improvements between his first visit in 1842 and his second in 1853. In addition to new hotels, shops with European goods, cleaner streets, 'the waste ruinous look of the place is giving way to something a little more modern and habitable'. Schools had been set up by the missions, Muslims were less fanatical ('single ladies are permitted to live quietly in the heart of the Moslem quarter, without any man-servant or other protectors', marvelled Bartlett) and under the enthusiastic auspices of the British consul, James Finn, and his wife, various projects had been launched designed to improve the material condition of the Jews by employing them in agriculture. Unfortunately one of Mrs Finn's schemes – to sell off small pieces of 'Holy Land' from a site they had bought outside Jerusalem to trusting clergymen in England – led them heavily into debt with the co-religionists of those whose poverty they had hoped to remedy. Bishop Gobat, with whom Finn was on the worst possible terms, partly because of Gobat's clumsiness in trying to proselytise among oriental Christians, called for an investigation into Finn's affairs and the consul was obliged to leave Jerusalem for the consular backwater of Trebizond.

The condition of Palestinian Jews was increasingly the concern of emancipated Jews in western Europe, in particular the patriarchal British Jew, Moses Montefiore, who visited Jerusalem on several occasions in the nineteenth century. Towards the end of the century the influx of persecuted, Zionist-inclined Jews from eastern Europe aroused the sympathy, among others, of the eccentric Laurence Oliphant, who first came to Palestine in 1879 to try to find a suitable

8. (opposite) The Khasne at Petra, 1843. Lithograph from a sketch by Lady Louisa Tenison, published in her *Sketches in the East* (1846)

9. The Carmelite convent on Mount Carmel, where many tourists stayed on arriving in the Holy Land. Watercolour by A. Schranz, 1837, an artist who was employed by several tourists, including Lord Castlereagh, to record their tours of the Middle East

site for a colony of eastern European Jews.* In 1882 the Oliphants, having failed to persuade the Sultan to grant them land for their project, set up house in Haifa, joining the strange community of expatriate mystics, prophets and fanatics who had chosen to settle there. As Gertrude Bell wrote, 'there must be something in the air of Mount Carmel favourable to mental derangement of a special kind – at any rate if you want to commence prophet you take a little house in Haifa; you could scarcely begin in any other way'.

Apart from the Oliphants, who had now turned their attention to the Druzes and were trying to convert them to their particular version of mystical union with God, there was also Charles Gordon, fresh from several months' leave in an isolated village not far from Jerusalem, spent studying the Bible and Thomas à Kempis; in his *Reflections suggested in Palestine*, published posthumously, Gordon

---

*Oliphant had had an adventurous career which had covered much of the world – Ceylon, Nepal, China, Japan, the Crimea and Europe – before he became involved with an American mystic, Thomas Lake Harris, who persuaded him to come to America to serve Harris' brotherhood, a self-sufficient community bound by Harris's extraordinary creed of passionate, in his case usually sexual, union with God.

expounded several dubious topographical theories and drafted prophetic projects, such as a canal from Haifa to Aqaba which would let the waters of the Great Sea into Jordan and thereby fulfil a prophecy of Ezekiel's. Another of Oliphant's acquaintances was Baha'ullah, the successor to the Persian Bab, who had been exiled to Palestine with his followers. Oliphant was responsible for introducing him to a party of American tourists in search of new spiritual truths, who were later instrumental in setting up a branch of the Babi sect in America. E. G. Browne also visited Baha'ullah in 1890.

Tourism in Egypt flourished from the early years of the century; by 1812, when Muhammad Ali had suppressed the last vestige of Mamluk opposition tourists were relatively well isolated from the hazards of travel by using the Nile, and could impart their own comforts without being inflicted with the *modus vivendi* of the local inhabitants – 'a donkey-ride and a boating trip interspersed with ruins', wrote Amelia Edwards. Plague was always the great drawback to travel in the Middle East, particularly in Egypt, but outside the danger months of April, May and June the risk was minimal. As far back as 1642, William Lithgow in Cairo noted that it was considered a good plague year when only 300,000 died and in 1835, the year of Kinglake's visit to Cairo, he estimated that at the height of the epidemic at least 1,200 were dying each day. Quarantine was imposed on travellers from the Middle East to Europe, either at Malta or Marseilles. Some found this pleasant enough; Thackeray for instance found the seventeen days of 'prison and quiet' a much needed rest after two months' hectic sight-seeing.*

A typical stately tour was made as early as 1818 by Lord and Lady Belmore, their family and their physician, Dr Richardson (who published an account of it). The Belmores landed at Alexandria and sailed up river to Cairo, where the consul, Henry Salt, took them under his wing. No tour was complete without a visit to Muhammad Ali, who confided to the Belmores his belief that the English came to see ruins in Egypt because they had nothing to look at in their own country. At Thebes on the way up river, tying up by a sycamore which must have been in danger of falling into the river from the number of visitors who mention tying their boats there, Belmore commissioned a Greek, Athanasi, who was working for Salt, to collect antiquities for him and on his return 'the noble traveller, who put a number of Arabs constantly at work, set an example of the most

---

* The threat of plague was considerably diminished by the end of the century as a result of improved sanitary conditions in India which reduced the number of rats aboard ships from the Far East.

commendable industry and perseverance to the whole party' in his zealous excavations. It was quite common for wealthy tourists to be allotted a piece of land at Thebes on which they could excavate. Lady Belmore and the rest of the party meanwhile amused themselves with visits to local harems, another essential feature of a Middle East tour.

The development of the Overland Route increased the number of tourists; hotels were built and transport, especially between Alexandria and Cairo, improved. Thackeray's tour in 1844 was arranged both on sea and on land by P & O. Harriet Martineau visited Egypt in 1846–7 and even she, with her utilitarian outlook, decided that there were few things gayer than a trip to Cairo. Shepheard's Hotel, where she stayed, arranged details for sight-seeing in Cairo – hiring donkeys for Miss Martineau and her party to go riding before a good English breakfast – and produced a magician for their entertainment, the one who had so impressed Edward Lane that he had introduced him in *Modern Egyptians*, though he was dismissed by Miss Martineau as a mere mesmerist. Like all tourists, she climbed the Kheops Pyramid – accompanied by an Arab with a camp stool to help her up the higher steps (Cook's tours were later to include fees for all entrances to monuments 'but not payment for extra assistance in climbing the Pyramid'). More diligent than many of her fellow tourists, Miss Martineau declared of her journey up river that she was hardly able to sit down to breakfast unless she had first explored a temple. Her visit to a harem, however, was rather a failure because none of the inmates could understand why she was not married.

Wintering in Egypt became very popular in the middle of the century, the Prince of Wales establishing the fashion in 1872, when he chose to convalesce in Egypt after an illness. 'The English milord, extinct on the Continent, has revived in Egypt and is greatly reverenced and usually liked', wrote Lady Lucy Duff Gordon, herself quite the most romantic tourist to visit Egypt, where she lived on and off for seven years trying to cure or at least survive tuberculosis. Her letters from Egypt to her family achieved a tremendous vogue when they were published in 1865 and in many later editions, one of which even rated an introduction by George Meredith. The picture which the letters paint of Egypt is not particularly original, but they had a far greater appeal as the letters of a young woman dying in a strange and exciting land which few of her readers had visited; and the touching allusions to health – 'I now feel so much like living on a bit longer that I will ask you to send me a cargo of medicines', she wrote shortly before her death – have an almost calculated innocence.

In her house at Luxor, originally built by Henry Salt into the ruins of the temple, Lady Duff Gordon was reasonably secure from prying tourists and indeed welcomed the occasional visitor with news from England. Only a few years later, however, the great triumphal progresses of Cook's tours revolutionised the tourist scene. Cook, as a devout Christian, may have been inspired to extend his activities to the Middle East by Buckingham, whom he knew in connection with temperance work. In 1869 thirty-two ladies and gentlemen went up the Nile and thirty of them continued to the Holy Land. By the 1870's the Holy Land tour was a meticulously organised progress that protected its members from the rigours and discomforts of contact with the country as far as possible. It generally lasted thirty days. Visitors slept three to a tent and there were also two dining tents and three cooking tents to each expedition, all of which had to be taken down and pitched for each halt. Prayers were said morning and evening, on one tour – as an added attraction – 'by the famous traveller and Eastern explorer, just escaped from a brigand sheik in the land of Moab, Dr Tristam'. During the day visitors travelled by horse or mule and specially designed carriages were introduced for those who did not want to ride. By the 1890's Cook's were managing to house a thousand tourists under canvas at one time. Royalty from all over Europe put themselves in the hands of Cook's for their visits to the Holy Land, the most celebrated of such occasions being the Kaiser's visit in 1898 (during which Gertrude Bell noted he had given orders that no one was to be forbidden to come and gaze upon him). This was the time when the Kaiser tried to enter Jerusalem by the celebrated Golden Gate, which legend says will not be opened for anyone to pass through until the second coming of the Messiah; the legend was recalled only just in time and the Kaiser re-directed.

In Egypt, Thomas Cook's son, John, gained experience of the Nile to establish the company as one of the most knowledgeable users of the river, by transferring the wounded from Cairo to Alexandria after Tel el-Kabir, taking Gordon to Korosko in 1883 and transporting Hick's abortive expedition to rescue Gordon the following year. Cook's own boats had already earned a reputation for floating luxury and a later steamer launched in 1890 contained electric light, daily newspapers, breakfast with porridge, afternoon tea and a reading room, as well as entertainment by members of the crew after dinner. There was a special Cook's hotel at Luxor to cater for invalids attracted by Lady Duff Gordon's descriptions of the winter sun. Cook's would also arrange for tourists to travel independently up the Nile on *dahabiyahs*, the local boats, such as that described by Amelia Edwards; this was one of the largest –

about a hundred feet long, sleeping eight – and had ample space for a dining-room with a piano and a large saloon. This was the height of Egyptian tourism; at Abu Simbel, unearthed by Belzoni eighty years earlier, Miss Edwards found a 'fleet of *dahabiyahs*' ranged along the shore and 'three sketching tents' in front of the temple, their occupants obeying the instructions of their guide books to take 'notebook and pencils to record incidents and describe scenes to which memory will look back with fond pleasure in after years'.

These guide books, written by some of the leading authorities of the period on the Middle East, were among the best books on the area. *Murray's Guides to Egypt* were written by Wilkinson, Cook's by Wallis Budge. Their scope was astonishing (though the *Murray's Guide to Syria and Palestine* modestly deferred to the Bible as the 'best handbook' to the area) : Gertrude Bell travelling in the Jebel Druze – not exactly on the tourist track – finds a local Druze shaikh mentioned in Murray as a suitable contact. They provided enormous lists of provisions for the Nile traveller – among them foot-tubs, a broom and tin for sweeping the cabin, books and measuring instruments – hotels where they existed, where to excavate, what to look out for and what to copy. Never go ashore without an escort, they warned, as a result of which the riverside towns and villages fortunate enough to be near ruins became populated by a hereditary class of dragomans, passed on by recommendation from one tourist to another, just as they themselves passed on the skills of guiding 'the peach-fed standardised' tourist, as Ronald Storrs unkindly called the winter visitors, to their sons and grandsons. Early *Murray Guides* catered for the leisurely tourist, who was considering spending several months in the area and required advice on renting houses in Cairo, no doubt seeing himself as a follower in the worthy tradition of Lane and J. F. Lewis the artist. Murray recommended sending three or four Egyptians through the rooms first to carry off the fleas. It is interesting to note that by the 1870s tourists are advised against wearing native dress unless they speak Arabic fluently – it merely makes them look foolish. In the first half of the century native dress of some kind had been essential to a traveller's security.

15 Artists in the Middle East

Architecture, landscape, costume – these were the most popular subjects for the pictorial representation of the Middle East from the
sixteenth century onwards. Constantinople figured most frequently
at first, the Ottoman sultans attracting a number of European
artists – French, Italian, Flemish, German – whose rare but magnificent volumes started crazes for costumes *à la Turque* and fantastic
oriental architecture. Outside Constantinople, in the earlier period
covered here, the artist was primarily a traveller with greater or
lesser academic interests, often better with his pen than his pencil
and considerably at the mercy of the untravelled engraver, while
the engraving itself might be subsequently used by an artist who had
never been anywhere near the Middle East.

The outstanding artist to visit the Middle East in the earlier period
was the Dutchman, Cornelius de Bruyn, whose drawings of his two
journeys in the Levant and in Persia provided the contemporary
Englishman with the most complete picture of the area available at
the time. Few British artists, however, ventured as far even as Constantinople and the pictorial record was supplied by merchants,
pilgrims and other travellers whose often limited skill was hampered
by the difficulties of sketching in Islamic countries where representation of the human figure was forbidden. George Sandys illustrated
his travels with some quaint engravings and Henry Maundrell was
one of the earliest visitors to attempt anything like an accurate sketch
of ruins he passed on his way to and from Jerusalem. Sir John
Chardin's travels were also entertainingly illustrated.

Many of the great volumes of eighteenth century travel in the
Middle East were illustrated by their authors, though with occasional
insertions by other more professional artists if they were available.
Alexander Russell's *Natural History of Aleppo* was illustrated with
magnificent plates particularly in the second improved edition produced in 1794 after his death by his brother, in which some of the
finest were by an Anglo-German artist, George Ehret. Jonas
Hanway's highly observant record of Nadir Shah's conquest of north-
west Persia was illustrated by the author with a variety of scenes
gruesome enough for any sensationalist; Charles Perry drew most of

the illustrations for his *View of the Levant* and Drummond's drawings of ruined cities in his *Travels* were among the first to include
rather inaccurately dressed Turkish peasants to give an impression
of scale.

The decline of Ottoman power and of European fear of that
power in the eighteenth century coincided with the fashion for the
exotic and unfamiliar, the nearest examples of which were the
strange elaborate ritual of the Sultan's court and its setting along the
Bosphorus. France led the way in the ensuing fad for all things
Turkish and it was principally French artists who exploited the
magnificent subject matter in Constantinople and its surroundings.
Not until the last quarter of the eighteenth century, under Sir Robert
Ainslie, did the British embassy begin to rival the French
ambassador's patronage. By then all the principal embassies had
their paid artists and Ainslie's contribution to British enlightenment
took the form of a series of volumes of 'views' by his talented artist
Luigi Mayer – of Egypt, Palestine and the Ottoman dominions in
Europe and Asia – published as aquatints between 1801 and 1810.

Many of the gentlemen travellers who were visiting the Levant in
ever increasing numbers by the end of the eighteenth century were
competent artists: in the days before photography most people of
leisured affluence could draw a little and often very well. Sometimes,
however, they employed artists to accompany them. These had often
been trained as architects and were principally interested in the
stylistically fashionable Hellenistic world, an influence on their work
reflected in neo-Greek buildings all over London and the main provincial cities in the early nineteenth century. Wood and Dawkins
early on set the fashion for this kind of expedition when they took
with them to the Levant the Italian draughtsman and architect,
Giovanni Battista Borra, whose minutely detailed drawings published
in Wood's accounts probably had the greatest immediate impact on
architectural fashion. In 1763 Lord Baltimore toured the Levant
with his Anglo-Italian artist, Francis Smith, and the same year
Nicholas Revett took the young topographical artist, William Pars,
to gaze upon the Hellenistic ruins of Asia Minor, financed by the
Society of Dilettanti. The Society also sponsored one of the most
important antiquarian–architectural expeditions of the early nineteenth century, that of Sir William Gell; Gell was an able artist
himself but also employed such architect-draughtsmen as John Peter
Gandy-Deering (who later wanted to plant the English countryside
with lodges modelled on Egyptian pylons).

Napoleon and Denon marked a turning point in the development
of interest in the Middle East, the one politically and the other
culturally. Denon was able to take advantage of the presence and

1. View from Alexandria Troas, c. 1801, from Sir William Gell, *The Topography of Troy* (1804)

2. A Graeco-Roman tomb in Asia Minor, c. 1810. Watercolour by J. P. Gandy-Deering, architect companion of Sir William Gell. The antiquities he saw on his travels had a considerable influence on his later architectural designs

progress of Napoleon's victorious army through the length and breadth of Egypt to record what he saw in such detail and with such depth of interest and sympathy as to awaken Europeans for the first

3. Thomas Hope, 1798, who travelled widely in the Middle East during the 1790's and published a book of designs, *Household Furniture*, in 1807 which had a considerable influence in the Regency period. Portrait by Sir William Beechey (National Portrait Gallery)

time to the splendours of ancient Egypt. England had begun to flirt with Egyptian styles even before Napoleon's expedition, though principally under French influence and stylistically it never became much more than a flirtation. Thomas Hope was an amateur artist who spent several years in the 1790's among the ruins of the eastern Mediterranean, collecting antiquities which he later displayed in two large houses in London and Surrey against suitably designed backgrounds – a sketch of Hope's drawing-room shows sphinxes real and fake in all directions; and in his influential *Household Furniture*, published in 1807, he included a number of his own designs for furniture using Egyptian motifs. Decoration seemed better suited than architecture to Egyptian influence; Hope himself counselled against the too lavish use of a style which seldom, he

4. Design for a chair, from Thomas Hope, *Household Furniture* (1807)

5. Design for an Egyptian room, from Hope's *Household Furniture*

considered, beautified Egyptian monuments. An Italian architect, Agostino Aglio, who travelled with the neo-classical architect William Wilkins in Greece and Egypt between 1801 and 1805, also put his impressions to good use in Covent Garden Opera House, Drury Lane and the famous Garden Pavilion in the grounds of

Buckingham Palace. But the celebrated Egyptian Hall in Picadilly, where Belzoni had his exhibition in 1821, was an example of how superficial the Egyptian craze really was, a marvellous heteredox mixture of styles which made Sir John Soane's condemnation of the 'puerile imitation of Egyptian styles' particularly apt.

Interest in Egypt itself, however, continued to grow and the tradition of good draughtsmanship in the service of antiquarian exploration was maintained by Henry Salt, who was appointed British agent and consul-general in 1815 and remained there until his death in 1827. After training as a professional artist Salt had travelled to India and Ceylon and twice to Abyssinia, subsequently producing a finely illustrated account of the latter and his second journey there. In Egypt he spent most of his time organizing the collection of antiquities, by Belzoni and others, and ensuring that some kind of pictorial record was kept of their discoveries. Belzoni himself em-

7. Francis Arundale. Europeans still needed to travel in native dress and one of Arundale's companions, Joseph Bonomi, describes fitting himself out with the right garments in the Cairo bazaar. Frontispiece engraving of a portrait by Percy Williams, from Arundale's *Illustrations of Jerusalem and Mount Sinai* (1837)

6. (*opposite*) Street scene in Cairo. Watercolour by William Simpson, who was extremely skilled as a rapid observer and draughtsman, a style well suited to the genre scenes of which he was so fond. He was in Egypt on his way back from India where he had gone on behalf of *The Illustrated London News*

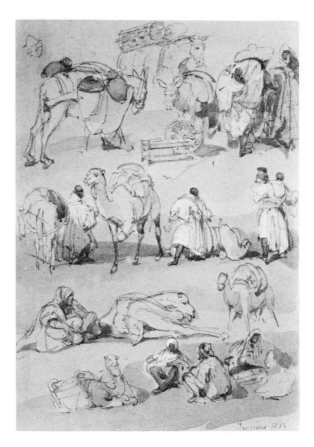

8. Sketches in pencil and watercolour by David Roberts R.A., 1833

ployed Alessandro Ricci for one summer to help him prepare a model of Seti's tomb and Ricci later provided many of the illustrations for Belzoni's *Operations*.

During the 1820's and 1830's the dealer-collectors began to be replaced by more serious Egyptologists more intent on the record than the hoard. Robert Hay was typical of the new generation and was wealthy enough to employ a number of artists to make the record in which they were greatly assisted by the use of the *camera lucida*, a means of reflecting an image on to paper which Frederick Catherwood in particular among Hay's party used to great effect. Other artists who worked with or for Hay included Joseph Bonomi who had trained as a sculptor and Francis Arundale who had studied architecture and also painting under Pugin. Arundale first went to Egypt in 1831 and spent some nine years in the Middle East. During

9. Tomb of Al-Adel Tuman Bey in Old Cairo. Watercolour by Owen Jones (1809–74) of a subject which demonstrates Jones' interest in the decorative features of Islamic architecture

this time he accompanied Bonomi and Catherwood to Palestine where they were the first artists to win permission to enter the Muslim shrine of the Dome of the Rock in Jerusalem. Bonomi appears time and time again in any survey of early nineteenth century Egyptology – on an expedition, arranging an exhibition, publicising Egyptology, helping Wilkinson and Lane (both of whom were good amateur artists) to illustrate Wilkinson's *Ancient Egyptians* – and rounded off a distinguished career as curator of the Soane Museum, guardian of one of the most exquisite specimens of Egyptian art in Britain, the alabaster sarcophagus of Seti 1 which Belzoni had excavated.

Owen Jones also joined Hay's party, an architect-decorator of great significance in Victorian decorative art who spent some time in the 1830's touring in Egypt, Constantinople and Spain, producing

10. Blind Arab with a teasel, watercolour by Egron Lundgren

many drawings and water-colours of great charm. His Egyptian experience led to his appointment as joint decorator for the ornamentation of the Crystal Palace at Sydenham in 1852 where Bonomi joined him in the design and decoration of the Egyptian court.

On the whole there was little creative art in the works of these men: that was not their task. What they were doing, under generally uncomfortable conditions*, was what the camera today can do in a

* Hay in his tomb at Thebes lived comfortably enough, however, with a Fuller's cream freezer, a cuckoo clock, and a patent apparatus for roasting, baking, steaming and boiling meat.

matter of moments – building up such a comprehensive record that modern archaeologists still refer to the forty-nine volumes of Hay papers in the British Museum to check on ruins which have since disappeared.

Their sketches moreover provided the engraver back in England with some of the earliest topographical water colours of the area. This was the hey-day of the engraver, who was in great demand to prepare the heavy ornamental tomes of the Victorian drawing-room, similar to the modern coffee-table book. Sometimes the engraver and the publisher were the same person, such as the Finden brothers who published and engraved such popular picture books as Finden's *Landscape Illustrations of the Bible, Life and Works of Lord Byron* and *Moore's Beauties*. Fisher's *Views of Constantinople*, Miss Pardoe's *Beauties of the Bosphorus* and a dozen similar publications, with engravings by the Findens and others, fed the fashion for the exotic. In many cases the engravings were made from drawings by established artists who had worked them up from 'sketches taken from nature on the spot' either by less well-known artists or by amateurs. Many of the final artists had never been near the scenes they were employed to compose – Turner, Harding, Prout, Cattermole and Callcott among them. For others, such as David Roberts, this kind of composition may have provided the inspiration that later took them out to see for themselves the places they had been drawing at second hand. The standard of even the original sketches was very high, their artists including Charles Barry the architect, William Page, Catherwood, Wilkinson and Bonomi. Barry, educated in the classical tradition of architect, felt a qualified admiration for Egyptian architecture, writing of Karnak that 'although it cannot be judged by the strict rules of Architectural Proportion and Symmetry yet when in the midst of such a vast assemblage of columns the effect it produced upon me was the most impressive I ever experienced'.

A new class of professional topographical artist was appearing by mid-century to cater for this market, again often with the background of architectural draughtsmanship, hence the prevalence of ruins in so many of their compositions. William Bartlett, Thomas Allom, William Purser, William Page and William Leitch were familiar names to the public of their day. Bartlett was by far the most indefatigable of these artists and his output the most prodigious. Before he died in 1854 at the age of forty-five, on his way home from his fifth trip to the Middle East, he must have produced well over a thousand drawings which were engraved and published in a dozen or more books. He was as competent with the pen as with the pencil and brush, accompanying his illustrations of mountain scenes, rushing torrents, romantically costumed figures and ruined

11. A halt in the desert, watercolour by J. F. Lewis R.A. Lewis lived as a Turk in Cairo from 1842 to 1851

castles with suitably melodramatic notes – 'savage as is the seclusion, it is in the heart of a territory of exceeding beauty and fertility, where a ruthless hand and licentious heart could find ample indulgence', ran one such description. Palestine was his happiest hunting ground, where he assiduously traced and retraced biblical footsteps, missing in the process no detail of religious, secular or contemporary life and history. He also contributed to a still more popular version of topographical art – the dioramas. These were collections of enlarged views, painted from the sketches of such artists as Bartlett, Bonomi and David Roberts, described by one enthusiastic promoter as 'the embodiment of the poetry of oriental travel', which were sent round the country for the benefit of those who could reach neither London nor the Middle East to see the places for themselves.

The revelation and elucidation of the past were obviously worthy subjects but as conditions of travel improved (or the hazards became better known and more easily guarded against) the Ottoman dominions began attracting professional artists less exclusively interested in the past. Some of these, such as William Muller, David Roberts and Edward Lear, still concentrated on the topography of the area; others, such as John Frederick Lewis and David Wilkie, were more interested in developing the image of the 'mysterious east' – in portraits, street scenes, costume rather than buildings and landscape.

12. The silk mart at Bursa. The import of silks was important in Anglo-Turkish trade in the seventeenth and eighteenth centuries and Bursa was the centre of the trade. Lithograph by J. F. Lewis from an original drawing by Coke Smyth, from Lewis, *Illustrations of Constantinople*

Muller went to the Middle East in 1837 aged twenty-five and died eight years later so that all his paintings seem to be drawn through the eyes of youth, whether they are catching a light, sketching the stone of a column, fastening upon a character in a street or bazaar or wondering at the Cairo slave market, 'one of my favourite haunts'. He was back in south Turkey in 1843–4 at the suggestion of Sir Charles Fellows who wanted a record of his excavations and the journey produced some of Muller's finest water-colours though possibly failing to fulfil Fellows' technical requirements, and it is this element of imagination which distinguishes the second generation of artists from the architect-draughtsmen of the earlier years. 'Imagine

a precipitous crag', Muller exclaimed in one letter, 'a lower spur of
the mountains thrust out into the valley ... crowned with myrtle,
wild olive and arbutus ... then fill the air with the music of the
dancing streams on their way to the valley below, and you will have a
faint idea of the situation of the ancient Tlos'; no earthly paradise
was more suited to his palette.

Edward Lear travelled extensively in Egypt, Sinai, Palestine and
Syria between about 1848 and 1858, an artist more at home among
the crags of Sinai, the 'astonishingly grand' red cliffs of Petra and
the hills and villages of Palestine than in the monotonous flatness
of the 'sad, stern uncompromising' Egyptian landscape. He captures
the light, the angularity of trees and rocks, something of the intrinsic
character of an unfamiliar world which eluded so many other
artists. 'Oh Master!' exclaimed his servant Giorgio at Petra, 'we
have come to a world where everything is made of chocolate, ham,
curry powder and salmon.'

Both Roberts and Lewis had already established reputations for
their drawings in Spain where they had travelled in the early 1830's.
Roberts had extended his journey to Tangier, a first experience of

13. Street scene at the Bab el-Luk, watercolour by J. F. Lewis, 1856. This
is typical of his crowded scenes of life in Cairo, probably worked up from
the many sketches he made during the nine years he lived there.

the Arab world that may have inspired his later journey through
Egypt and the Levant. This journey, between September 1838 and
May 1839, resulted in a comprehensive and enthusiastic record of
all he saw, providing him with material for paintings for many years
to come and also for the six splendid volumes of lithographs (by his
friend Louis Haghe) – *The Holy Land, Egypt and Nubia* – which gave

14. Halaku Mirza, uncle of Nasir u'd-Din Shah, who was living in exile in
Constantinople when Wilkie made this sketch of him. It seems clear from
subsequent sketches that in the face of this Persian prince Wilkie felt he
had found the ideal type to represent Jesus Christ. Lithograph by Joseph
Nash from Wilkie's *Original Sketches*

him lasting fame. Possibly because of his early training as a theatrical scene painter, he was the more architecturally-minded of the five artists, as is clear from the detail of his drawings of such widely differing subjects as the mosques of Cairo (which he was allowed to paint inside as long as he did not use hog's bristle brushes), the ancient temples and monuments of Upper Egypt and Nubia, the

15. Study for the *Ecce Homo.* Pontius Pilate is here shown with Arab features rather than the conventional Roman. Lithograph by Nash from Wilkie's *Oriental Sketches*

ruins of Petra and the classical buildings of Baalbek. The third volume is mostly devoted to Cairo, 'this most wonderful of all cities . . . unequalled in the world for the picturesque'.

Lewis was in Cairo a few years after Roberts and his interest in the Orient took a rather different turn. Lewis set out for the Middle East in 1839 and reached Cairo in 1841; three years later he was found by Thackeray living the life of a well-to-do Turk ('a lotus-eater', said Thackeray) in a typical Turkish house, surrounded by all the appropriate trappings and amenities. He did not return to London until 1851 – an absence of twelve years during which he amassed the sketches from which he was able to make such a success-ful living for the rest of his life. To the modern eye the original sketches probably have greater appeal than the highly finished paint-ings and water-colours, brilliant in light, colour and detail, of street scenes, markets, harems and schools of Egypt that stirred Ruskin's admiration so deeply. Lewis was a skilled animal painter and one of the few artists to draw a respectable camel.

David Wilkie died, like Bartlett, on the homeward journey off Malta so that the only original works that survive from his travels

16. Head of an Arab, oil sketch by Frederick Lord Leighton, P.R.A. (1830–96). Leighton used sketches such as this in his later religious paintings

are sketches of which only one – a portrait of Muhammad Ali –
was completed as an oil painting. His many sketches were a mixture
of picturesque and religious subjects. The most impressive were
concerned with his search for 'types', regardless of race (even the
ladies of the British consular service had to put on Turkish dress
before he would paint them) that fitted his idea of Christ and his
happiest sketches provided the appropriate background to his New
Testament conception. Palestine, wrote Wilkie, 'represents a new
field for the genius of Scripture painting to work upon'.

Much of Wilkie's work was typically inspired by the religious
revival of mid-nineteenth century Britain, evidenced in the Middle
East by the growing number of visitors to Palestine. Scholars and
divines with wives and daughters streamed through the Holy Land
busy with pen and pencil. And artists came too, to paint for the
revival. William Holman Hunt, the young Thomas Seddon,
Frederick Lord Leighton followed Wilkie's admonition that 'a
Martin Luther in painting is as much called for as in theology' and
went to the Middle East to acquire that familiarity with the background of their paintings which their colleagues among the Pre-
Raphaelites considered so important a part of their pictures. Not
everyone was prepared to leave the comfort of a Kensington studio
to live on the shores of the Dead Sea in the height of summer, as
did Hunt when seeking the light on the hills of Moab for his
'Scapegoat'. But Hunt did not find it easy to satisfy his ambition
to have genuine orientals for the figures in his paintings; he was
constantly frustrated by the suspicions of Jews and Muslims alike
when it came to being painted.

Frederick Leighton included Damascus in his tour where Richard
Burton was then consul (Leighton painted his portrait at this time).
It was Burton and another expatriate resident of Damascus, the
celebrated Lady Ellenborough (married now to a Syrian shaikh)
who helped Leighton amass a considerable collection of Islamic and
Arab antiquities which he installed in the Damascene hall of his
Kensington home, creating a great sensation when it was opened to
the London public in the 1870's.

It is easy to forget, in studying the numerous accounts, drawings
and paintings of the Holy Land, how much of that country and
other parts of the Middle East were still being explored. The
journals and letters of the more intrepid artists such as Lear, Roberts
and Bartlett make it quite clear that expeditions to Sinai and Petra
were not undertaken lightheartedly. Fellows excused his many
accounts of his excavations in south-west Turkey by the fact that the
area was so little known. Burton's sketches of Arabia are important
not for their skill, which was limited, but for their illustration of so

17. Bayazit on the slopes of Mount Ararat, sketched in 1836 by F. C. Lewis the Younger (sometimes known as 'Indian' Lewis to distinguish him from his more famous brother J.F.) on his way through Turkey to Persia

unfamiliar an area. This is particularly the case in Mesopotamia and Persia, both of which suffered from a dearth of artistic portrayal. Buckingham sketched rather inaccurately as he went along though travelling 'native' as he did he must have risked the same dangers

18. The monastery of Mar Saba, original pencil and wash drawing by
Hercules Brabazon (1821–1906)

as Burckhardt and Burton in Arabia when it came to sketching or
writing about Muslims and their countries. Chesney's account of
his expedition down the Euphrates included a number of illustrations, some by members of the expedition (all of whom were supposed to produce drawings regularly during the journey). Archaeologists in Mesopotamia helped to fill some more blanks. Layard was
too preoccupied with excavating for more than the occasional sketch
and the British Museum supplied him with a professional artist,
Frederick Cooper, for his second expedition. After a year or so
Cooper's health broke down and most of the illustrations in Layard's
accounts were acknowledged to be by the Rev. S. C. Malan, although
Cooper, whom Layard never liked, actually did the majority.

In Persia the only British artist of real consequence to produce
drawings of high quality and permanent interest was Sir Robert
Ker Porter; James Morier and James Baillie Fraser were both
competent amateurs but their drawings bear little comparison with
the magnificent water-colours which illustrate Ker Porter's *Travels
in Georgia, Persia, Armenia, etc.*, published in 1829. Most of these
suffered at the hands of the engravers and they must be seen in the
original for the beauty to be appreciated. Ker Porter visited the

Middle East at the request of the President of the Russian Academy of Science (Ker Porter was living in St Petersburg and Moscow at the time) who was particularly anxious to have accurate drawings; time and again Ker Porter stressed his determination to draw with absolute accuracy (his brush more obedient in this respect than his pen), berating his predecessors for producing finished, as opposed to accurate, drawings. Finest of all are his costume drawings and sketches – sad Persian peasants propping up Sassanian ruins, picturesque guides, 'a windy day in Tehran which gave an opportunity of seeing the boots of the females', a wrestler, the chief executioner – subjects generally difficult to portray, whose appearance and expression make Ker Porter one of the best illustrators of nineteenth-century Persia.

For any pictorial record at all of the less accessible regions of the Middle East we are dependent on the talents of serving soldiers and sailors. Officers of the East India Company, of the Bombay Marine, the Indian Army and the British Army often drew with considerable skill. Several of the more interesting drawings – of the Arabian peninsular and the surrounding waters for instance – were done in the course of duty by naval surveyors whose normal job was to draw plans or elevations of what they saw and who often extended their skills to recording actual operations in which they might be participating. Captain Moresby of the *Palinurus* produced excellent drawings of his official Red Sea survey of 1829 and Lieutenant Rundle showed remarkable skill in his water-colours of the capture of Aden in 1839. Many of these drawings were published as lithographs and those of another Indian army officer, Lieutenant Temple – *Sixteen Views of Places in the Persian Gulph* – are best known as coloured aquatints.* The soft colours, the reflections in the water, the quaint scenes of boat building in picturesque harbours, did something to counter the tales of gun-running and slave-dealing which coloured the written accounts.

* See above, p. 148.

16 The Plaint of the Reed

The greatest contribution of the Middle East to nineteenth-century English literature was the provision of an abundance of ideas and forms for English writers to draw upon when breaking away from earlier conventions. As George Eliot wrote, 'no act of religious symbolism has a deeper root in nature than turning with reverence to the East ... the East is the land of the morning'. To an age which loved to hear of outlandish places, but which often destroyed the exotic by pursuing the material, 'death hath no repose warmer and deeper than that of orient sand', amongst whose grains the Victorians could glimpse the vanishing myths of earlier civilisations.

Oriental literature to most people – then as now – meant the *Alf Lail wa Laila*, the *Thousand and One Nights*, more commonly known as the *Arabian Nights*. Many of these tales were told in verse, the rich, warm, imaginative poetry of Persia and Arabia, where poets were thought worthy to advise kings and spoke the oldest living languages in the world. Arabia had inspired a chapter of English literature noted for its agonising realism but the world of the *Arabian Nights* evoked a world of dreams and the tales told by the beautiful Princess Shahrazad to fill the thousand and one nights of King Shahryar were the recreation of kings, barbers and cooks, the manner by which favourites restored themselves to grace or philosopher poets undertook the education of young princes, walking in the evening on aromatic hill sides.' 'Tales, marvellous tales', wrote James Elroy Flecker,

> Of ships and stars and isles where good men rest,
> Where never more the rose of Sunset pales,
> And winds and shadows fall towards the West.

Long before the first direct English translations of the *Thousand and One Nights* in the 1830's, the Arabian tale had become a popular medium for lugubrious Gothic fantasies and sentimental romances. French still being the recognised language for translations of authentic oriental tales,* William Beckford first published his *Vathek* in French

---

* See above, p. 92.

in 1786, there demonstrating the degree to which the oriental framework could be adapted to suit the fashion for melancholia well garnished with exotic imagery. Beckford, who had read all the available orientalia of the period and had briefly studied Arabic and Persian, familiarised his readers with the paraphernalia of Arabian story-telling – genii, houris, the Hall of Eblis, Prince of Demons (a hall 'so lofty and spacious that they took it for an immeasurable plain', which Beckford had modelled on the great Egyptian hall in his home at Fonthill), customs of harems and the superstitions of their masters. The story of the proud and sensual Caliph Vathek, 'who for the sake of empty pomp and forbidden power, had sullied himself with a thousand crimes', Nouronihar the beautiful princess whom he seduces, Carithis his evil mother and Gulchenrouz the lovelorn poet is as typical of the *Thousand and One Nights* as any of Shahrazad's actual stories.

Robert Southey's *Thalaba the Destroyer*, published in 1800, was, in spite of its classical style, clearly inspired by *Vathek*. Southey described its unusual metre as 'the Arabesque ornament of an Arabian tale', though a metre further from Arabic or Persian verse could hardly be found. The poem lacks Beckford's harmony of phrase and imagery, owing to Southey's fundamental dislike of the hyperbole and intricacies of oriental literature, which he described as 'worthless' in one of his notes to *Thalaba*. Around the tale of the youth Thalaba, who descends to the Domdaniel ('a seminary for evil magicians under the Roots of the Sea') to slay the power of evil, Southey wove an impressive tapestry of second-hand oriental learning and the extensive footnotes at the bottom of each page quote all the familiar authorities – Hakluyt's travellers, Greaves, Pococke and Niebuhr among them.

In spite of *Thalaba's* artificiality it enjoyed a considerable success and from it developed the far more popular poetry of Thomas Moore and Byron. Moore used sources similar to Southey's but with greater effect, seizing the opportunity offered by William Jones' translations of oriental poetry to replenish the overworked classical imagery of contemporary literature. Moore's most celebrated work, *Lalla Rookh*, was published in 1817. It is a collection of verse tales told to the heroine Lalla Rookh, an Indian princess, by the young poet Feramorz during her journey to be married to the King of Bokhara; naturally the beautiful maiden falls in love with the sorrowful poet and at the moment of her marriage discovers him to be none other than her betrothed. Byron generously told the author that he had 'caught the colours as if you had been in the rainbow, and the tone of the East is perfectly preserved'. Moore leaves nothing out of his fairy tale – doe-eyed houris blush, nightingales sing, youths languish

1. The grand procession of the sacred camel, bearing the canopy for the Prophet's tomb in Mecca, passing through the streets of Cairo at the start of the annual pilgrimage to Mecca, coloured aquatint from the Rev. Cooper Willyam, *A Selection of Views in Egypt, Palestine, etc* (1822)

for love of dark tresses glimpsed through the lattice of the harem. His readers were as enchanted and spellbound as Lalla Rookh's bridal procession, as they followed the poet through the heavy scent of jasmine and roses, along valleys lush with streams, willows and the fruits of paradise – 'places of melancholy, delight and safety, where all the company around was wild peacocks and turtle-doves'. Some of the many subsequent editions were illustrated by the famous Finden brothers – with portraits of moustachioed Persians in the decorous arms of exquisite maidens dreaming in tropical gardens, over-shadowed by the monstrous phantoms of oriental imagination.

Lalla Rookh enjoyed tremendous popularity on publication, running to five editions within the first year. One of the verse stories, *The Paradise and the Peri*, was dramatised and the whole book was translated into Persian. A contemporary of Moore's eulogised the translation:

> I am told, dear Moore, your lays are sung,
> (Can it be, you lucky man?)
> By moonlight in the Persian tongue
> Along the streets of Isfahan.

Nowadays it haunts the back shelves of second-hand book shops and opinion follows Curzon's criticism, that 'a heavy weight of responsibility lies at the door of Moore, whose descriptions of Persia are about as much like the original as the Alhambra at Leicester Square is like the exquisite palace of Boabdil'.

Moore's friend Byron was deeply attached to the image of himself as the great oriental traveller, even though his knowledge of the Orient was confined to Constantinople, the Bosphorus and of course the Hellespont:*

> The European with the Asian shore
> Sprinkled with palaces; the ocean stream,
> Here and there studded with a seventy-four;
> Sophia's cupola with golden gleam;
> The cypress groves; Olympus high and hoar;
> The twelve isles and more than I could dream,
> Far less describe, present the very view
> Which charmed the charming Mary Montagu.

Byron wrote several poems with oriental backgrounds after his visit, though he relied more on the recognised authorities than on his own limited experience for details. How right Moore was when he wrote after the publication of *The Giaour* (which just preceded his own *Lalla Rookh*), 'never was anything so unlucky for me than Byron's invasion of this region, which when I entered it, was as yet untrodden and whose chief charm consisted in the gloss and novelty of its features; but it will now be over-run with clumsy adventurers'. Byron was certainly acquainted with William Jones' translations of Arabic poetry, to judge by the notes to his poem, and it may be more than coincidence that he reflects the same melancholia and introspection which is often so typical of Arabian poets. Byron and Moore satisfied the same eagerness for the unfamiliar as characterised the paintings of Ker Porter in Persia, the wanderings of Lady Hester Stanhope in the Levant, and the turgid volumes of endless travel published by their friends Edward Dodwell and John Hobhouse.

Several improvements on Galland's translations of the *Arabian Nights* were published during the eighteenth and early nineteenth

* Canning, who was in Constantinople when Byron arrived with his friend John Cam Hobhouse in 1810, saw enough of the poet to prejudice his later opinion of Byron's image of the Orient: Byron wanted to join in the ambassador Adair's farewell procession to the Sultan and 'arrived in scarlet regimentals topped by a profusely feathered cocked hat and ... asked what his place, as a peer of the realm, was to be'; having been told that he would have to walk at the end of the procession because he was not a member of the embassy, 'his lordship walked away with that look of scornful indignation which so well became his fine imperious features'. He later apologised and joined the procession as a private individual.

2. Egyptian dancing girls, engraved from a drawing by E. W. Lane and published in his *Manners and Customs of the Modern Egyptians* (1836)

centuries, but no English translations were published until the 1830's. Henry Torrens published an incomplete edition in 1838 and Edward Lane's fuller, but still expurgated, edition appeared between 1838 and 1841. Lane 'thought it right to omit such tales, anecdotes, etc. as are comparatively uninteresting or on any account objectionable': he intended his translation to replace Galland's, which he considered both indecent and ill-informed. As one might expect of the author of *Modern Egyptians*, Lane's tales are more informative than they are romantic; the bazaars and streets of Baghdad where the Caliph Harun al-Rashid (who appears with his *vazir* Jaafar in many of the stories) used to wander at night, the manners of the court and the daily life of the Middle East are described as accurately in Lane's translation (and sometimes more vividly) as in any traveller's account.

Selections from the *Nights* were published throughout the century, many of them plagiarised versions from Lane or Galland, losing some of their freshness if little of their popularity in the endless repetition. Collections of fairy tales also copied the unique narrative form of the tales, their brevity and precision; R. L. Stevenson, for instance, wrote *New Arabian Nights* and *More Arabian Nights* in which, as Burton rightly pointed out, 'the only visible connection with the old *Nights* is the habit of seeking adventures under a disguise'. George Meredith's *Shaving of Shagpat* used the familiar ingredients with a deceptive sureness of touch.

The great difference between Lane's version and the sixteen-volume edition published by Richard Burton between 1885 and 1888 emerges in Burton's preface, when he describes his aim, 'to preserve intact, not only the spirit, but even the *mécanique*, the manner and matter'. Torrens' and Lane's versions he described as 'garbled and mutilated, unsexed and unsouled'. Burton set out to remedy the ignorance with which he considered the stories were generally read by copious footnotes, 'a repertory of Eastern knowledge in its esoteric phase'. He was among the first to recognise that the greatest Arab poets and scholars held the *Thousand and One Nights* in as much disdain as the scandalised Victorians; Shahrazad's tales were not intended to represent stately conventions of literature or *mores* but the seedier, racier life of the streets, the gossip of the harem, the lust, fraud and obscenities of life. Since these exist, however much of a blind eye people may like to turn to them, argued Burton and the Persian and Arab story-tellers who preceded him, they might as well be enjoyed. It is difficult not to do so in such an encyclopaedia of knowledge as Burton's, accumulated over a life spent travelling through so much of the world; moreover it is written with a superb and quite unexpected enthusiasm and humour for someone who had suffered as many disappointments as Burton.

3. The whirling dervishes, by an unknown artist

The great masterpiece of literature about the Middle East is James Morier's *Hajji Baba*. Morier was one of four sons of Isaac Morier, British consul in Constantinople, three of whom entered the diplomatic or consular services. James first went to Persia in 1808–9 and returned a few years later after accompanying Mirza Abul Hassan to London. In 1824 the 'ripened product of his Persian experiences and reflections' was published in the form of *Hajji Baba of Isfahan*. Many travellers turned to the fictional orient, using their first-hand knowledge to describe the tales they had overheard in the caravanserai or the coffee house, illustrating society and manners more evocatively than in their travelogues. But the notorious rogue of a barber's son, Hajji Baba, was the most successful in stripping the orient of its glamour and showing its trimmings for the tinsel they often were.

The book had an immediate and lasting success in England. Curzon, who was surely qualified to judge, described Hajji Baba as 'a Persian of the Persians; typical not merely of the life and surroundings, but of the character and instincts and manner of thought of his countrymen'. In relating the career of his hero – through the gamut of barber, Turcoman slave, vendor of smoke, dervish, doctor's assistant, executioner, holy man, scribe, merchant and finally assistant to an ambassador – Morier covered every aspect of Persian life, himself so steeped in oriental experience, expression and thought that he deceived the reader as easily as his hero cheats his clients.

Hajji Baba entertains not only as a satire but also as an historical document. For a generation better acquainted with Persia than most – through Morier's own travels and those of Ker Porter, Malcolm, Ouseley and Baillie Fraser – *Hajji Baba* set the scene for the political interests revolving round Anglo-Russian rivalry in Persia in the first half of the nineteenth century. The figures that move across the stage are not 'pasteboard creations' but living personalities, disguised only by name, with whom Morier was in daily contact in Tehran – the uxorious Fath Ali Shah, the grand vezir, the court treasurer, the poet laureate and of course Mirza Firouz Khan, who under his real name of Mirza Abul Hassan Khan was Morier's Persian ambassador. By liberally scattering his pages with quotations from Persian literature, Morier revealed his own and the average Persian's high esteem of their great inheritance and led his readers to share in it.

The anger of the Persians that an outsider could write so well about themselves is best demonstrated by the letter Morier received from Mirza Abul Hassan on its publication. 'What for you write *Hajji Baba*, sir? King very angry, sir. I swear him you never write lies; but he say, yes – write. All people very angry with you, sir. That very bad book, sir. All lies, sir. Who tell you all these lies, sir?

4. Persian musicians, engraving from Morier's *Second Journey*

What for you not speak to me? Very bad business, sir. Persian people very bad people, perhaps, but very good to you, sir. What for you abuse them so bad?' It is interesting to note that the Persian translation which was made at the end of the century contained more material than Morier's original, aimed at the Persian intelligentsia and according to E. G. Browne contributed in a small way to the climate of opinion which led to the revolution of 1905.

Morier's other novels, using his Persian experiences, have been eclipsed by *Hajji Baba* over the years, but enjoyed no little success on their first publication. Baillie Fraser, another Persian traveller, supplemented his rather laborious books of travel with *Allee Neemroo*, *Buchtari Adventurer*, and *The Khan's Tale* – more to the taste of the contemporary reading public. Malcolm's *Sketches of Persia*, a lightly satirical description of Persia by a fictional traveller, was rated by Curzon as highly as *Hajji Baba* and essential reading for diplomats or travellers visiting Persia.

An oriental background was used as a literary device in some of the nineteenth century's most famous novels, among them those of Benjamin Disraeli who visited the Levant in 1830–1 and managed to bring his travels into three of his subsequent novels, two of which – *Contarini Fleming* and *Alroy* – he began while in the Middle East. The East filled him with delighted enthusiasm and flighty musings about his own oriental ancestry. Constantinople with its 'cypress groves and mosquish domes (shades of Byron), where the 'meanest merchant in the Bazaar looks like a Sultan in an Eastern fairy tale', was 'like life in a pantomime or Eastern tales of enchantment', he wrote to his sister. How attracted he felt by the luxurious indolent life of the Turks – 'a life accompanied by a thousand sources of mellowed pleasure'. His impressions of Jerusalem, though bearing little resemblance to other travellers' accounts, make splendid reading in *Contarini*: 'nothing could be conceived more wild, and terrible, and desolate than the surrounding scenery, more dark, and stormy and severe; but the ground was thrown about in such picturesque un-dulations, that the mind, full of the sublime, required not the beautiful.' It is difficult to banish the suspicion that Disraeli need not really have gone to Jerusalem to produce so melodramatic a description.

The expansion of travel and the publication of so many descrip-tions of travel introduced unfamiliar subjects to contemporary writers in England who had either no intention or no chance to visit the Middle East themselves. Shelley, Keats and Leigh Hunt, for instance, were so stimulated by the excavations of pharaohnic Egypt by Belzoni and others that they decided to compete in composing poems on the Nile.* Shelley's version was erudite and classical:

> Month after month the gathered rains descend
> Drenching yon secret Aethiopian dells,
> And from the desert's ice-girt pinnacles
> Where Frost and heat in strange embraces blend
> On Atlas, fields of moist snow half depend.
> Girt there with blasts and meteors Tempest dwells
> By Nile's aerial urn, with rapid spells
> Urging these waters to their mighty end.

Keats' poem is the least successful and one of his most awkward compositions:

> Son of the old moon-mountains African!
>   Chief of the Pyramid and Crocodile!
>   We call thee fruitful, and that very while,
> A desert fills our seeing's inward span;
> Nurse of swart nations since the world began,
>   Art thou so fruitful? or dost thou beguile
>   Such men to honour thee, who, worn with toil,
> Rest for a space 'twixt Cairo and Decan? . . .

---

* Shelley's *Ozymandias* was actually composed the year before.

Interestingly it is Leigh Hunt, generally the least impressive poet of the three, who most successfully breaks away from the classical conventions to evoke the exciting discoveries of the previous fifteen years:

> It flows through old hush'd Egypt and its sands,
> Like some grave, mighty thought, threading a dream;
> And times, and things, as in that vision seen,
> Keeping along it their eternal strands.
> Caves, pillars, pyramids, the shepherd bands
> That roamed through the young earth – the flag extreme
> Of high Sesostris, and that southern beam,
> The laughing Queen, that caught the world's great hands.

Matthew Arnold knew both Kinglake and Layard and used Alexander Burne's *Travels in Bokhara* for his *Sick King in Bokhara* and John Malcolm's *History of Persia* for *Sohrab and Rustum*, the tragic tale of the brave and noble Sohrab slain by his father, Rustum, who did not recognise him on the battlefield:

> As those black granite pillars, once high-rear'd
> By Jemshid in Persepolis, to bear
> His house, now, mid their broken flights of steps,
> Lie prone, enormous, down the mountain side –
> So in the sand lay Rustum by his son.

Rustum was the Hercules of Persian folklore, whose exploits were celebrated in the *Shahnama* or *Book of Kings* of the great Persian poet Firdausi. Arnold's epic poem captured some of the elegiac nature of Firdausi's poetry; it is adorned with the long elaborate similes of oriental verse and the abundance of names he introduces (and revels in as Marlowe did nearly three hundred years earlier) gives an impression of familiarity with a legend so much a part of Persian folklore.

In 1772 William Jones published the translation of a Persian song by the fourteenth-century poet Hafiz:

> Sweet maid, if thou would'st charm my sight,
> And bid these arms thy neck infold;
> That rosy cheek, that lily hand,
> Would give thy poet more delight
> Than all Bocara's vaunted gold,
> Than all the gems of Samarcand.

Jones' example made the translation of Persian, Arabic and Turkish poetry a fashionable exercise among oriental scholars and the influx of manuscripts, resulting from the British conquest of India at the end of the eighteenth century, suddenly made available the works of poets revered with religious fervour in their own countries but hitherto hardly known at all in Europe. Jones tried to associate East and West together in the world of literature and enjoyed comparing Persian poets and sages with the masters of European literature – Homer, Petrarch and Shakespeare. 'Persia has produced more writers of every kind, and chiefly poets, than all Europe together', he wrote in his *Essay on the Poetry of Eastern Nations*; 'the Asiatics excel the inhabitants of our colder regions in the liveliness of their fancy, and the richness of their invention', and he described the 'softness and love of pleasure, that indolence and effeminacy' which made the Persians the prey of other nations but also, in the intervals of peace, enabled them to 'sink into a state of inactivity and pass their lives in a pleasurable yet studious retirement':

> Speak not of fate: ah! change the theme,
> And talk of odours, talk of wine,
> Talk of the flowers that round us bloom:
> 'Tis all a cloud, 'tis all a dream;
> To love and joy thy thoughts confine.

It was just this state of inactivity which visitors to Persia in the nineteenth century so deplored – a state of moral and physical torpor. But Jones' demonstration of the riches of Arabic and Persian poetry evoked an unexpected delight in the Victorians, their enjoyment of it unspoiled by their disapproval of Persian corruption and brutality.

Jones also demonstrated the variety and scope of oriental metres, delighting in versifying his translations in the metres of the originals, sometimes at the expense of the translation's beauty but sometimes with such success that English poets adopted the metre for their own verse. An example of this is Jones' translation from Arabic of the *Muallakat*, the famous pre-Islamic odes which according to legend were hung in the Kaaba at Mecca.* The most celebrated imitation of the long couplets into which Jones translated the odes is Tennyson's *Locksley Hall*. Both this poem and the oldest ode of the *Muallakat* – by Imr al-Qais – open with a lover standing before the deserted dwelling of his faithless mistress, a common theme in Arabic verse. Jones' prose translation opens:

---

* A later translation of the *Muallakat* was by Lady Anne Blunt, versified by her husband and published in 1872.

'Stay – let us weep at the remembrance of our beloved, at the sight of the station where her tent was raised, by the edge of yon bending sands between Dahul and Haumel.'

Tennyson begins:

> Comrades leave me here a little, while as yet 'tis early morn;
> Leave me here, and when you want me, blow upon the bugle horn.

Nowhere perhaps was the Persian 'softness and love of pleasure, that indolence and effeminacy' ensnared as inescapably as in the epicurean quatrains of Omar Khayyam – as translated by Edward Fitzgerald:

> I sometimes think that never blows so red
> The Rose as where some buried Caesar bled;
>   That every Hyacinth the Garden wears
> Dropt in its lap from some once lovely Head.

How foreign to the industrious Victorians were these languid verses and how they delighted in Omar Khayyam's pleasure-seeking. Fitzgerald was an unconventional Victorian with few ambitions; in his youth he travelled round Europe and in his middle age settled in Suffolk to 'plain living and thinking' and for amusement began to learn Persian – from Jones' Persian Grammar. His teacher was one of the great Persian scholars of the century, Edward Cowell, and it was Cowell who from Calcutta sent Fitzgerald a manuscript of Omar Khayyam, an eleventh-century astronomer and mathematician of Khurasan.

Fitzgerald began working on his translation in 1857 and published it in a small cheap edition two years later, when it lay for a year or more collecting dust in book-shops. Dante Gabriel Rossetti and Algernon Swinburne claimed to have discovered it first – in a second-hand bookshop – and showed it to their friends; in a letter some thirty-five years later Swinburne described their discovery of this, the first edition of many: 'I know none to be compared with it, for power, pathos and beauty – in the same line of thought and work, except possibly Ecclesiastes; and magnificent as that is, I can hardly think the author comparable to Omar either as philosopher or poet.'

Swinburne was writing at the time to decline an offer of membership of the Omar Khayyam Club, only one of the many Omar Khayyam ploys which swept late Victorian England. It was parodied in the *Golfer's Rubaiyat*, *Rubaiyat of William the Warlord* and

Rubaiyat of Omarred Wilhelm; there was an Omar Khayyam calendar, with quotations for each month: a concordance with spiritual interpretations; a birthday book; and an Omar Khayyam rose at Kew, grown from seeds sent home from Omar Khayyam's grave at Nishapur by William Simpson, the *Illustrated London News* artist. Travellers in north-west Persia visited his grave, to the puzzlement of local inhabitants, though Curzon wrote that its condition would greatly shock Omar Khayyam's English admirers – 'it stands in a neglected garden, which once contained flower beds, and rivulets of water, but is now a waste of weeds.'

To Fitzgerald himself, now signing himself Edward FitzOmar, the enthusiasm was startling, though he died before seeing his friend Tennyson's clumsy eulogy of 'your golden Eastern lay'. For Fitzgerald the appeal of the quatrains lay in their emphasis on the transience of life and its beauties – 'Unborn Tomorrow, and dead Yesterday, Why fret about them if Today be sweet?' 'I suppose very few people have ever taken such pains in translation as I have,' he wrote, 'though certainly not to be literal. But at all costs a thing must live: with a transfusion of one's own worse life if one can't retain the original's better.' Some say Omar wrote his 'slightly bibulous musings' as a form of relaxation, certainly not be taken seriously, while others interpret each traditional symbol of beauty – roses, streams, nightingales and women – in the light of Persian mysticism. Burton, another great translator of oriental verse, said that a line had to be drawn between 'unendurable inaccuracy and intolerable servility' and Fitzgerald has often been castigated – mostly recently by Robert Graves – not only for an inaccurate translation but also for ignoring the allegorical implications of the quatrains. But as Fitzgerald himself said, 'better a live sparrow than a stuffed eagle', and it is to Fitzgerald the poet rather than to Omar the Sufi astronomer that the beauty of the English translations is due.

Fitzgerald has eclipsed most other translations of Persian or Arabic poetry, but it would be difficult to pass on without mentioning Gertrude Bell's translation of the Divan of Hafiz – 'no European who reads his Divan,' she wrote, 'but will be taken captive by the delicious music of his songs, the delicate rhythms, the beat of the refrain and the charming imagery.' Gertrude Bell learnt Persian during her visit to Persia in 1892, three months after her arrival writing to a cousin of the pleasures of lying in a hammock in a Persian garden reading the poems of Hafiz in the original. Though many Persian linguists have tried their hands at translating Hafiz, no one perhaps captured so well the spirit of the poet:

Songs of dead laughter, songs of love once hot,
Songs of a cup once flushed rose-red with wine,
Songs of a rose whose beauty is forgot,
A nightingale that piped hushed lays divine:
And still a graver music runs beneath
The tender love notes of those songs of thine,
Oh, Seeker of the keys of Life and Death!

Omar Khayyam, Hafiz and their translators reflected the joy and luxury of the East; through the poetry of James Elroy Flecker – much of it written from his home on Mount Lebanon – runs the strain of 'wandering and pain', hardship and violence which was present in so many of the better travel accounts. Flecker joined the Levant Consular Service after leaving Oxford and was sent to Beirut in 1911. His hatred of the 'banishment of hot Beirut, the steaming harbour, the formal consulate, the slow sourness of boiled cabbage' in his hotel embittered the most successful of his poems and he admitted to a friend in 1913 that 'I loathe the East and the Easterns and spent all my time there dreaming of Oxford. Yet it seems – even to hardened orientalists – that I understand.' Of one of his finest oriental poems, *The Gates of Damascus*, Flecker wrote, 'I consider this to be my greatest poem   it was inspired by Damascus itself':

Four great walls has the city of Damascus,
And four Grand Wardens, on their spears reclining,
All day long stand like tall stone men
    And sleep on the towers when the moon is shining.

Flecker began his verse drama *Hassan* when he was on leave in Corfu in 1911. The story of Hassan, the confectioner of Baghdad, is a typical 'Arabian night', with the Caliph Harun al-Rashid and his *vazir*, the faithful Jaafar, wandering in disguise through the night. T. E. Lawrence, who knew Flecker in Beirut, described his feeling for Arab town life – 'the satins and silks, perfumes, sweet-meats, grocers and Syrian boys' – and this is the setting which Flecker built so carefully round his characters. But the scene where the young lovers Rafi and Pervaneh are tormented by their agonising quandary – whether to enjoy one last night of love before dying the most tortuous death the caliph can devise or to be parted for ever, Rafi to go free and Perveneh to spend her days in the caliph's harem – erases the tawdry trappings of a century of pseudo *Arabian Nights*. The same drama includes the magnificent war song of the Saracens – 'We are they who come faster than fate: we are they who ride early or late': – and the merchants' songs overheard by the

5. Gertrude Bell (1868–1926), traveller and archaeologist. Watercolour by Flora Russell, 1887

disillusioned Hassan and his friend the court poet as they decide to leave Baghdad and make the journey to Samarkand:

> Sweet to ride forth at evening from the wells
>   When shadows pass gigantic on the sand,
> And softly through the silence beat the bells
>   Along the Golden Road to Samarkand.
>
> We travel not for trafficking alone:
>   By hotter winds our fiery hearts are fanned:
> For lust of knowing what should not be known
>   We make the Golden Journey to Samarkand.

'For what land leave you the dim-moon city of delight?' asks the watchman of the merchants and receiving the reply, 'We make the Golden Journey to Samarkand', he turns to console the women:

> What would ye, ladies? It was ever thus.
>   Men are unwise and curiously planned.

Nowhere else perhaps in the literature inspired by the Middle East has a writer – in spite of himself – captured the whimsical nature of British ventures in the area.

6. A room in the house of the Mufti, Cairo. This magnificent house was
particularly popular with foreigners living in or visiting Cairo. Watercolour
by Frank Dillon, c. 1860

There were indeed many whose interest in the Middle East was solely because of its trade; others posterity has liked to think were inspired by Flecker's 'hotter winds' to seek for its soul. But the vast majority were never really involved in the area at all – travelling, writing, painting, digging, independently of its real moods and politics. It would be a mistake (though one commonly made by their admirers) to liken these visitors to the Middle East too closely to Flecker's merchants and pilgrims; all too often the fireside contemporaries of these 'curiously planned' wanderers surrounded them or their writings with an aura that adheres, however uneasily, in later generations. This is particularly true in the case of Lady Hester Stanhope, and the Victorians were particularly guilty. 'All experience is an arch wherethro' Gleams that untravelled world', mused Tennyson's Ulysses, an opinion qualifying him as a Victorian idol. The difference between Flecker's caravan setting out to seek the Golden Road and the British travellers is that the former were obliged to explain to the sensible, sceptical watchman their loftier motives of travel. The characters of this book suffer from being attributed with lofty motives to the exclusion of more whimsical ones, largely due to their own marvellous literacy which spun entrancing webs around their readers.

7. The 'Sweet Waters of Asia', a popular and fashionable retreat for Turks and Europeans alike. Watercolour by William Purser

17 Epilogue

By the end of World War I the British in the Middle East had
become Britain in the Middle East. British political interest continued until the end of the 1950's to be primarily influenced by
communications with India and after 1947 with the Far East, with
oil supplies only assuming an importance of their own during and
since World War II. During this period the Middle East became
second home to large numbers of British administrators, technicians
and military personnel, many of whom came to the Middle East via
India (sometimes literally, more often metaphorically), hence the
frequent mistake made at home in Britain that more of the area
than Aden once belonged to the British Empire.

For many British in the area between 1914 and 1958 (when the
Iraqi revolution finally terminated British responsibilities) there
was generally much more fraternisation between British and local
inhabitants than in India, though they were on better terms in some
places than in others. In Egypt, the most firmly controlled country,
the British community never quite threw off Cromer's condescend-
ing shrug towards the Egyptians though developing better relations
with the Turkish–Syrian elite. In Palestine the British were bogged
down in the morass of racial hostility created by arrangements for
the Jewish homeland. In Iraq they were on such good terms with
the Sandhurst-educated, polo-playing aristocracy that they badly
misjudged the bitter enmity of the opposition. In Persia up to 1935
the provincial anarchy was such that few British went far outside
their posts and relations with the Persians suffered for a long time
from the latters' bitterness at the Anglo-Russian power struggle that
threatened the country's survival. Only perhaps in the Persian Gulf,
where the British presence on land was thinner than elsewhere
(though considerably thicker on water), was a mutual respect
maintained.

Familiarity does not necessarily breed contempt but it can lead
to a certain scepticism which often characterised British social and
political attitudes towards a Middle East slowly finding its feet after
the dissolution of the Ottoman Empire and the establishment of
national boundaries. Between the wars, however, the British

presence in Egypt, Iraq, Palestine and southern Arabia worked quite successfully; enough of the British still believed in the imperial mission, regardless of the fact that the area was not part of the empire, often they were visibly improving the standard of living in those countries and it was quite common for the local ruling class to feel closer to their British 'advisers' than to the increasingly vociferous nationalist or left-wing (or both) movements. Some of those movements developed into political parties during and after World War II and eventually succeeded not only in ridding their countries of the British presence but also in shattering what remained in the minds of the British public of an orient that was mildly but not obsessively exotic.

In the nineteenth century, and even today, the semitic Muslim lands have often been called the 'Near' East – nearer in culture as well as mileage than the Indo-European 'Middle' East. Given the 'Indian' route into the area it is not surprising that the Arab east – its religion, its history, even its way of life – should have seemed more acceptable, closer to our own classical Christian heritage than India and even Iran. The fact that much of the 'Near' East is dotted with Greek and Roman ruins as well as Egyptian, Phoenician, Mesopotamian and Hittite has attracted many travellers who have come to it via the classical Mediterranean but yearned Byron-like for a more exotic environment than that beautiful blue and gold landscape.

The romantic attachment of the British for the area did not easily survive their acquiring responsibilities there; that it did was largely due to that peculiarly British tradition of traveller who, following the luminous vapours despite the mire, believed in travel for its own sake and needed no worthier qualifications than stamina and great literary fluency. Style was as important a part of the tradition as content, as Kinglake and Doughty demonstrated in the nineteenth century. More recent practitioners in this tradition include T. E. Lawrence (despite the semi-professional reasons for his wartime presence in the Middle East), Freya Stark and Wilfred Thesiger and – in a slightly different vein but no less influential as far as his countrymen's idea of the area was concerned – Lawrence Durrell; Durrell, though no indulger in the mire of travel, is a master of the luminous vapour and his Alexandrian quartet magnificently sustained the Levantine mystique when it had fallen to a low ebb after Suez.

Although all four found employment in the Middle East none came because of it. Lawrence first went to the Middle East as an Oxford undergraduate to study Crusader castles and subsequently archaeology in Syria. Thesiger came to his Middle East via Africa and a mission to Abyssinia in 1930. Freya Stark never left Europe until she was thirty-four and learnt Arabic in the course of a long illness 'in the hopes that . . . it might lead me . . . to some sort of fairy-land of my own'. And Durrell came, like so many, in the wake of diplomacy and war and never really left.

It is the special gift of certain writers to recreate for us their fairy-lands, however swiftly these tend to disappear into thin air if we ever trespass on the reality and these four writers – three of them writing about areas in which few of us are likely to travel extensively and one indulging in an Egyptian successor to Flecker's *Hassan* – were able to counter the harsh realities of civic and political involvement. To the modern reader, nurtured on the gruesome hardships of the contemporary travelogue, their style is often nostalgically purple but still fascinating. Listen to Lawrence: 'for years we lived anyhow with one another in the naked desert, under the indifferent heaven. By day the hot sun fermented us; and we were dizzied by the beating wind. At night we were stained by dew, and shamed into pettiness by the innumerable silence of stars.' etc., etc., etc. Thesiger is better: 'A cloud gathers, the rain falls, men live; the cloud disperses without rain and men and animals die. In the deserts of southern Arabia there is no rhythm of the seasons, no rise and fall of sap, but empty wastes where only the changing temperature marks the passage of the years. No man can live this life and emerge unchanged.' No man, it was once thought, could read about it and remain unchanged. Durrell is in a gentler world. 'Landscape-tones: brown to bronze, steep skyline, low cloud, pearl ground with shadowed agate and violet reflection.' The truth of the period is sounded by Freya Stark. 'I never imagined,' she wrote to a friend in 1928, 'that my first sight of the desert would come with such a shock and enslave me right away.'

Among the British experts in the Middle East have been the archaeologists and historians. The absence of historical appreciation persisted in many respects until the rude awakening of World War I. Greater academic interest in the Middle East has helped to develop a national, or, on a larger scale, racial pride which was barely emerging at the end of the period covered by this book. National and international interest in the mounds of dust and rubble that dot the Middle East and have been excavated by the archaeologists grew slowly at first but now Mesopotamia, Jericho and Pharaohnic Egypt have been brought to Britain by television and the returning package tourist, Iran has celebrated its 2,500th birthday and the World of Islam has been unveiled. This is an age where facts go further than stylish prose and the new political clout that the oil countries of the Middle East discovered in their hands in the

1970's is supported by the well-publicised history of previous glories.

And yet, as Cardinal Newman mused, 'I used to wish the Arabian Tales were true.'

Bibliography

This list omits most of the contemporary, first-hand accounts mentioned in the text or illustrations, except where they are particularly valuable commentaries on British involvement in the Middle East. Although the bibliography is arranged according to chapters, the sources mentioned often overlap from one chapter to another.

1 The Middle East: Ottomans and Safavids

A. J. Arberry (ed.), *The Legacy of Persia*, 1930
Sir Henry Blount, *Voyage into the Levant*, 1637
Sir John Chardin, *Persia and Other Eastern Nations*, 1724
H. A. R. Gibb and Harold Bowen, *Islamic Society and the West*, Volume 1, *Islamic Society in the Eighteenth Century*, 2 parts, 1950, 1957
Jonas Hanway, *An Account of British Trade over the Caspian Sea*, 1753
P. M. Holt, *Egypt and the Fertile Crescent*, 1966
Richard Knolles, *General History of the Turks*, 1603
E. W. Lane, *Manners and Customs of the Modern Egyptians*, 1836
Bernard Lewis, *The Middle East and the West*, 1964
Sir John Malcolm, *History of Persia*, 1815
P. M. Sykes, *History of Persia*, 2 volumes, 1930
Sir Arnold Wilson, *A Bibliography of Persia*, 1930

2 The Lord of the Golden Horn

Samuel Chew, *The Crescent and the Rose*, 1937
Richard Hakluyt, *Principal Navigations*, 1598–1600
Hakluyt Society publications: accounts by John Sanderson, 1931; Peter Mundy, 1907–36; Thomas Dallam and Dr Covell, 1893
Levant Company archives in the Public Record Office, State Papers 105 and 110
Lady Mary Wortley Montagu, *Letters*, 1727
Boies Penrose, *Travel and Discovery in the Renaissance*, 1952
Samuel Purchas, *Purchas His Pilgrims*, 1625
George Sandys, *Relation of a Journey*, 1652
A. C. Wood, *History of the Levant Company*, 1964; this contains an excellent bibliography

3 The Turkey Merchants

Chew, Hakluyt, Penrose, Purchas, Sandys, Wood
Ralph Davis, *Aleppo and Devonshire, Square,* 1967
Christine Grant, *The Syrian Desert,* 1936
Charles Johnson, *General History of the Pirates,* 1724
Roger North, *Lives of the Norths,* 1826 edition
Charles Perry, *View of the Levant,* 1743
Joseph Pitts, *A Faithful Account of the Religion and Manners of the Mahometans,*
    1704
Richard Pococke, *Description of the East,* 1743–5
Alexander Russell, *Natural History of Aleppo,* 1757

4 The Grand Sophy

Chardin, Hakluyt, Hanway, Penrose, Purchas
John Bruce, *Annals of the East India Company,* 3 volumes, 1810
Cornelius de Bruyn, *Travels,* 1737
Sir John Chardin, *Travels,* 1686
East India Company Court Minutes, in the India Office
Sir William Foster, *The Embassy of Sir Thomas Roe,* 1926
    England's Quest for Eastern Trade, 1933
    English factories in India (calendar of documents)
    (ed.), *Letters received by the East India Company,* 1896–1902
Hakluyt Society publications: accounts by John Jourdain and Pedro
    Teixeira
Thomas Herbert, *Some Yeares Travaile,* 1634
D. G. Hogarth, *The Penetration of Arabia,* 1904
Karsten Niebuhr, *Travels,* 1792
Boies Penrose, *Urbane Travellers,* 1942
Sir Arnold Wilson, *The Persian Gulf,* 1928

5 Not for Trafficking Alone

Chew, Blount, Hakluyt, Purchas, Wood
Lionel Cust, *History of the Dilettanti,* 1855
John Greaves, *Miscellaneous Works,* 1737
Mary Hervey, *Thomas Howard, Earl of Arundel,* 1921
William Lithgow, *A Most Delectable and True Discourse of a Painful Peregrina-*
    tion, 1614
Henry Maundrell, *A Pilgrimage from Aleppo to Jerusalem, 1697* (1703)
Fynes Moryson, *Itinerary,* 1617
Sir Thomas Roe (ed. Samuel Richardson), *Negotiations at the Ottoman Court,*
    1740

6 Flowers of Luxuriant Fancy

Chew, Greaves, Knolles, Wood

A. J. Arberry, *Aquatic Jones*, 1946
  British Orientalists, 1943
  Cambridge Arabic, 1948
G. M. Clark, *The Seventeenth Century*, 1947
A. Conant, *The Oriental Tale in England*, 1908
Edward Gibbon, *The Decline and Fall of the Roman Empire*, *1776*
  Autobiography, 1796
Sir John Mandeville, *Travels*, 1900 edition

7 *The Middle East in the Nineteenth Century*

Holt, Lewis, Sykes, Wilson
Peter Avery, *Modern Iran*, 1967
E. G. Browne, *A Year Among the Persians*, 1927
George Curzon, *Persia and the Persian Question*, 1892
R. L. Greaves, *Persia and the Defence of India*, 1959
Bernard Lewis, *The Emergence of Modern Turkey*, 1961
John Marlowe, *Anglo-Egyptian Relations 1800–1953*, 1954
K. S. Salibi, *The Modern History of Lebanon*, 1965

8 *The Red-Hot Horseshoe*

Holt, Lewis, Salibi
E. B. B. Barker, *John Barker: Syria and Egypt under the Last Five Sultans*, 1876
Isabel Burton, *The Inner Life of Syria*, 2 volumes, 1876
Sir Edmund Hornby, *Autobiography*, 1929
S. L. Poole, *Stratford Canning*, 2 volumes, 1888
William Russell, *Diary in the East*, 1869
David Urquhart, *A History of Lebanon*, 2 volumes, 1853

9 *The Veiled Protectorate*

Holt, Marlowe, Russell
George Baldwin, *Political Recollections Relative to Egypt*, 1801
W. S. Blunt, *Diaries*
James Bruce, *Travels to Discover the Source of the Nile*, (1768–73)
Lord Cromer, *Modern Egypt*, 2 volumes, 1908
  Abbas II, 1915
  Ancient and Modern Imperialism, 1910
E. M. Forster, *Alexandria*, 1922
H. L. Hoskins, *British Routes to India*, 1928
Sir Ronald Storrs, *Orientations*, 1937

10 *The Great Game*

Avery, Browne, Curzon, Greaves, Wilson
Valentine Chirol, *The Middle Eastern Question*, 1903
Philip Graves, *Sir Percy Cox*, 1941

Sir John Malcolm, *Sketches of Persia*, 1827
James Morier, *A Journey Through Persia to Constantinople*, 1815
James Morier, *A Second Journey Through Persia to Constantinople, 1810–6*, 1818
   Hajji Baba of Isfahan, 1824
George Rawlinson, *Sir Henry Rawlinson, a memoir*, 1898

11   The Road to India

Avery, Baldwin, Greaves, Hoskins, Marlowe
William Ainsworth, *A Personal Narrative of the Euphrates Expedition*, 1888
Constance Alexander, *Baghdad in Bygone Days*, 1928
Francis Chesney, *The Euphrates Expedition*, 2 volumes, 1868
Frederick Goldsmid, *Telegraph and Travel*, 1874
H. F. B. Lynch, 'The Karun River', *Proc. Royal Geog. Soc.*, 1891
Thomas Waghorn, *Particulars of an Overland Route*, 1831
Sir Arnold Wilson, *South-West Persia: A Political Officer's Diary, 1907–14*,
   1941

12 Luminous Vapours

Browne, Curzon, Hogarth
Gertrude Bell, *Letters* (ed. Lady Bell, 1927)

13 Old Desolate Places

Poole, Rawlinson
James Baikie, *A Century of Excavation*, 1924
Giovanni Belzoni, *Operations and Recent Discoveries*, 1820
Dominique Vivant Denon, *Travels in Lower and Upper Egypt*, 2 volumes, 1802
   Description de l'Egypte, 12 volumes, 1808–25
J. J. Halls, *Life and Correspondence of Henry Salt*, 2 volumes, 1834
Seton Lloyd, *Foundations in the Dust*, 1947
Who's Who in Egyptology

14 The Noisy, Odd, Capricious Stream

James Finn, *Stirring Times*, 2 volumes, 1878
Philip Henderson, *Laurence Oliphant*, 1956
Dr C. L. Meryon, *Memoirs of Lady Hester Stanhope*, 1845
   Travels of Lady Hester Stanhope, 1846
Murray's Handbooks, 1847, etc.
John Pudney, *The Thomas Cook Story*, 1953
W. M. Thackeray, *From Cornhill to Cairo*, 1865
A. L. Tibawi, *British Interests in Palestine, 1800–1901*, 1961

15 Artists in the Middle East

James Ballantine, *David Roberts*, 1866

W. Holman Hunt, *Pre-Raphaelitism*, 1905
Edward Lear, *Letters*, 1907
  Later Letters, 1911
Sir Robert Ker Porter, *Travels in Georgia, etc.*, 1821–2

16 *The Plaint of the Reed*

Arberry, Bell, *Letters*
Sir Richard Burton, *The Thousand and One Nights*, 16 volumes, 1885–8
The Cambridge History of English Literature
Edward Fitzgerald, *Letters and Literary Remains*, ed. W. Aldiss Wright,
  1902–3
Marzia Gail, *Persia and the Victorians*, 1951
Marie de Meester, *Oriental Influences in Nineteenth-Century English Literature*,
  1915

Index

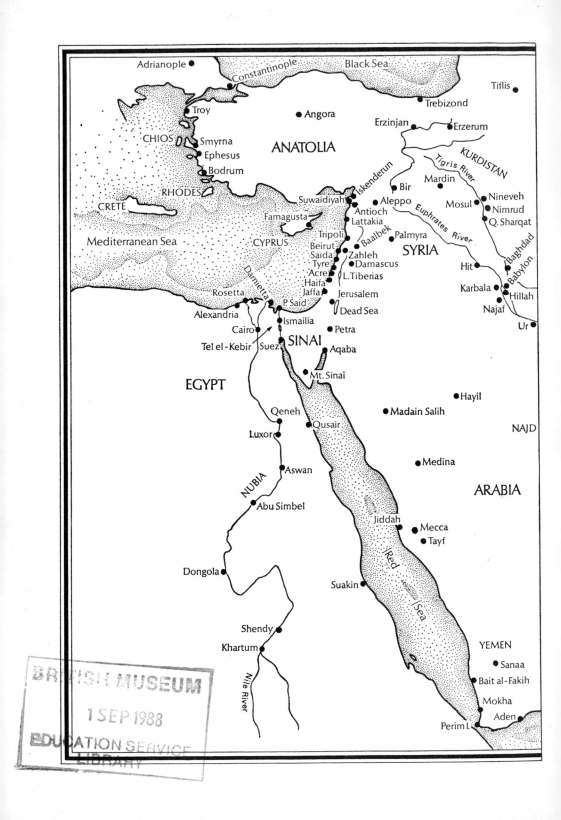

Adrianople

Constantinople
Black Sea

Tiflis

Troy

Angora
Trebizond

CHIOS
Smyrna
Erzinjan
Erzerum

Ephesus
ANATOLIA
KURDISTAN

Bodrum
Tigris River

RHODES
Iskenderun
Bir
Mardin
Nineveh

CRETE
Suwaidiyah
Aleppo
Mosul
Nimrud

Famagusta
Antioch
Euphrates River
Q. Sharqat

Mediterranean Sea
CYPRUS
Tripoli
Lattakia

Beirut
Baalbek
Palmyra
SYRIA
Baghdad
Babylon

Saida
Zahleh
Hit

Damietta
Tyre
Damascus

Rosetta
Acre
L. Tiberias
Karbala
Hillah

Alexandria
Haifa
Najaf

Jaffa
Jerusalem
Ur

Cairo
P. Said
Dead Sea

Ismailia
Petra

Tel el-Kebir
Suez
SINAI

EGYPT
Aqaba

Mt. Sinai
Hayil

Qeneh
Madain Salih
NAJD

Luxor
Qusair

Aswan
Medina

NUBIA
ARABIA

Abu Simbel
Jiddah
Mecca

Tayf

Dongola
Red Sea

Suakin

Shendy
Sea

Khartum
YEMEN

Nile River
Sanaa

Bait al-Fakih

Mokha
Aden

Perim I.